William Shakespeare, Richard Simpson, J. W. M Gibbs

The School of Shakspeare

William Shakespeare, Richard Simpson, J. W. M Gibbs

The School of Shakspeare

ISBN/EAN: 9783744685542

Printed in Europe, USA, Canada, Australia, Japan

Cover: Foto ©Thomas Meinert / pixelio.de

More available books at **www.hansebooks.com**

THE
SCHOOL OF SHAKSPERE.

THE SCHOOL OF SHAKSPERE

INCLUDING

'THE LIFE AND DEATH OF CAPTAIN THOMAS STUKELEY,'
WITH A NEW LIFE OF STUCLEY, FROM UNPUBLISHED SOURCES;
'NOBODY AND SOMEBODY;' 'HISTRIO-MASTIX;'
'THE PRODIGAL SON;' 'JACK DRUM'S ENTERTAINEMENT;'
'A WARNING FOR FAIR WOMEN,'
WITH REPRINTS OF THE ACCOUNTS OF THE MURDER;
AND 'FAIRE EM.'

EDITED,

With Introductions and Notes,

AND AN ACCOUNT OF ROBERT GREENE, HIS PROSE WORKS, AND
HIS QUARRELS WITH SHAKSPERE,

BY RICHARD SIMPSON, B.A.

AUTHOR OF
'THE PHILOSOPHY OF SHAKSPERE'S SONNETS,' THE 'LIFE OF CAMPION,' ETC.

IN TWO VOLUMES.—VOL. I.

London:
CHATTO AND WINDUS, PICCADILLY.
1878.

[All Rights reserved.]

Bungay:
CLAY AND TAYLOR, PRINTERS.

CONTENTS OF VOL. I.

	PAGE
PREFATORY NOTICE	vii
APPENDIX: THE STORIES OF THE PLAYS OF 'CAPTAIN STUCLEY' AND 'NOBODY AND SOMEBODY'	xiii
BIOGRAPHY OF SIR THOMAS STUCLEY	1
THE FAMOUS HISTORY OF THE LIFE AND DEATH OF CAPTAIN THOMAS STUKELEY	157
NOBODY AND SOMEBODY	269

NOTICE.

THE lamented death of the Editor—the learned, researchful, ingenious, refin'd and sweet-natur'd Richard Simpson—has depriv'd these volumes of his Preface, his final revision, and the further notes he would doubtless have added to the texts. He left the whole of the Introductions and Texts ready for the press before he quitted England for the journey to Rome, whence he never return'd, and during his illness he saw the first sheets of vol. i, up to p. 288, through the press. Unable myself, from press of other work, to take up my late friend's task, and not succeeding in inducing Mr P. A. Daniel to do so, or Professor Craig to persevere in it, I at last secured the aid of Mr J. W. M. Gibbs—an old helper in Elizabethan work, and a dramatic critic of some standing—and he has, with mere overlook from me, seen through the press and revised the rest of the sheets, has written short sketches of the Plays and some notes, and added the excellent index at the end. The trouble and care he has given to the work deserve warm acknowledgment.

The present volumes are the main portion of that 'School of Shakspere' which Mr Simpson started by his edition of *A Larum for London*, in 1872 ; and they include all the plays (except *Mucedorus*,[1] ed. Delius, 2s.) that he named as most important

[1] See Mr Simpson's Paper on it in *The New Shakspere Society's Trans.* 1875-6, p. 155.

in the original Prospectus of his Series. As this Prospectus states his aims in projecting the Series, it follows here :—

'Under the title of *The School of Shakspere*[1] may be included all those plays which were acted by the Lord Chamberlain's (afterwards the King's) company during Shakspere's connection with it, and other plays, acted by other companies, which have been assigned to him by tradition, or with which there are plausible grounds for connecting him. Of these plays it is proposed to reprint those which are not to be found in the collected works of the old dramatists, or in the usual miscellaneous collections, such as Dodsley and Hawkins.

'I. These reprints are necessary for completing our idea of Shakspere as a writer and thinker. For a play is not to be looked upon as an isolated literary effort, but as a part of an organic system, like an article in a review or a newspaper. To understand Shakspere's influence, we ought to consider as a whole the dramas introduced on his stage while he was connected with it, and also the dramas acted at the rival theatres. The stage in his day was the great means for inculcating opinions on all practical subjects; we ought therefore to be able to say, not only how Shakspere wielded this weapon as a private dramatist, but how he wielded it, as necessarily the presiding genius, the *Johannes factotum* as he was called, among his fellows.

'II. These reprints are necessary also for completing the collection of works which more or less owe their origin to Shakspere's hands. The recognized works of Shakspere contain scarcely any but those which he produced for the Lord Chamberlain's or King's company of actors. But, in 1592, Greene tells us he had almost a monopoly of dramatic production, and had made himself necessary, not to one company, but to the players in general. It may be proved that he wrote for the Lord Strange's men, and for those of the Earl of Pembroke and the Earl of Sussex. It may further be shown[2] that some at least of the so-called spurious or doubtful plays assigned to him by tradition are early productions of his pen, written for these companies.

'III. The plays acted by companies for which Shakspere was "factotum," even when written by other dramatists, often contain alterations and additions, which the company's poet would naturally be called upon to make. Such additions and alterations clearly

---

[1] As Mr Simpson rightly alterd his spelling of 'Shakespeare' to 'Shakspere' in later life, that spelling is printed here.

[2] This of course I do not admit.—F.

from his hand[1] may be found in the play of *Sir Thomas More*, first printed by Mr Dyce for the [old] Shakespeare Society. They ought therefore to be counted as "parcel works" of Shakspere, and to find a place in his "School."

'In accordance with this programme the Editor intends to reprint some of the rarer plays of the classes specified, with Introductions to justify their claims to be recognized as members of Shakspere's School. The first play thus reprinted will be *A Larum for London*, or *The Siege of Antwerp*, with the proof that it is referred to by a contemporary writer, founded on a pamphlet by Gascoyne, and written chiefly by Marston, under the direction of Shakspere. The next will be *The Life and Death of Captain Thomas Stukeley*, with proof of its connection with the former play, and with a new life of Stucley from unpublished sources. Other plays will be *Mucedorus, Faire Em, Histriomastix*, with the *Prodigal Child, Nobody and Somebody, A Warning for Fair Women*, and the like. There remain other series of plays intimately connected with the School of Shakspere, which will be printed if the series attains a moderate success. These series are :—1. The Martinist and Anti-Martinist plays of 1589 and 1590, which drove Shakspere for a time from the stage; and 2. The plays connected with Ben Jonson's controversy with the players and player-poets in 1600—1603.'

Mr Simpson accordingly contends that Shakspere either had a hand in, or was closely connected with, most of the plays of his 'School,' including those in the present volumes, while *Histriomastix* was written, first by Peele, and then by Peele and Marston, against Shakspere and his 'School' of *factotum* got-up plays. Another purpose of Mr Simpson's was, says Mr Gibbs, 'to show the relations of the then political parties to the writers for the Elizabethan stage. And in this regard the editor's labours must be viewed as supplementary to his very full and suggestive papers "On the Political use of the Stage in Shakspere's Time," and "On the Politics of Shakspere's Historical Plays," contributed to the *Transactions of the New Shakspere Society* (*Trans.*, 1874, pp. 371—441).

'*Stucley*, the first play here given, is a fairly spirited stage pro-

[1] This of course I do not admit.—F.

duction of the popular biographical order; and Mr Simpson thinks he traces four hands in its composition, the strongest being Shakspere's (v. I. pp. 139—141). Among the proofs of this position ne points out that the play is a glorification of Stucley, as an idol of the military or Essex party to which Shakspere is known to have leant. The long prefatory *Biography of Stucley* tends to this end also, in so far as it shows, more fully perhaps than has ever before been shown, the truly adventurous career of the hero, and so lets us into the secret of why that and other notabilities of the gallant and dashing, if not very honest or otherwise admirable, Essexian party, were so popular, and got to have their names and deeds reflected from the stage, or "mirror" of the time, and that by the great showman, or "mirror"-up-holder of his age, Shakspere. For other reasons the long *Biography of Stucley* will be found valuable:—First, as giving much information on the Irish Catholic plots of rebellion against Elizabeth, with their interweaving of Spanish-Papal projects for invading Elizabeth's dominions; and, secondly, as showing how much the buccaneering of the early days of Elizabeth was countenanced by, and interwoven with, the political exigencies of the time, and how even more countenanced and liked it was by the time's populace. The information as to the Irish Catholic intrigues will be found to be in no small degree supplementary to Mr Simpson's *Life of Campion* and other similar works.

'*Nobody and Somebody*, the next play given, is included, chiefly for these reasons:—

'(1) That it is in the German collection of English plays (published in 1620) played by Shakspere's company in Germany (about 1600, as Herr Cohn supposes; see v. I. p. 274); (2) That the allusion in the *Tempest* to "the picture of Nobody" has reference to it; and (3) That the character of Lord Sycophant, contained therein, is a stinging satire on Essex's (Shakspere's hero and patron) great enemy, Lord Cobham.

'*Histrio-Mastix* has already been alluded to, and Mr Simpson has more fully accounted for its presence in this work in his "Introduction," v. II. p. 3. Its two chief ingredients of value are,— (1) The view it gives us of the Stage and the Players, as the original author (Peele) has exposed them for castigation; and (2) The more particular view and castigation given in its later, or Marston-added-to version, of the leading Player, Post-haste, who is supposed to be meant for Shakspere, the monopolizing Player-poet, or *Johannes Factotum*, of Greene and Peele and Nash's frequently expressed aversion.

'*The Prodigal Son* is an excerpt from the interesting German collection of English plays which are supposed to have been played by Shakspere's company when in Germany (and to have been in part written by Shakspere; see v. I. p. 356; v. II. pp. 12, 13); and it owes its reproduction here chiefly to the allusions made to it in the before-going *Histrio-Mastix*, as explained more fully in Mr Simpson's "Introduction" to the latter play (v. II. pp. 12—15, etc.).

'*Jack Drum*, Mr Simpson assumes to be one of the series of plays which relate to the quarrel of Jonson with Marston and Dekker, and he thinks it to be in the main written by Marston. He connects it with Shakspere by the supposition that Planet, the Jaques-like character therein, "to whom the sceptre of criticism" seems to be conceded, is meant for Shakspere (see v. II. p. 131).

'*The Warning for Fair Women* comes in chiefly as being a play of the Lord Chamberlain's company (*i. e.* Shakspere's), and as containing the possible origin of some of the ideas worked up in the play-incident of *Hamlet* (see the Introduction, v. II. p. 212).

'*Faire Em*, Mr Simpson views as having greater claims to consideration in connection with Shakspere than any other play in the present collection. He, in fact, in his long Introduction (pp. 339 —405, v. II.) seeks to show: (1) That the play is not by Greene, as is most commonly supposed; (2) That it is by Shakspere—

though to some extent written by him in derisive imitation of Greene; and (3) That its derisive intent was accepted and resented by Greene.

'Mr Simpson at first intended to include in the present collection *The Cobbler's Prophecy*, by the puritan writer Robert Wilson (1594), and *The Pedlar's Prophecy*, attributed by Mr Simpson to Robert Crowley, the calvinistic author-printer and epigrammatist[1] who became Vicar of St Giles without Cripplegate early in Elizabeth's reign, and was buried there in June 1588, but considerations of space have finally compelld the exclusion of both these plays. Robert Crowley, by the way, was the writer whom Greene accused Shakspere of writing with. In his *Farewell to Folly*, Greene calls Shakspere (as Mr Simpson supposes) "Theological poet," and says he is one "that cannot write true English without the help of clerks of parish churches," besides making other allusions to "the Sexton of St. Giles" in connection with Shakspere's work. See v. II. pp. 378-9.'

The texts of the plays are from Mr Simpson's copies, and have been collated with the originals, of which they are trustworthy reproductions, except in a few details of spelling, as 'scums' for 'scummes,' &c. The old punctuation and defective metre he occasionally left uncorrected.

Mr Simpson's account of Robert Greene and his prose works is the best I know. The early blank-verse poet whom Greene at first abuses, I suppose to be Marlowe, and not Shakspere.

But however any reader or critic may differ with Mr Simpson's views, I feel sure that he will hold these volumes a most useful and valuable contribution to the knowledge of the Elizabethan stage and time.

F. J. FURNIVALL.

14 *Sept.* 1877.

[1] See his 31 Epigrams, Voyce of the last Trumpet, &c., in the Early English Text Society's Extra Series, 1872, price 12*s*.

APPENDIX.

THE STORY OF THE PLAY OF *CAPTAIN STUCLEY* BRIEFLY TOLD.

AT the play's opening, its hero, Stucley, is a young but five-years'-gone student of the Temple. He, however, dislikes the law, and has become a roistering city gallant and spendthrift. He then marries the daughter of the rich Alderman, Sir Thomas Curtis. With his wife's large dowry he first pays his extortionate creditors, Cross the mercer, Spring the vintner, Hazard the tennis-keeper, &c., and then equips a troop, with himself as Captain, to go against the rebels in Ireland. Only three days after his marriage, and much against the wishes of his wife, his father, and his father-in-law, he and his troop set out. At Dundalk, Stucley finds the town beleaguered by O'Neil's rebels. In a sortie made by the garrison and Stucley's troop, the rebels are routed; but Stucley and his party, pursuing the advantage further than the rest, get shut out from the town on the retreat into it for the night. The town's governor is Captain Herbert, a sometime roistering associate of Stucley, but now his enemy. Finding Stucley shut out, Herbert, from mere personal spite, keeps him out. Disgusted with such treatment, Stucley at once abandons Ireland, and with his troop, and rebel spoil of horses, cattle, &c., ships for Spain. It is then shown that the Irish rebels have been so completely routed that the leaders, O'Neil and Mackener, are about to give themselves up, and to sue for mercy. Ere they can do so, however, the two are met by the two Scots, Oge and Busk, and are by them killed. Arrived at Cadiz, Stucley is imprisoned by the Governor, because he will not yield as customary tribute five of his horses. But the Governor's wife, smitten with the Captain's handsome person and gallant bearing, releases him for a time, and so enables him to get an order from King Philip freeing him altogether from the Governor's power. Stucley then speedily finds great favour with

Philip II., by whom he is sent on an embassy to Rome. For this service Philip promises the Englishman 5000 ducats, and sends that sum, minus 20 ducats, after him. When the amount thus clipped reaches Stucley, he spurns it with his foot, at the same time sending Philip a rebuke for his 'niggardice' (p. 242), the spirit and words of which very well illustrate the Captain's proceedings throughout the play. But although Stucley refuses, under the circumstances, Philip's pay for the embassy to Rome, he proceeds with that embassy. The Pope makes him Marquis of Ireland; for which country, after a time, Stucley sets sail. But landing, on his way, in Portugal, just as King Sebastian's expedition to Barbary is afoot, the Captain is induced to join the King in that expedition. 'Heaven, displeased with their rash enterprise' (as chorus says in the play), displays 'a fatal comet in the air;' but this, instead of being taken as a warning, is viewed as prognosticating success. Ultimately, Stucley and his Italian band, Sebastian and his Portuguese power, and Muly Mahomet, one of the princes of Barbary, fight the battle of Alcazar, against Abdelmelek and Muly Hamet. The battle is a victory for the latter, King Sebastian and Muly Mahomet getting killed, and Stucley getting wounded. Stucley, thus wounded and a fugitive, is then killed by the remainder of his own Italian followers, because he has brought them to the disaster of Alcazar; and with its hero's death the play ends.—G.

THE STORY OF THE PLAY OF *NOBODY AND SOMEBODY* TOLD BRIEFLY.

ARCHIGALLOES, King of Brittayne, is dissolute and a tyrant. He despoils his subjects of their wives and their goods, and meets all objections with an imperious, 'What we will, we will.' For his misdeeds, and for the encouragement he gives to like misdeeds practised by his Court, Cornwell and some other honest Lords resolve to depose the King, and to enthrone in his stead his virtuous brother Elydure. The unambitious Elydure at first refuses to accept the crown; but finally his ambitious wife and the patriot Lords persuade him, and Archigalloes is dethroned and banished, and Elydure reigns in his stead. Soon, however, Elydure meets his banished brother, a ragged wanderer; and so touched is the King with his brother's wretchedness and repentance, that he gives back the crown, and persuades the Lords to again take Archigalloes for their King. The latter, almost immediately after his restoration, dies, and Elydure again comes to the throne, this time by lawful succession. Peridure and Vigenius, two other of his brothers, then conspire against Elydure, and dethrone and imprison him. Peridure and Vigenius at first propose to reign jointly; but Elydure dethroned, they speedily quarrel for mastery, and fighting for the same they kill each other. Elydure is then, and for the third time, crowned King. Nobody and Somebody are chief characters in what is rather the sub-plot than the main-plot of the play, and they are personified abstractions. Nobody is the familiar myth who, everywhere as well as in this play, gets blamed for most of the ill that is done, and Somebody is he who actually does the ill. Somebody does and instigates ill all through the play, and Nobody gets execrated for the ill that is done. This state of things, of course, constitutes the satire upon the writer's time which is sought to be conveyed by the play. But in the end Somebody formally charges Nobody, in a long trial-scene before King Elydure, with all his own (Somebody's) malpractices. This enables Nobody to completely turn the tables upon his defamer by showing that all these malpractices must have been *Somebody's*, for 'If *Nobody* should do them, then should they be undone.' Somebody is then punished. Much of the comedy of the play lies with the two Queens of Archigalloes and Elydure, and with the obsequious courtier, Sicophant. Each Queen, when in power, is so bent upon putting her sister in the most abject subjection, that their frequent changes of place keep them in a continual, and continually augmenting, state of the fiercest feminine antagonism and reprisal. Lord Sicophant's allegiance, and with it his fulsome flattery, comes and goes precisely as power comes and goes to and from the ruling personages in the play. In the end, however, as he is proved to have been in league with Somebody, and largely implicated in that arch-criminal's card and dice, and other innumerable cheatings and villanies, in so far as these have prevailed in the Court, Lord Sicophant gets his meed of punishment along with Somebody.—G.

P.S. A reviewer of this book (*Athenæum*, Sept. 22, 1877, p. 357) says, on *Jack Drum*,

"'Thy masters nose shalbe thy lanthorne and candle light' may, perhaps, be accepted as taken from Falstaff's address to Bardolph; and, 'Reioyce Brabant, thy brother will not liue long, he talkes idlely alreadie,' notes the same fact or superstition concerning death which in more poetical shape is expressed in 'a babbled of green fields.' The lines commencing 'Yes, yes, and would complot ten thousand deaths,' are very much in the style of Marlowe."

THE SCHOOL OF SHAKSPERE.[1]

AFTER the acuteness and learning of Malone, and the industry of Mr Collier and Mr Halliwell, it is not probable that much new matter regarding Shakspere will ever be discovered; or that any farther direct references to him or his works will be found in the remains of his times. Still there are whole fields of Shaksperian criticism which have hardly been touched. While the literary bearings of his works have been thoroughly examined; while every tale or ballad or older drama which he made use of has become known; and while his obscure phrases and words have been abundantly illustrated from the writings of his day, his works have not been studied, either by themselves, or in their connection with those of other dramatists produced on the same or on a rival stage, as the exponents of a school of opinion and policy, standing in the closest connection with the chief movements of contemporary history. Burke saw that this connection must exist when, congratulating Malone on his history of the stage, he wrote: "The stage may be considered as the republic of active literature, and its history as the history of that state. The great events of political history, when

[1] Introduction profixed to the reprint of "A Larum for London" (*Longmans*, 1872), intended by Mr Simpson to form No. I. of "*The School of Shakspere.*"

not combined with the same helps towards the study of the manners and characters of men, must be a study of an inferior nature." It cannot however be granted that Malone, or his successor Mr Collier, has succeeded in raising the history of the stage to any very dignified place in general English history. Yet during its palmy days the English stage was the most important instrument for making opinions heard, its literature the most popular literature of the age; and on that account it was used by the greatest writers for making their comments on public doings and public persons. As an American critic says, " it was newspaper, magazine, novel—all in one."

Hence the rival theatres of the Elizabethan age may be expected to exhibit the same phenomena as the rival journals of the present day. In both alike we have to look for the opposing views which distinguish the opposite schools of political thought. It is strange that hitherto no attempt has been made to classify the dramas, acting companies, and dramatists of the sixteenth century in a way that would enable us to place them in their true position with regard to the history, or to the less important rivalries of their day.

After 1594 this classification becomes easy; for then the chief London actors became agglomerated into two great rival companies, which were sufficiently permanent to establish a history and character of their own, and important enough either to throw smaller unions into the shade, or so to attract them as to bring them within the spheres of their respective influences. These companies were the Lord Chamberlain's and the Lord Admiral's. Of the first, Shakspere and Richard Burbage were the presiding geniuses. Of the second, Philip Henslowe and Edward Alleyn were the managers. The very names will suggest the characters of the two companies. While Shakspere secured for the one an artistic, philosophic, and political unity, the illiterate and commercial character of Henslowe naturally led him to sacrifice all unity and consistency to the readiest means of present popularity. Hence the distinct character of the dramas brought out by the rival companies. When we regard them as a whole, those of the Lord Chamberlain's company are characterised by common sense, moderation, naturalness, and the absence of bombast, and by a great artistic liberty of form, of matter, and of criticism; at the same time they favour liberty in politics and toleration in religion, and are consistently opposed to the Cecilian ideal in policy, while they as consistently favour that school to which Essex was attached. Through its constant adherence to its principles this company more than once found itself in great difficulties.

In the dramas of the Lord Admiral's men there is no such unity to be found; they are constant only in their inconstancy. Henslowe appears to have looked about with a keen eye for the conquering cause, and to have hired dramatists to make his stage its advocate. When Essex was first in disgrace at Court, but was still superlatively popular with the citizens, Henslowe's stage echoed his popularity; when he fell, he was Phaethon and Judas. Not that Henslowe always hit exactly the lucky mean. Sometimes, in trying to outdo a rival popularity, he would overleap his steed and fall on the other side, as was his mishap in the matter of Nash's drama, *The Isle of Dogs*. In a great many instances the choice of subjects for Henslowe's stage may be shown to have been determined by the dramas produced with success by the rival company. As he and Alleyn contracted with Streete the carpenter to erect the Fortune playhouse and stage "in all proportions contrived and fashioned like the playhouse called the Globe," so they seem to have contracted with their dramatists to furnish them with plays after the model of the same theatre. Hence the whole English drama during a certain period might be called the school of Shakspere—his school, either through his direct management in his own theatre, or through his indirect influence in that of his rivals.

Before 1594, however, this marked division of the London stage did not exist; the companies did not hold together long enough, nor during their existence did they preserve enough personal identity, to gain for any one of them a special character and history of its own. Sometimes one company came to the front, sometimes another. The two companies mentioned existed indeed, but had not yet conquered their position; neither had Shakspere as yet devoted his services exclusively to one of them. During the year 1592 Lord Strange's company eclipsed all rivals, having probably collected the chiefs of companies usually in rivalry into a transient fellowship. Other prominent companies were those of the Earl of Sussex (1589), the Earl of Worcester (1590), and the Earl of Pembroke (1592). For all these Shakspere can be shown to have written during the first part of his career. According to the well-known epistle annexed to Greene's *Groatsworth of Wit*, Shakspere, by 1592, had become so absolute a *Johannes factotum* for the actors of the day generally, that the man who considered himself the chief of the scholastic school of dramatists, not only determined for his own part to abandon playwriting, but urged his companions to do the same. We see by Nash's preface to Greene's *Menaphon* in 1589, that even then a similar strike had been discussed amongst the playwrights; and it may be shown that Lodge had vowed that same year not again to sully his pen with plays. Greene in 1592, when he urges Marlowe, Peele, and Nash to be faithful to their determination, says he knows two more who have come to the same resolution; and for the retirement of all these six dramatists (including himself) he gives but one reason,—the monopoly which Shakspere had established with the players.

It is clear, then, that before 1592 Shakspere must have been prodigiously active, and that plays wholly or partly from his pen must have been in possession of many of the actors and companies. For the fruits of this activity we are not to look in his recognised works. Those, with a few exceptions, are the plays he wrote for the Lord Chamberlain's men. Many of these plays doubtless were, like *Henry VI.* or the *Taming of the Shrew*, new versions of older dramas of his own. Others were first written by him for the Lord Chamberlain's, or as it became after 1613, the King's company. But as before 1594 he had been "factotum" for the players, inserting speeches where occasion required, altering them where they could not endure the censure of the Master of the Revels or of the audience, writing apologetical scenes when offence had been given, and the like; so doubtless after that period he performed services of the same kind for the company he was connected with.

There are thus two kinds of Shaksperian remains which may be recovered, or rather assigned to their real original author, by the critic and historian. First, the dramas prior to 1594, which are not included in his works; and secondly, the dramas over the production of which he presided, or with which he was connected as editor, reviser, or adviser. A good many plays have been assigned to him by tradition more or less authoritative, some of which are printed at the end of several editions of his works, under the name of spurious or doubtful plays. There are other anonymous plays which are stated on the title-pages to have been acted by his company of players, and which therefore belong at least to his school. There are other anonymous plays which internal evidence will compel us to assign to the same owners. All these plays ought to be studied together if we would form a right idea of the school of Shakspere.

But to render this study possible to the ordinary student we want reprints of many of these plays. Some of them may be found at the end of certain editions of Shakspere, others of them are included in the ordinary editions of the old dramatists, others have been reprinted by various literary societies, and by Delius and Moltke (for Tauchnitz) in Germany. But there remains a balance of very important plays which either have never been reprinted at all, or have become almost as rare in reprint as in the original. Of these plays I propose to publish a series, with an introduction to each piece, showing its connection with the school of Shakspere, and containing such other historical illustrations as may seem necessary to define its place.

RICHARD SIMPSON.

1872.

Biography of Sir Thomas Stucley.

SOME BALLADS AND A PLAY ON THE SUBJECT OF HIS LIFE.

CAPTAIN THOMAS STUCLEY was the third son of Sir Hugh Stucley (died Jan. 6, 1560), of Affton, on the river Taw, near Ilfracomb, Devonshire, by his wife Jane, daughter of Sir Lewis Pollard one of the Judges of the Common Pleas. Prince, in his Worthies of Devon, tells us that the Judge was born about 1465 and died about 1540, and had by his wife, Elizabeth Hext, two-and-twenty children, eleven sons and eleven daughters; and that the daughters were all married 'to the most potent families in the county; most of them knights, as the first to Sir Hugh Stucley, the second to Sir Hugh Courtenay of Powderham, the third to Sir Hugh Pawlet of Stamford Peverel, the fourth to Sir John Crocker of Lineham, &c. So that what is said of Cork in Ireland, that all the inhabitants therein are akin; by these matches almost all the ancient gentry in the county became allied.'

It appears that Sir Lewis Pollard died, not in 1540, but on the 21st of October, 1526. That his children, who lived to be recorded in the Visitations, were eleven in all; five sons—Hugh, Richard, John, Robert, and Anthony; and six daughters—Grace, Elizabeth, Jane, Agnes, Thomasin, and Philippa. I cannot discover any Hugh

Courtenay of Powderham, or any intermarriage of the Courtenays and Pollards in the generation in question. But Elizabeth, the second daughter, was married in succession to Sir John Croker and Sir Hugh Trevanion, of Carey-hayes, in Cornwall. Grace, the eldest daughter, does not appear to have been married at all. Possibly she was the nun of Canon Leigh, called in religion Margaret, to whom her father, alone of his daughters, left a legacy in his will.

The father of Sir Hugh Stucley was Sir Thomas Stucley (died Jan. 30, 1543), a Knight of the body to King Henry VIII., in 1516, and whose name is found on the sheriff roll for Somerset and Dorset in 1518 and 1519, and on that for Devon in 1520. His wife was Anne, the daughter and heir of Sir Thomas Wood of Bingley. He was a person of great wealth, and of very wide connections in the county. The list of the men whom he appointed trustees of his estates in 1535 contains the names of Sir Richard Grenville, Sir Philip Champernoun, Sir John Chamond of Trenoke, Cornwall, Sir Hugh Pollard, John Arundell Trerysse, George Carew, Hugh Pawlet, Henry Fortescue, Edward Danyard, John Cobleigh, Thomas Tremayne, Nicholas Dennis, Lewis Savile, Humphrey Keynes, Alexander Goode, Edmund Sperot, Roger Arundell Trerysse, Richard Fortescue, Gregory Grenville, Edward Thorne, Richard Chamond, Nicholas Furse, and Thomas Clotworthy.

In Benolt's Visitation of Devon, A° 22 of Henry VIII., the family name of the Stucleys of Affton is spelt *Steretchley*, and that of the Stucleys of Trent, Somerset (who were identically the same persons), *Strevokley*. There is also another family name, Stratcheley of Stratchley, which seems to have been originally the same. Two of the names in Sir Thomas Stucley's long list of connections just given, seem only related to him through the Stratchleys. Thus

Edward Thorne's mother was Jane, daughter of William Stratchley, and he was married to Agnes, a daughter of Sir John Chamond; and Edmund Sperot's mother was Anne, daughter of Wm Stratchley, and he was married to Jane, daughter of Sir Roger Grenville, another of whose daughters was also wife to Thomas Tremayne. But it would be endless, if not also unprofitable, to trace the interlacings of the Devonshire families; at this period they seem to have been very prolific, and to have married generally within the county; there is no need of the fable of Sir Lewis Pollard's eleven daughters to explain their affinities. Cousinhood, however, was claimed in cases where it cannot be accounted for by the pedigrees as they stand. Thus the Spanish ambassador, Don Guerau, wrote to Philip II. in 1572, that the famous Sir Humphrey Gilbert was first cousin 'primo hermano' to Thomas Stucley, a relationship in no wise borne out by the known pedigrees of the two men.

Hugh Stucley, the father of our Thomas, was sheriff of Devon in 1544. Like his son, he was a man of military instincts. Lord Russell, who was then commissioner of array for the Western Counties, wrote thus about him to the Council, from Dartmouth, July 10, 1545: 'Whereas Master Hugh Stuycklye, Sheriff of Devonshire, hath upon your commandment laid out certain sums of money for the conduct and prest money of such mariners as he took to go to Portsmouth [which was then menaced by the French Fleet, and where Henry VIII. then lay], I shall very heartily desire .... he may be allowed thereof with such expedition as you shall think convenient. I can do no less than commend him for such painful diligence and desirous mind to serve which I have well noted in him in this little time which I have been in the county. There hath not passed one day this eight or nine days in which he hath not been on horseback to travel to and fro to see the kings bulwalks and fortresses, some already on making, some newly devised, some fallen in decay to be repaired, in such places where he either by his office either otherwise might have to do. If your lordships shall think it good to give him thanks therefore (although he look for none) no doubt you shall not only cause him to rejoice to have employed his labour so, but also you shall much encourage many other gentlemen to do their uttermost to follow such examples as other doth give before them.' (State Papers, Henry VIII., Vol. i.)

By his wife, Jane Pollard, Sir Hugh Stucley was father of four sons and four daughters; Lewis, Anne, Mary, Elizabeth, George, Thomas, Hugh, Agnes. Lewis was married when his grandfather, Sir Thomas, settled his estates in 1535, and though he does not then seem to have had a male heir, he must have had daughters. One of them, Mary, was married successively to Tristram Larder, and to Sergeant Prideaux. The latter died in 1558, leaving three children; the woman who had time to be twice married, and to have this family by her second husband, in 1558, was probably born some years before 1535. If, then, her father Lewis was born about 1510 (which would make him 25 years old in 1535), it is presumable that his brother Thomas, the subject of the present sketch, was born sometime before 1520.

In common with most heroes of the stage and of popular ballads, Stucley's life has been surrounded with a complete cloud of traditions. Of the two following details one is taken from Peele's *Battle of Alcazar*, a play published in 1594, but acted long before, and therefore probably written within about ten years of Stucley's death in August, 1578. In this play Stucley is a Londoner by birth, and he beguiles the moments between his murder and his death with the story of his life, beginning thus:—

> In Englands London, Lordlings, was I born
> On that brave bridge, the bar that thwarts the Thames.

The other surmise I do not find in any author previous to the Irish historian, Philip O'Sullevan, who, in his Compendium of the Catholic History of Ireland (Lib. iv. c. xv. p. 112), tells how, when James Geraldine went to Rome to get aid for an attack on the English in Ireland (in 1577), he found there Friar Cornelius O'Melrian, Bishop of Killaloe, an Irishman, and Thomas Stucley, 'who by some was said to be an illegitimate son of Henry VIII., King of England; by others, son of an English Knight and an Irish lady; by others, Irish by both parents, who either from anger at the English, or from religious motives, or desiring war and revolution in hopes of gain, or aspiring to reign, being perhaps a man of royal blood, was supplicating in the name of the Irish for succour against the English.' It is possible, though no record appears in history, that this should be so. Stucley's birth must have occurred at the time when the king, tired with his wife Catherine, was as yet ranging among favourites who were contented with something less than a crown as the price of their kindness. Elizabeth Tailbois had been succeeded by Mary Boleyn; and as Mary Boleyn was married to William Carey at Court and in the presence of the king, Jan. 31, 1521, it is clear that some one else had already succeeded to her place. But there is no proof that Hugh Stucley's wife ever ranked as a royal mistress, except a surmise that might result from the peculiar terms of intimacy which her son Thomas always found himself able to assume towards royal personages. After a short service with Henry II. of France, the king called him 'notre cher et bon amy.' On his return to England the Duke of Northumberland treated him with the same jealousy with which he might have treated Henry Fitzroy, Duke of Richmond, if he had been still alive. At Mary's accession she recommends him warmly to the Duke of Savoy, through whom he is introduced to Charles V.; he writes familiar letters to Mary; he tells Elizabeth that when he is ruler of Florida he will write to her 'in the style of princes—to my dear sister;' when he flies to the Court of Philip, and afterwards to Rome, he is treated with more distinction and expense than any other of the English exiles, even than the Countess of Northumberland, the Earl of Westmoreland, or Sir Francis Englefield. And the Archbishop of Cashel, in his protest against this treatment, dwells repeatedly on the fact that he is a private gentleman, whose elder brother, and heir of his father, also lives as a private gentleman in Devonshire. The reception given by Philip to Stucley was similar to, though more royal than, that given by him in 1588 to Arthur Dudley, who professed to be a son of Queen Elizabeth and the Earl of Leicester. (Ellis Letters, 2nd Series, iii. 136.) The mere rumour and opinion of such a relationship between Stucley and Henry VIII. would go far to account for the welcome he always had at various courts, without containing in itself any evidence of the truth of the thing asserted. There is no trace that Stucley ever asserted of himself that he was of royal blood. And this is one very important point in which his character, rightly seized by the author of the following play, differs from that of the bastard Falconbridge in Shakespeare's *King John*. Both are great swaggerers; but in neither is swagger connected with cowardice; both are consummate soldiers as well as thorough braggarts. Neither ballad writer nor dramatist had an idea of claiming royal descent for his hero, unless we so understand the speech of Vernon in the play, sig. E verso :—

> 'Doubtless, if ever man was misbegot
> It is this Stucley; of a boundless mind,
> Undaunted spirit,' &c.

I have found no authentic information of his education. His name does not occur as a member of either University. The dramatist supposes him to have been a member of the Temple, and bred for the law; the ballad-writer says that he was a servant or retainer to 'a Bishop in the west;' while the Archbishop of Cashel, in his more authentic biography, says that he was a retainer to the Duke of Suffolk till his death. The Archbishop perhaps thought to make King Philip believe, as Mr Froude understood him, that Stucley was connected with the Greys, and that he took part in Wyat's rebellion; this, however, Stucley could not have done, as will appear further on. The Archbishop must have meant that he was brought up as a retainer in the family of Charles Brandon, Duke of Suffolk, who died in August, 1545.

As a retainer of the Duke of Suffolk, Stucley would naturally follow his master to the siege of Boulogne. In the year 1544 Henry VIII. raised two armies, one under the command of the Duke of Norfolk, the other under the Duke of Suffolk, the Lord Chamberlain, the Earl of Arundel, Sir John Gage, Sir Anthony Browne, and other Captains, among whom were Sir Hugh Paulet and Sir George Pollard, near connections of Stucley. On the 19th of July this second army encamped on a hill to the east of Boulogne, and after some sharp skirmishes they gained first 'the old man' (Grafton's Chronicle), and shortly after the lower town. On the 14th of July the King crossed over to Calais, and encamped to the north of Boulogne, which was so assaulted that scarcely a house was left whole. After a month's siege the town was surrendered, the soldiers and inhabitants evacuating it to the number of 4454. On the 18th of August the King entered the town, and received the keys from the Duke of Suffolk. Two days afterwards he surveyed it, and ordered the church of Notre Dame of Boulogne to be plucked down, and a mount erected in its place, to strengthen the town.

The English were not allowed to hold it in peace. Soon the Dauphin attacked it, occupied the lower town, slew many in their beds, but was soon repulsed. In February, 1545, M. de Bees, with 15,000 men, came against it, but was put to flight by the Earl of Hertford (afterwards Duke of Somerset), Lord Lisle, Lord Grey, and others. In June a French army of 20,000 men came against it, and built a fort, which continued to be a great annoyance to the English, and a fruitful cause of continual skirmishes and alarms. Another fort was to have been built on the road between Calais and Boulogne, but 7000 men were landed from England and prevented them. All this time 'many great skirmishes were daily between the Bullenois and the French Bastilion; and one day the one part lost and the other gained, and likewise the losers regained: but in one skirmish were lost xvi English gentlemen and lxxx other, although there were slain but three rascal Frenchmen. And in this skirmish was slain Sir George Pollard. And in a like journay was slain Sir Ralph Elderkave, Captain of the light horsemen; but yet a great multitude of Frenchmen at that time lay on the ground.'

So things went on, till in April, 1546, peace was concluded between England and France. But Charles Brandon was dead since August in the previous year, when Stucley seems to have attached himself to the Earl of Hertford. He had powerful friends at Boulogne. His uncle Sir Hugh Paulet was treasurer to the army, and was knighted for the capture of Bray. This Paulet in 1540 had been made Supervisor of the manors and lands of Richard Whiting, the last Abbot of Glastonbury. Paulet's brother-in-law, Richard Pollard, another uncle of Stucley's, had been one of Cromwell's three commissioners in September, 1539, to discover the hidden treasures of the Abbey; and in 1541 he was employed to search the houses of Queen Catherine Howard's kinsfolk for evidence of her irregularities.[1] Stucley's connections therefore would lead him to enter the service of Lord Hertford, afterwards the Protector Somerset, with whose principles their conduct well agreed.

Stucley, however, may not have been present all this time at Boulogne. There is an entry in State Papers, Henry VIII. Vol. I. p. 785, just after April, 1545, 'Mr Stucley is spoken unto, and gone to put himself in order to be in Berwick Castle.' At this time the French threatened to turn the tables on the English, and to become invaders instead of invaded. In August of the same year,

[1] The following account of the end of Sir Richard Pollard is given in a MS. by John Hooker, *alias* Vowel, Harleian 5827, fol. 162 verso, 'The greatest and most principal park [in Devon] was Okehampton park, which was parcel of the Earldom of Devon, and was disparked in King Henry VIII.'s time by means of Sir Richard Pollard, Kt. For he had persuaded the King that if the parks were disparked, there would grow thereby a great benefit to the commonwealth both in tilling and pasture, with sundry other commodities. Whose speeches the King crediting and believing, granted his commission unto him for disparking all the said parks belonging to the said Earldom. All which he did. In the end the King, when he was disappointed of his expectation and found no such good commodities nor benefits to ensue as was promised, and also not liking the discontentments of the gentlemen of the county which by these means were debarred of the recreations and pastimes, he was very much grieved, and called the said Sir Richard Pollard before him, and so chid and fell out with him, that he took it in such grief as he never enjoyed himself, but died.'

Stucley's brother George is recorded to have been Captain of the George of Totness, a vessel of 40 tons and 32 men, for the wing of the fleet. But after the alarm of invasion had subsided Thomas Stucley must have returned to Boulogne, where we find him, in the first year of Edward VI., holding the post of King's standard-bearer, with the fee of six shillings and eight pence a day. In those days his uncles and cousins were in full employment, either at Boulogne or on sea. In August, 1548, the Admiral (Lord Seymour) commissioned Sir Peter Carew (whose brother, Sir George, drowned in the Mary Rose, 1545, had married Stucley's aunt, Thomassine Pollard), Sir T. Dennis, and Sir R. Grenville to see that Devonshire sent out its quota of privateers to take French ships.

After the surrender of Boulogne by treaty in March, 1550, Stucley returned to England and came to Court, where he attached himself to the service of the Protector Somerset. In May, 1550, he and Sir Thomas Shelly conducted the Marquis of Maine to Scotland and back. The Marquis was one of the French hostages for the performance of the treaty, but he was permitted to take that journey, under surveillance, in order to comfort the Queen of Scots on the death of the Duke of Guise. The entries of Stucley's expenses in this employment are in the Council-book.

We next hear of him at the Court of Henry II. of France, at Amboise, from which place Sir John Mason wrote to the Council, April 22, 1551, that Mr Dudley (probably Robert, subsequently Lord Robert and Earl of Leicester) and Mr Stucley had been made very much of, and intended to return to England in seven or eight days.

As one of the retainers of the Protector Somerset, Stucley would naturally have been one of those who, according to the information of Sir Thomas Palmer, were to revolutionize the government. The plot was just such a one as suited Stucley's dare-devil disposition. The gendarmerie upon the muster day were to be assaulted by 2000 men under Sir Ralph Vane, and by a hundred horse of the Duke of Somerset's, besides his friends who were to stand by, and the idle people who, it was hoped, would take his part. [After this was done, the Protector intended to run through the city and proclaim 'Liberty, Liberty.' But the plot was exploded by the commital of Somerset and his chief accomplices to the Tower on the 17th of October, 1551. Stucley was too much compromised to remain in England. He therefore once more crossed the sea to the French court, and devoted his sword to the service of Henry II. He must have fought in the famous campaign of Henry against the Emperor Charles V. in 1552, when Metz was taken by fraud, and the country and the towns were overrun which were the scenes of the French reverses of 1870. Stucley may have been in the out-posts, where skirmishes were going on throughout the winter; or he may have held a post nearer the King, perhaps in his Scottish body-guard; wherever he was he managed to gain the friendship and confidence of Henry, as is proved by the following letter with which he armed himself when he ventured to return into England in August, 1552:

'Henry II. of France to Edward VI. of England.

'Most high and mighty prince, our most dear and beloved good son, brother, cousin, gossip, and ally, we most affectionately and heartily recommend to you our dear and good friend Thomas Stucley, an English gentleman, who during these wars has ever behaved himself well and valiantly in our service. He has given

us to understand that he had a very great mind and desire to
return into England, which we have willingly permitted and granted
him, as we are greatly pleased with his service, and the duties which
he has always well performed about our person. But since he fears
that he is in some fault for having heretofore departed out of your
Realm without asking your leave, we beseech you, most high and
mighty prince, our very dear and beloved son, brother, cousin,
gossip, and ally, for our love and at our prayer to forgive him this
fault, and to take him back to your good favour and service, assuring you that so employing him you shall find that you are well
served. Therefore praying the Creator, &c.—

    'Written at Follembray, the 3rd day of August, 1552
       your father, brother, cousin, gossip, and ally *Henry*.
                (and below) Bochatel.'

    The warmth of this letter might of itself raise a suspicion that
there was some unexpressed intention in recommending Stucley to
the English government; and it is manifest by Stucley's first act
after his return what that intention must have been. Henry, con-
fiding in the military abilities of his new friend, had talked with
him upon the best means of conquering Calais and invading
England, and had sent him to the English court in order that he
might in an underhand way second the proposed conquest. But
Stucley had not yet suffered sufficiently at his countrymen's hands
to forget that he was an Englishman. And he thought that he
could use his information for the double purpose of forewarning his
countrymen and regaining the favour of his government. He
therefore presented himself at Court on the 16th of September,
1552, and there, according to the King's entry in his journal,
'declared how that the French King, being wholly persuaded that

he could not return again into England, because he came away without leave upon the apprehension of the Duke of Somerset his old master, declared to him his intent,' that as soon as he had made peace with the Emperor he would besiege Calais, which he thought easy to be captured if he seized the sandhills and Risbank, for then he could famish the town and bombard the market-place; moreover that he would land in England in an angle about Falmouth, where the fortifications were weak and the people discontented with the new religion; and that at the same time the Duke of Guise would invade the country in the north, with the Scots.

The Duke of Northumberland, suspicious as he must have been of any friend of Somerset, could not help writing to Secretary Cecil the next day to require his immediate repair to Court, because 'such matter is come forth as God is to be praised for,' and (MS. Dom. Sep. 17) on the 19th September Cecil took Stucley's examination. The examinant said that 'having been in France and there entertained of the French King very gently, he learnt from him and others things of great importance intended against England, and that it was to give intelligence of this that he returned from France.' He then explained the plan which the King proposed to adopt in besieging Calais; and it was the very plan by which six years afterwards Calais was actually taken. But, he continued, the capture of Calais was only of use to Henry as a stepping-stone to the conquest of England, for which he laid down the following plan. 'First, the Scots were to enter Northumberland in force. Then the Duke of Guise with one army would land at Dartmouth, where they would be victualled from Brest, while Henry himself with another army would land at Hellforth, so as to take Falmouth on the weak side, by land, not by water. This done, he would by proclamation restore the old Mass, and the full liberties of the people. And even though he could do no more, yet he could hold Dartmouth and Falmouth, and fortify himself there, and take Plymouth, and hold those three places as the English held Calais; and he could victual them as easily as the English victualled Calais.'

Moreover, to keep him from suspicion, Stucley said that the King offered to send him to Venice till peace was made with the Emperor, when he should be recalled, and so advanced and married as to allure others in the west country to the French King's service. And when this peace was made, Henry hoped that the Emperor would consent to the invasion of England, to punish it for its neutrality, and to force it to confess their common faith. And so the troops that had been employed against the Imperialists would be ready for the fresh enterprise against the English.

When Cecil asked how he was introduced to the French King, Stucley replied that it was through the Constable Montmorency, who first broached the subject, and then, finding that Stucley had some ideas about it, took him to the King. This Montmorency, it is to be remembered, was the General to whose talents all the successes in the campaign of Alsace and Lorraine had been due, and by whose trickery Metz was taken. Stucley, as we shall find was afterwards the case, seems here also to have first gained the friendship of the General by his military talents, and then, through him, the friendship of the King.

The probabilities of this intelligence struck Cecil so forcibly, and he was on other grounds so doubtful of the intentions of Henry, that he meditated sending Stucley back to France to 'continue his practices there for more intelligence.' But a more flashy idea seems to have sparkled in the less statesmanlike Machiavellianism of Northumberland; by which not only the intelligence might be used, but also the treasury spared the great expense of the reward promised to Stucley, which was the payment of all his debts. It was to tell the French King what he had been accused of and to ask him whether it was true. The reply might be true or false, but at least it would give Northumberland time to carry out his own schemes at home. Hence on the 21st of September a letter was sent to Pickering, the ambassador in France, 'only,' as the young King wrote, 'to try Stucley's truth,' and to ask whether he had told any of this matter to the ambassador. 'Ye shall understand,' wrote Cecil in the name of the Council, 'that Thomas Stucley returned hither about the latter end of August, and, upon some demand made, hath uttered matters of great importance, alleging that he disclosed some part of them to you, and enquiring whether you have ever advertized us of them.' Then followed a general outline of the information. 'This he saith he had of the French King himself, with whom he entered into such credit, as we here be somewhat amazed how to interpret the tales, and how to judge of the man. For some trial of him, we wish to know for certain whether he has ever uttered the like matter to you, as he says he has. You never wrote about it to us, though you wrote to the Duke of Northumberland for Stucleys return to his country with his kings favour. Wherefore, for our better judgment of the man and his strange tales, we pray you to certify us what intelligence he hath at any time given you of this manner of matters, and of others also; and the same to send in cipher to us, as ye shall think needful.' (Cotton MS. Galba. B. 12.)

On the 7th of October the Council received Pickering's answer. Stucley had never said a word to him on these matters; and moreover he was certainly advertized and believed, that Stucley never heard the French King speak such a word, and never was in credit with him or with the Constable, excepting once, when he was interpreter between Montmorency and some English prisoners. Hereupon Stucley was committed to the Tower, and the French ambassador was told how he was imprisoned for slandering the French King, as other runagates do daily. This latter clause was added, says the royal journalist, ' to make him suspect the English runagates that be there.' A letter to the same effect was sent to Pickering, who on the 11th of October went to Rheims to see Henry, and to declare to him what Stucley had revealed, and how he was imprisoned for it. Henry thereupon protested his own good meaning in the amity, railed at Stucley's ingratitude, lewdness, and ill-demeanour, and thanked the English government for its gentle proceeding in uttering the matter, and refusing to be led with false bruits and tales. (Edward VI. Journal.)

About this time the Duke of Northumberland wrote to tell Cecil how the French ambassador had shown his satisfaction. He sent his secretary to speak privately to the Duke, and to tell him that ' never thing declared hearty love nor assured friendship more than the princely handling of Stucley's false reports, and that this kind of princely dealing should never be forgotten in the King his master's heart. Also he desired nothing so much as that the amity should be preserved, and that the punishment of such a false man might without delay be prosecuted. And this,' adds the Duke, ' was uttered with such plenty of good words as the like I have not heard.' (MSS. Foreign, Oct. 1552, No. 38.)

Though Stucley's information was probably genuine, he was only sent to the Tower for his pains. It may however be, that the plan for the assault on Calais and the invasion of England was Stucley's own, the fruit of his unquestionable military genius; which, with his impotence of reserve, he had communicated to Montmorency and the King; then, to salve the wound he had given to his patriotism, he was obliged to reveal it to the English Government as if it was the deliberate intention of the French, instead of a mere vague project which he had put into their heads. In the Tower he seems to have laid for a few months, not however without bringing his hard case before the Council; for in January, 1553, Northumberland wrote to the Secretaries of the Council, Petre and Cecil, that among other weighty affairs they should take order for Stucley's *dépêche*. By this time probably the Duke had begun to suspect that there was some truth in the information; Cecil thought so; and his advice must have been corroborated by the reply of Chamberlin, the ambassador at the Emperor's court at Brussels, who, when told that the jealousies raised by the information were calmed by the assurance of Pickering that it was only falsehood and imposture, drily answered that he thanked God that all things were so well as their Lordships reported.

But Northumberland had other matters than Stucley to think of. By the beginning of the year it was manifest to him that the days of Edward VI. were numbered, and he was thinking how he could set aside the will of Henry VIII., and place on the head of his daughter-in-law, the Lady Jane Grey, the crown that was to go to the Lady Mary. During these intrigues Stucley probably remained in prison, or if he was released, as he could not venture to return to France, he offered his sword to the Imperialists. Whether he was at the siege of Terouenne in June, or at the capture of Hesdin, the first exploit of Emmanuel Philibert, Duke of Savoy, in July, is doubtful. It is certain, however, that Mary on her accession in July wrote to that prince in his favour, and that the English soldier must, before the cessation of the campaign in October, when the hostile armies went into winter quarters, have won golden opinions from him. Early in December Stucley was at the Emperor's court at Brussels, apparently in the suit of Drury, the English envoy. For after Drury had written to Lord William Howard at Calais an account of the taking of Vercelli by the French, Stucley supplemented the letter by sending immediate intelligence of fresh news which somewhat modified the gravity of the first. While he was writing, Howard said he received another letter from Mr Stucley at Brussels, saying that fresh news had come of the taking of Vercelli by the Imperialists, who however had not recovered the booty. Stucley added that the loss was deeply lamented in the Court, especially by the Emperor and the Queen of Hungary. (MSS. Foreign, Dec. 4, 1553.) Two months afterwards we find Stucley as Captain of a band, at St Omers, from which place he wrote to Queen Mary, Feb. 3, 1554 (MSS. Foreign), 'May it please your gracious goodness to be advertised, that whereas I addressed my last letters unto your highness, signifying the same [in] what state of favour and service I stood with the Emperor's Majesty by the means of your good cousin the Duke of Savoy, " and offering to employ myself and my whole charge in any service you might command, so now I do most humbly submit myself unto your clemency and beseech you so to employ me at any time. And as it hath pleased your Majesty to commend me in such sort, as both mine entertainment, and the great courtesy I find in these parts proceedeth through your most gracious goodness," so now, having obtained the copy of an important letter from the French King to his ambassador in England, I send it by a gentleman of my band, whom I beseech you to tender being a gentleman of such honesty, wit, and experience, as ought to be commended to your Majesty. I beseech you to vouchsafe me with answer by the bearer at your highness' pleasure.'

The letter of the King of France expresses his displeasure at the engagement of Philip with Queen Mary, as the English will be sure to declare war against France in the spring: but as he hears that the Governor of Cornwall intends to oppose Philip's landing, he directs his ambassador to give all encouragement to the project, and to inform him what enterprise is on hand, that he may second it with another attempt on his own account. He also wants an account of the ships which he hears the Queen is preparing to escort the King of Spain, and of the time of their sailing, to give the French an opportunity of surprising him by sea; he also orders him to be diligent in his attendance at Court, and to send over his news as expeditiously as possible. This was about the time of Wyat's rebellion in England; and doubtless the rumour of that rising was the reason why Stucley was so urgent with the Queen to employ him and his band in England. As he was now, and had been for months, in the service of the Emperor, it is clear that he had no part—as Mr Froude was led to suppose by the authorities whom he followed—in the treason of the Duke of Suffolk and the disturbances in which the Carews and others of Stucley's cousins were implicated with Wyat. All danger had however passed by, and Stucley's presence was not required in England. He remained therefore, during the campaign of 1552, with the Duke of Savoy, who with a very inferior army held in check the gigantic forces of Henry II.

and prevented them from doing proportionate damage, raised the siege of Renti and laid waste Picardy with fire and sword, in revenge for similar outrages of the French in Artois. By October Stucley was again in winter quarters, and, as twice before, employed his leisure in writing to the Queen; this time 'from the Emperor's camp beside Hesdin, the 9th of October':

'Whereas in two several letters addressed by me unto your grace, I advertised you of my service and advancement in this foreign country, and also acknowledged the infinite goodness I had received of your habitual clemency; so now, encouraged with the good hope of your *continue* of favour towards me, I make bold to write, beseeching your grace, that like as toforetime you remembered your poor subject and servant in his most distress and calamities, so now you would tender my poor suit. Whereas the Duke of Savoy, my very good Lord, understanding his repair towards your majesty to be very shortly, and having of long time used my poor service in all turns wherein he was pleased to employ me, whereby I am manifoldly increased with his favour and inestimable good opinion, hath commanded me to prepare for mine attendance upon his highness with expedite speed. Now he knoweth not my poor and miserable stay there; nevertheless I offered myself as one that would be ready to accomplish his commandment. So it is that the case stands *indirect* with me, being endangered to divers in credit of such great sums as my very small power shall never attain to discharge or satisfy, unless you of your mere mercy provide for me in that behalf. For whereas in the service of your grace's noble father Henry VIII., and your brother Edward VI., I consumed that for which I am in credit, and not in any private use or charge upon myself, your brother the late king had accorded to me, for one service

which I achieved at my departure out of France, to give me my
whole debts. Which service, as it appeared, after redounded to my
utter undoing, if your Majesty had not of your mere bountifulness
considered the cruel entreatment which the late Duke of Northumberland had used towards me. This was the only ground of the
enemy's displeasure and indignation, and is like to be cause of my
perdition, if I do fall into his hands. Partly for this cause, partly
because I must look forward to ceasing my service here (where
I am before an enemy, of whom if I be taken, I despair utterly
of grace or liberty), and to returning to my native country,
where I intend to lead my life, I am constrained to have recourse
unto you, beseeching you to relent my miserable condition, to
tender mine earnest request, and to take order that I may attend
on the Duke in England, exempted from all danger and arrest
by reason of my debts. And that the Duke's good opinion of
me may be increased, and your Majesty's letters of commendation may be seen to have taken just place in the furthering of
me to so great a prince, if I may verify the praise you have
bestowed on me as well in my native country as I have been
agreeable to him in the Emperor's service.' (MSS. Foreign,
Oct. 7, 1554.)

The result of this letter was that on the 23rd of October a
Patent was issued giving security and freedom from arrest for the
term of six months, from November 1 to April 30, to Thomas
Stucley gentleman, son of Sir Hugh Stucley knight of Devonshire
(Patent Roll, 1 and 2 Phil. and Mary, Pt. 2). No use was made
of this privilege for two months, probably through the delays of the
Duke. At length his train reached Calais, on the way to England,
and Stucley wrote from that place, 'this Friday, at night, the 20th

of *Dessembar*, 1554,' to Sir Thomas Cheney, Lord Warden of the Cinque Ports, at Dover:

'The Duke of Savoy, arriving here at 3 of the clock at afternoon, doth intend, God willing, to come over into England, so soon as the wind doth serve him. I would not fail to give your lordship *knowlytte* that he hath at the least fifty gentlemen of *repetasyon* with him, as I believe his whole train will be at the least two hundred *hores* [horse]. He hath divers noblemen with him. He hath commanded me to attend upon him, so that if you have any *sarvis* to command me you shall find me ready.'[1]

We may conclude, then, that Stucley spent the last days of 1554 and the first days of 1555 at Mary's court, in attendance on the Duke of Savoy. From this time till the death of Mary we have but few distinct notices of Stucley; but in these few years we must place his first buccaneering experiments, and his marriage. A sketch, or rather caricature of his life, presented in 1570 to the Court of Spain by an envious ecclesiastic, gives us to understand that he served the Duke of Suffolk, the father of Lady Jane Grey, and implies that he took part in his treason. But, as we have seen, he was then abroad, serving under the Prince of Piedmont. The story goes on to say that after Suffolk's death Stucley somehow got a ship, and turned pirate, and was captured in Ireland, and sent over as prisoner to England, and confined for some time in the Tower; and that, having got his freedom, he mended his ruined fortunes by marrying the heiress of Alderman Curtis. His only incarceration in the Tower of which I have seen any authentic record is that

---

[1] MSS. Foreign. Stow tells us (Chronicle, p. 626) that on the 27th of December the Duke with other Lords were received at Gravesend by the Lord Privy Seal and other, and so conveyed along the river of Thames under London Bridge to Westminster.

which he suffered for his information to Northumberland of the designs of Henry II. against Calais and England. But it is highly probable that between 1555 and 1558 he did become a buccaneer, and did incur suspicion of piracy, if not disgrace. On the other hand, I have failed to find the faintest evidence of his having joined the Carews and Killegrews in their conspiracies against Mary. It is more likely that he served under the person who was most active in putting down the attempts of the Western gentlemen; this was his uncle, Sir Hugh Paulet, who had married a sister of his mother's, and who evidently always took the liveliest interest in his career. If therefore he did become a buccaneer, he was probably one of those who prematurely robbed French vessels before declaration of war in 1556. (MS. Domestic, Mary, June 13, 1556.) He was not one of those who took advantage of the proclamation of July 8, 1557, licensing all English subjects to fit out ships to molest the French and Scots, the public enemies, because at that time he was marching with the English contingent under Lord Pembroke and Lord Robert Dudley, which had some small share in the Duke of Savoy's splendid victory at St Quentin over the army of Henry II.[1] But he was successful enough at sea also to have complaints made against him, probably for flying at all he saw, and making little distinction between Frenchman or Fleming, Scot or Spaniard. But whatever the complaints were, the Lord Admiral reported on the 14th of July, 1558, that he did not 'find matter sufficient to charge Stucley withal' (MS. Domestic, Aug. 27, 1558).

During the latter part of the year 1558 he was em-

[1] (MSS. Dom. Addenda, Sept. 3, 1574. Edward Woodshaw to Burghley says Stucley knows him 'because I served here when he was in credit with the Emperor Charles, and at the camp of St Quentin, and did good service to Lords Leicester, Bedford, Rutland, Pembroke, &c.')

ployed to attend upon a distinguished visitor to England, some
Spanish Admiral who on his departure from 'Dartamua' (Dartmouth) on the 7th of November wrote to the Queen on his behalf.
In return for the attendance and civility Stucley had shown him on
his journey, he humbly kisses the Queen's hands for what she has
done to Stucley in the case of his nephew. 'I have since heard,'
adds the Admiral, 'that there remain five brothers, for whose education the rents of his father are necessary; I humbly beseech your
Majesty, if it can be done without injustice, that you would order
that the captain should be assisted with these during the usual
time, that he may educate them conformably with their quality, and
that he may better serve your Majesty, for, to my mind, he is of
sufficient parts to deserve employment, and when occasion offers if
your Majesty lays your commands on him, I am certain that he will
know how to act in a way to deserve your Majesty's favour.' (MSS.
Foreign.)

This document shows Stucley as the head of a family, educating
his great-nephew Thomas Prideaux, and his younger brothers.
Concerning this nephew a warrant is extant from Queen Mary to
Sir Francis Englefield, Master of the Wards (MS. Domestic, Mary,
Vol. 13, No. 68), which after reciting that 'our right well-beloved
cousin the Marquess of Saria hath made earnest suit unto us that it
might like us to grant unto this bearer, our servant Thomas Stucley,
Esq., freely the wardship and marriage of the son and heir of
Sergeant Prideaux, lately deceased,' proceeds to direct Sir Francis
Englefield to see it done. A comparison of these two documents
would enable those whom it concerns to make out the illegible
signature of the Spanish letter dated from Dartmouth. Sergeant
Prideaux had married Stucley's niece Mary, daughter of his eldest

brother Lewis, and widow of Tristram Larder; so that Thomas Prideaux was his grand-nephew.

Stucley was unmarried in 1552, when he returned from France, where Henry II. proposed to match him with some great heiress; but he found in London what he had missed in France. Westcote indeed (View of Devonshire, edited by Dr Oliver, p. 271) implies that he more than once made such a marriage; 'by rich matches he got so good an estate as might have qualified a moderate mind to have lived bountifully and in great esteem, equal to the chief of his house.' But at this time he must have been married to Anne, the grand-daughter and heiress of Alderman Sir Thomas Curtis; this event, in the eyes of the authors of the following drama and ballad, was the beginning of his public life; but it is very evident that he was an experienced captain before he married. The Alderman died about a year after Queen Mary, on the 27th of November, 1559, and one of the correspondents of Challoner, the ambassador in Spain, writes to him, dating his letter on the 25th of November, 1559 (MSS. Foreign): 'The Alderman Curtes is dead, and by this time is busy Stucley in the midst of his coffers, having married his daughter or niece.'[1] Shortly afterwards, on the 6th of January, 1560, his own father, Sir Hugh Stucley, died also.

A libelous account of Stucley, drawn up by an unknown hand,

---

[1] The *Inquisitio post mortem* does not tell us of the wealth of the Alderman's coffers; only of his eight messuages, garden, and orchard in Lime Street, Mark Lane, Fenchurch Street, and Lombard Street, of the yearly value of £155 13s. 4d. He died, it says, on the 27th of November, 1559; Anne Stucley, now the wife of Thomas Stucley, is his nearest relation, being daughter and heir of Thomas Curtis, son and heir of the said Sir Thomas Curtis, Kt, and she is of the age of twenty-one years and over. (MS. P. M. 2 Eliz. Pt. 1, No. 106.) The old man died without a will. Sir Thomas Curtis was Lord Mayor from Nov. 1557 to Nov. 1558.

but corrected throughout by Lord Burghley in the year 1583, may be found in a paper of that date in the Record Office (MSS. Domestic, Eliz. Vol. 164, No. 85). It briefly relates his life up to this time, and says that he was known to have 'deceived the French King, the Connestable and the old Duke of Guise, and flying thence for fear of punishment, used the same sleights and falsehoods towards the Emperor Charles, commonly pretending himself to be a man of value and livelihood, when in truth he never had in his own right one foot of land, but by borrowing in every place and paying nowhere; and at length getting a simple but rich merchant's daughter of London to his wife, wasted all in a few months.' Burghley was able to give a truer account than this, but as he desired to exhibit his dead follower as 'a famose man for lewdness,' he rather allowed his scribe to follow the account furnished by one Digby, a discarded servant of Stucley's, as will be shown in the proper place.

The death of Queen Mary does not seem to have altered Stucley's position. The first knowledge we have of him under Queen Elizabeth is in May, 1560, when musters were being taken through England in view of wars with Scotland and France. He seems to have been a kind of agent for Sir Thomas Parry, the Queen's Treasurer and Master of the Wards, with Sir Henry Neville, the Sheriff of Berkshire, who officially superintended the levies in Berkshire. Neville had difficulties in arranging for the command of the several companies, and he had named two captains, Ward and Barker, who happened to be retainers of the Earl of Arundel. The Earl refused to allow them to act, because he intended to employ them himself. And Neville was placed in great difficulties by his refusal. The following letter of Stucley to Sir Thomas Parry relates chiefly to this difficulty:

'I have *sey* the letter that your honour sent to Sir Harry Nevell with the copy of my Lord of Arundels, whereby I perceive that Mr Ward and Mr Barbar may not be appointed captains in these parts. I dare assure your honour that the want of them will be great, for there is none others meet to be appointed to that charge in all these parts; for that the men which Mr Lieutenant hath appointed for them dwelleth round about them, and to my judgment both my Lord of Arundel and my Lord Lumley should have had better service of 200 men than of 2 men. Mr Lieutenant commendeth wholly to your honours discretion, as one that presently knoweth not to whom to commit the charge of the *sodgers*.

'This present day Mr Lieutenant hath mustered at Windsor without the help of any justice or gentleman of estimation other than the mayor. I ensure your honour methinketh it is a thing much out of order that they should not be as ready to *sarve* the Queen's Majesty as they are to seek their own gain. I ensure your honour Mr Lieutenant's pains (and also his charges) is like to be great if he have no better help hereafter than he hath had this day in the beginning.

'This *berar* came whilst the *sodgers war* marching in order, who can declare unto your honour what order they were in. The people that we have mustered this day have been very *confyrmabell;* I pray God we may find the rest in like sort to the end . . . .

'To-morrow with God's grace we shall muster all the seven hundreds at Red Bridge.

'I pray your honour remember my suit touching Mr Brent's daughter.' The letter is dated Windsor, May 20, 1560.

As Parry was Master of the Wards, probably Stucley's suit for

Mr Brent's daughter was that he might have her 'marriage'—the sale of heiresses was a common source of revenue to courtiers in those days. It is however possible that Anne Curtis was dead, and that Stucley was already ready to repair his fortunes with another marriage. On the 25th of May Stucley wrote again to Parry to tell him of the progress of matters. As doubts were afterwards thrown upon his profession of being a Catholic, it is as well to note that he places the sign of the cross at the top of his letters, as was the Catholic usage of the time. 'Mr Neville the 23rd of this present mustered at Reading, where there was to the number of 1300 and above; the 24th of the same he mustered at Newbury, where there was 1800 and above; and this present day we mean to be at Abingdon, and to muster there; from whence I do determine with as much speed as I may to return to your honour with the true certificates of the note of such armours and weapons as shall furnish this country. I assure your honour that you shall have such a number of choice men as never no Lieutenant had heretofore out of this country. Mr Neville hath been very well accompanied with gentlemen both at Reading and Newbury. .˙. . I pray your honour, if any man sue unto you for Mr Brent's daughter, that it may please you to remember my former suit.' The letter is dated from Newbury. Neville does not describe the men or their numbers so glowingly as Stucley. At Reading, he says, 'we saw before us 1000 good men beside other rascal, no want but of armour.' At Newbury 'above 1500 men, but nothing so good of able persons as the other, full of people, but rascal, and very few armour.' On the 28th the musters were over, and Neville sent Stucley back to Parry. 'I need not trouble you more in writing, for that Mr Stucley this bearer can better report all things by word of mouth,' who I daresay is not a little glad of his return, for I think he has never better toiled in so short a time in his life, and I assure you took great pains ; I think he will not fetch up his sleep he hath lost this sen'night.'

Stucley was sent back to Neville, who wrote again to Parry on the 27th of June—'I have returned Mr Stucley again to you with our certificate;' the armour, he continues, is yet unbought; but 'I have sent my man with Mr Stucley with one hundred pounds to bestow and do the best they can ;' after it is bought it will be a fortnight before it gets to Abingdon, for it will be seven days coming to Reading by barge. All other things as beacons and the like are ready, and most parts of the shire have been hardly stretched. 'For the conduct money you write of, I may soon keep it safe, for it is but in a few lines of paper my Lord Treasurer wrote to me to pay it out of my nown purse, who may evil spare it. Further, sir, you shall not need to trouble Mr Stucley till I send for him, for assure you I will make as much haste as possibly I can. For you would not so fain have the musters past as I would, for then I would think to have one quiet day to go a wooing in.' Stucley reappears on the 2nd of July, when he had to communicate to Neville that Parry was not altogether satisfied with the certificate, and then he disappears from this scene in his career.

We next hear of him in April, 1561, when he seems to have been appointed to a captaincy in Berwick (MSS. Foreign, April 16). In those days the garrison of Berwick was the only nucleus of a standing army of professional soldiers for England ; the other forces were only militia, levied and mustered for special purposes on special occasions : but the Berwick troops were soldiers and nothing else. Perhaps it was in Berwick that Stucley gained his reputation as the model officer and the soldier's friend. But wherever he served, his 'royalty to men at arms' was a continual drain upon his riches; at this time however he had still enough left to entertain a distinguished Irishman, who late this year visited Elizabeth's court, where with his train of Kerns and Gallowglasses, clothed in linen kilts dyed with saffron or a readier substitute, he made the same impression as an Abyssinian embassy would make now. Shane O'Neill, whose history is the history of Ireland for the few years of his supremacy, left that island at the end of November, 1561, and remained at Elizabeth's court till May, 1562. He returned to Ireland on the 26th of that month. While he was at Court, he wrote to Elizabeth in 1565 (MSS. Ireland, June 18, 1565), 'Many of the nobles, magnates, and gentlemen of that kingdom treated me kindly and ingenuously, and namely one of the gentlemen of your realm, Master Thomas Stucley, entertained me with his whole heart, and with all the favour he could. But I perceived that his whole intention, and the benevolence he showed me, tended to this;—to show me the magnificence and the honour of your majesty and your realm.'

While Shane was in England, the King of Sweden's ambassador was likewise at Court to arrange a marriage between Elizabeth and his master. Lord Robert Dudley, who aspired to the Queen's hand, naturally intrigued against the match. Keyle, an Englishman who acted in the King's interests, gives us information about some slight share which Stucley took in this business. 'The king's cause,' he writes, July 27 (MSS. Foreign), 'was never so favoured by the Queen and Council, the nobility and commons, as at this time. . . . Lord Robert at my coming made very great

search for me to some of his friends, that he might speak with me
ere I dealt with the Queen and Council. But when he saw he
might not, he wrought marvellously to have had me in prison.
And seeing that would not prevail, he made his old friends Stucley
and Allen his means to trouble me, thinking thereby to have had
me in prison. But he has troubled himself in vain, wherefore he
is very angry, and now his cutters look as though they would do
some hurt, and I have been warned to take heed. . . . Lord Robert
had plain answer from the Queen's mouth in the chamber of presence (all the nobility being there) that she would never marry
him, nor none so mean as he, with a great rage, and great checks
and taunts to such as travailed for him, seeing they went about to
dishonour her; whereupon he made means to have leave to go over
the seas, which was easily consented unto. But he is not gone, nor
means to go, unless he hear of the king's coming.' In another
letter of the same date he says that Mr Allen and Mr Stucley, 'confederates of the bear,' [Lord Robert, whose cognizance was the Bear
and ragged staff] 'have used a piece of villany against him under
colour of friendship that it caused him to remember another quarrel
which his correspondent had told him of.' And by another paper
of August 6 we find that Stucley had moved Keyle to serve Lord
Robert, and when Keyle refused, then had requested him to be
godfather, with Lord Paget, to a child of his. Keyle agreed to
this, because, as he said, he wanted to have a Roland against an
Oliver; meaning, that he had a matter before the Lord Keeper
wherein Stucley and Mr Secretary were against him, so he thought
to make the Lord Robert his friend, that he might have a stay
against them. Another paper of the same date exhibits the pro-
fuse hospitality of Stucley's house, where Keyle often dined with

Allen and the Swedish ambassador. But it asserts also that while Keyle was absent in Sweden Stucley obtained some condemnation of him, so that he might not be able to return. And Stucley confessed that he did this because he durst do none other for Lord Robert's displeasure, and with the intention of cutting Keyle off from working what he came for, only to have the more credit.

It appears from this that Stucley was still a married man, and had a child born to him in 1562. The next year was that of his famous Florida project. This has always been considered to have been a serious design of peopling Florida; but the official papers extant regarding it exhibit it in a somewhat different light.

In 1563 Elizabeth seems to have made her first venture in the trade which subsequently proved so profitable to her, that of buccaneering. Tradition says that Stucley, having run through his money, was obliged to turn to some project to cure the weakness of his purse; and that the design of peopling Florida was chosen, because 'lusty Stucley' was one 'whose spirit was of so high a strain that it vilified subjection (though in the highest and chiefest degree) as contemptible, aiming (as high as the moon) at not less than sovereignty.' So he determined to found a colony where he could 'play rex; having the proverb often in his discourse "I had rather be king of a molehill than subject to a mountain."' (Westcote, p. 271. See also Fuller's Worthies, sub nom.)

In April, 1563, Sir Hugh Paulet, then employed at Havre which the English had seized, took occasion in a letter to Lord Robert Dudley to ask him 'to continue your friendship towards my nephew Thomas Stucley, who doth acknowledge himself to be greatly bounden unto you.' At this time Stucley was preparing his squadron. On the 14th of May Henry Cobham wrote to Challoner that his cousin Bernadine Young was going to Terra Florida with Stucley, who had furnished five ships and a pinnace (MS. Foreign). On the 10th of May he was at Havre, and received from Vaughan, one of the officers there, 'by command of the master of the ordnance, 2000 weight of corn-powder, and 100 curriers; and besides artillery to the value of £120 towards the furniture of his journey.' This was doubtless part of the Queen's investment in the venture, although she did not furnish the powder out of her own stores, but made one Bromefield go into debt for it with one Nicholas Williamson, a Dutchman (Ib. May 10 and June 5, 1563). On the morning of July 2 Lord Warwick informs Lord Robert Dudley and Cecil that Captains Lyggins and Stucley had arrived at Havre, and that the rest of their company were expected that night.

There is no record left of the warrant given to Stucley himself; but the following paper, sent by Cecil in the Queen's name to the Earl of Sussex, Lord Deputy of Ireland, June 30, 1563, shows plainly enough that the pretence of Florida was a mere mask to hide the real intention of privateering (Haynes, State Papers, p. 401): 'Where our servant Thomas Stucley, associated with sundry of our subjects, hath prepared a number of good ships well armed and manned to pass to discover certain lands in the west towards Terra Florida, and by our license hath taken the same voyage. Because it may so happen that for lack of favourable winds he may be diverted from his direct voyage, and be constrained to come to some ports or coasts of that our realm of Ireland; which if he shall, he hath agreed to do any service there it shall be thought agreeable by you for our purpose. We do will and require you, that if he shall happen to come to any part of that coast, that ye cause him and his company to be well used, and do direct him to do any exploit by land or sea with his company that you shall find and think meet to be done for our service. And if he shall also bring or send in to any port there any manner of French ships which he shall arrest to our use, we would that the same might be received, and the goods and ladings therein put in inventory, and laid up in safety, until by the further proceedings of the French we shall perceive what is meet therein for us to do.'

This warrant makes it probable that Florida was for countenance, to hide the reality of authorized buccaneering from the French, with whom Elizabeth was not at open war. We need not be surprised, then, at the announcement made by Cureton in Bilboa to Challoner in Madrid, in December (MSS. Foreign, Dec. 15, 1563), that the whole country was crying out upon the English ships, which within three months had taken a French ship on his way to Bilboa, laden with linen cloth, most of the goods Spanish, and worth 12,000 ducats; and another French ship of war worth 7000 ducats, also with Spanish goods; or that Stucley had cut out of a port of Galicia two French ships laden with Spanish goods worth 30,000 ducats. Another English resident in Spain, Oliver Leeson, wrote to Challoner from Seville with news more than a year old, in August, 1564 (MSS. Foreign, Aug. 24, 1564): 'They say the Queen has delivered certain of her ships to Mr Stucley, and he is bound to Florida with four or five ships; and to Hawkins and Cobham others, who are bound for Guinea and the Portugal Indies.' The notice is valuable, as showing the opinion that Stucley, Hawkins, and Cobham were all fitted out by the Queen for similar purposes, and with similar pretences. It is confessed that Hawkins and Cobham were meant to be buccaneers, and it is absurd to deny the like of Stucley. Perhaps this adds zest to the tale told by Fuller and Westcote: 'It was a common report, spoken by divers worthy credit, that Queen Elizabeth in the height of his intended project, demanded him pleasantly whether he would remember her when he settled in his kingdom. "Yes," saith he, "and write unto you also." "And what style wilt thou use?" "To my loving sister, as one prince writes unto another."'

If he was meant to be a pirate, he cannot be said to have failed in his mission. In December, 1564, Challoner writes from Madrid to Cecil (MSS. Foreign, Dec. 24, 1564): 'Stucley's piracies are much railed at here on all parts. I hang down my head with shame enough. Alas, though it cost the Queen roundly, let him for honours sake be fetched in. These pardons to such folks as be hostes humani generis I like not.' Challoner saw the difficulty of dealing with Stucley. The Queen had ventured on his success, and would not easily consent to forego her profits. However, by Michaelmas, 1564, she had made the sacrifice, and had given letters to Sir Peter Carew, himself one of Stucley's numerous cousins, to fit out two vessels to apprehend pirates in the Irish seas. How he succeeded will be seen from his own letter to the Council, dated April 17, 1565 (MSS. Domestic). After reciting the letters just named, he proceeds—'I thought it best for her Majesty's profit that such mariners and others as were to be employed in that service should serve without wages, for the spoil only to their own uses, her highness being charged with the victuals;' which arrangement was sanctioned by the Council, with further warrant that the 'Lord Admiral was well consenting that all his interest either in the pirates' vessels or goods should remain with the takers.' On this Carew commissioned the two vessels, and another, subsequently warranted, which first scoured the west coast of England without finding anything meet for their purpose, and then sailed over to Ireland, 'where they found a hulk of Stucley's in Cork Haven, which they brought away, himself being before their arrival there on the shore with the Lord Barrymore, having left certain of his men in the hulk to guard her, who being shot into, rowed unto the shore in their long boat.' The letter then describes how from Cork they went to Beere Haven, where they found that Haydon,—who was married to a sister of the O'Sullivan Beere,— Lysyngham, and Corbet, with other pirates, had fortified themselves in a castle belonging to Haydon's brother-in-law, and had some 500 Gallowglasses and Kernes, besides about 160 of their own soldiers. The pirates were attacked, and Lysyngham, it was reported, was shot, but the attacking ships were disabled and had to haul off. Carew goes on to say that he had a letter from the Admiralty ordering him to deliver the hulk to John Peterson, a Fleming; against this order he protested, first, because the mariners served for the spoil without wages, and this was their only booty, and if this was given up, they would presently make exclamation for the Queen's wages, which would amount to twice the value of the hulk, 'being three ships and 246 persons, some of whom had served for five, the rest for six months.' And, secondly, because 'it is to be duly proved that in the Townhall of Kinsale the Fleming affirmed before the Mayor that he had compounded frankly and freely with Stucley, without any compulsion or for fear.'

It is clear from the following letter written from Dublin, April 22, 1565, to Cecil, that Stucley had already landed to surrender himself to answer any charges against him, before Carew's ships had found his hulk in Cork (MSS. Ireland, April 22, 1565):

'The IX.th of March last I came into Waterford in the company of the Lord Viscount Barrymore unto the Lord Justice of the Realm, who hath commanded me to attend upon his L. until he know the Queens Mtys pleasure what I shall do; which I have and will most humbly obey. His L. telleth me that he hath written unto the Queens Mty how I came unto him, and to know her highness pleasure. I shall most humbly desire your honour of your accustomed goodness towards me, as this is not the first good turn I have sought and have received at your hands, so shall it not be the last, as I have occasion to use your honourable goodness. Even so I pray your honour to think that if ever it shall please God to send me habilitie I will never be unthankful to do you service in anything I can or may to my lives end. I insure your honour I have little left at this present but mine honesty, which I shall most humbly desire you to think well of; not doubting but when I shall by your good means be heard I shall be better judged of than I am at this present. Fearing to trouble your honour with too large a discourse by writing, I have sent unto my cousin Sir John Pollard [*a hole in the paper*]. easure to enform you of my doings, and also how my ship and goods was taken away, being before delivered to the Queens Mtys use for the trial of my doings. I pray Almighty God to preserve you, with my good Lady your wife, and all yours.'

After this he must have gone directly into England to answer the matters laid to his charge. These were not very great, if we may trust a paper of May 27, 1565 (MSS. Foreign): 'Specification of robberies committed at sea on Spanish subjects by Englishmen sailing from English ports with the patronage, permission, and authority of

the Queen, without finding any security.' On this list, No. 4 is
'a ship called the Trinity, Captain Martin de Goyas, from Zeeland to
Biscay, fell in with two English ships of war, commanded, one
by James Spencer, the other by a man of the Stucley family, about
June, 1563, and was robbed of linen cloths and other wares to the
value of 3000 pounds Flemish.' No. 37, 'a ship called the Fortune, Captain John Stevens of Middleburgh, from Nantes to Antwerp, fell in with a ship said to be Captain Thomas Stucley's, in
Feb. 1564, about Issant, and was taken to Ilfracombe, and there
robbed of plums to the value of 200 pounds Flemish, and the ship
itself was split and lost in the entrance of Ilfracombe harbour.'
Others of these robberies were committed by John Pollard, Anthony
Courtenay, and others unknown, some of whom carried their prizes
into Waterford. These probably belonged to Stucley's squadron.
The capture of Stucley was only a political act. Whatever damage
he had done to the French, he had done in accordance with his
instructions. But as the French were now to be reconciled, it was
necessary to sacrifice somebody to their exigencies. Accordingly
Cecil wrote to Smith, the English ambassador then at Bordeaux,
that ' Stucley was taken in Ireland, and Thomas Cobham in London,
he at the suit of the Spanish ambassador, Stucley by the Queen's
ships which were sent to scour the seas; and so, to any man's
knowledge, there was no English pirate left upon the sea' (MS.
Foreign, May 2, 1565).

Stucley, therefore, landed in Ireland, and went over to England
to answer whatever accusations there might be against him. He
must have been soon acquitted; for on the 23rd of June the Lord
Justice ' did not understand that he had committed any piracy upon
the coasts of Ireland or elsewhere,' and therefore prayed for his dis-

charge. Cecil, however, in 1583 represents this portion of his life, after his marriage, as follows; after wasting his property 'upon pretence of navigation to discover lands he became a pirate ; and so being in danger of punishment fled into Ireland.' Whether on his arrival in England he had to pass through the same burlesque ordeal as Cobham, I have not found. It is, however, worth while to show the kind of *Burleria* (as Burghley's strokes of the theatre were afterwards called) which Stucley possibly had to endure, for the satisfaction of the French ambassador, by what Cobham had to endure for that of the Spaniard. De Silva writes to Philip from London, July 16, 1565 (Froude's Simancas Transcripts, vol. B, p. 358), that 'Thomas Cobham was taken from prison and arraigned according to the process of the country; and being asked whether he would be judged by the laws of the realm, answered No; and persisting therein, was condemned to be returned to the Tower, to be stripped naked, his head shaved, the soles of his feet striped, and his arms and legs stretched, and so be laid with his shoulders on a sharp stone, and with a piece of artillery on his stomach, more than he could bear, but not enough to finish him at once, and to have, till he died under that torture, only three grains of bread and the foulest water in the Castle.' De Silva did not seem to wonder that great effort should be made to procure the reprieve of such a sentence. In fact, Thomas Cobham lived to return to his trade, and a paper of about 1570 is extant containing a complaint of some Bristol merchants that their ships are stayed in Spain, because of the capture of a Spanish ship by Thomas Cobham.

Although Stucley did not get into any great disgrace for his piracies—an action was entered against him in the Admiralty court, and he was enlarged upon sureties,—he did not come so well out of his money accounts with the Queen. She had given him ships and ammunition, and wanted to have her own with usury. But Stucley had 'little left save his honesty,' and the Queen was obliged to put up with a loss which she could never forgive. In these straits Stucley's old friends stood him in some stead. 'In return for all he did for me in England,' Shane O'Neill wrote to the Queen, June 18, 1565, 'I cannot do less than with all my might requite him with love, the fervency of whose love I then enjoyed. But it has been lately shown me that you are persuaded that he has done something that offends you and your laws. If it be true, alas and alas!' and he goes on to beseech the Queen to examine Stucley's case with equity, and to restore him to favour; 'he will be as grateful for any kindness shown to Stucley as if it had been done to himself.' Once more, he continues, 'I wish you would send Stucley to me that I might use his aid and counsel against your Majesty's enemies and rebels, and then I doubt not that your service in the North of Ireland will flourish so as has not been seen for many years past.' In another letter of July 28th Shane repeats his prayer, and adjures the Queen, by his services against the Scots, who had fortified themselves in Ulster, to be gracious to his friend Stucley.

Cecil, partly perhaps from his old friendship to Stucley, more from policy, because he thought he would be a useful instrument for dealing with O'Neill, at length took upon himself to listen to Shane's request. So he, with the Earls of Leicester and Pembroke, sent over warm recommendations in his favour to Sir Henry Sidney, who had succeeded the Earl of Sussex as Deputy in Ireland. Here is Cecil's letter:—

'Where Thomas Stucley the bearer sheweth to me his disposition to repair to your Lordship in Ireland, and having the letters of the Earls of Pembroke and Leicester to your Lordship in his favour, he also requireth mine, I could not deny such his request, although I know well the party himself may be welcome to your Lordship without any so mean writing as mine. Yet for the good will I bear the gentleman, and for that I am sorry to see his fortune not answerable to his good courage and hability to serve, I am so bold of your Lordship as to recommend him to you, being already his very good Lord, that if my weight may make his balance of your favour incline the more to his benefit, he may think that he hath not in vain required this my letter. 4 Nov. 1565.'

It is to be remembered that Cecil when he wrote this letter in 1565, had Stucley's piracies much more freshly in his memory than he had when he wrote his tract on the English justice in 1583, where he thus speaks of Stucley 'the rakehell': 'Out of Ireland ran away one Thomas Stucley, a defamed person almost through all Christendom, and a faithless beast rather than a man, fleeing first out of England for notable piracies, and out of Ireland for treacheries not pardonable.' The Earl of Pembroke appears now for the first time among Stucley's friends. This connection must have been formed while Stucley was serving with the English contingent under Pembroke in the campaign against the French in 1557, and in the battle of St Quentin.

Soon after Stucley reached Dublin he was employed in negotiations with Shane O'Neill. On the 26th of January, 1566, Shane wrote to the Council, asking that he might be sent to him. On the 30th the Council replied: 'We have satisfied your special desire; sending to you these bearers, Master Justice Dowdall and Thomas

Stucley, gentleman, whose coming and speech we understand you earnestly desire.' The messengers returned with Shane's answer, dated Feb. 5, and were immediately sent back to him. The report which Stucley brought back formed the foundation of the more dramatic parts of the following letter, in which Sidney exposes to Cecil the condition of Ulster (MSS. Ireland, 5 March, 1566): 'For Ulster, there tyrannizeth the prince of pride. Doubtless I believe Lucifer was never puffed up with more pride nor ambition than that O'Neill is; and he is at present the only strong and rich man in Ireland, and he is the *dangerust* man, and most like to bring the whole estate of this land into subversion, and to subjection either of himself or of some foreign prince, that ever was in Ireland since the first conquest of it. At me he will not come, and yet I have used all the good means and friendly offices that I could; and assure you, my Lord, and her majesty also, that since he will not come to me, he will come to no Englishman living.

'Which when I had cause to suspect, (that he would not come at me, I mean) I considered how I might decypher him in the *censyblyst* and preciseset manner that I could, which by letters I knew I should never do; for in the morning he is subtle, and then will he cause letters to be written either directly otherwise than he will do, or else so doubtfully as he may make what construction he list, and oft times his secretary penneth his letters in more dulce form than he giveth him instruction. But in the afternoon, when the wine is in, then unfoldeth he himself,—In vino veritas—and then showeth he himself what he is, and what he is like to attempt. And therefore I sent two gentlemen to him, Thomas Stucley and Justice Dowdall, both discreet, both faithful to the Queen, stout, assured to me, and grateful to him. And sure, very well they did behave themselves with him, both for the honour of the Queen, the quiet of the country, and his commodity if he had had the grace to understand it.

'He seemed at the first flexible, but yet very timorous to come, alleging the breach of sundry promises of safe passing and returning made to himself, his father, and other Irishmen, and though not doubting myself, yet fearing restraint of liberty by some commandment that might be in secret unwitting to me, and upon the sudden might be delivered to me by some enemy of his, which I might not disobey, but further [forthwith?] apprehend him and send him:—or some treacherous practice whereby he might be killed. Withal, urged still and earnestly the ratification of the peace made with him by Sir Thomas Cusack, and the granting of the petitions made for him to the Queen by the Dean of Ardmagh. And by that time that they had tarried with him a day or two, and that he had conferred with certain rakehells his *concelarys* (counsellors) he *gru* (grew) so absolute that, without grant had of those petitions and ratification of that peace, he would never come in to any deputy: and these had, if he came to any he would come to me. They affirmed my sincere meaning towards him, and that I would come to the nearest town or house to him in the English pale, with many persuasions for his benefit: but all to no purpose, for come to me he would not into any house or town but upon those conditions; howbeit, tarry he would for seven or eight days where he was, which was in a wood by a bog side. He lay there with above a thousand fighting men, and such a meeting I thought neither honourable, sure, nor to bring forth any good effect.'

Then Sidney explains why it would be neither dignified, safe, nor useful. As for the peace made by Cusack he had at the time

no copy of it; now he has obtained copies, one from her English
Council, the other from Shane, and finds them to agree 'as Luke
the Evangelist and Huon of Bordeaux.' Then he proceeds:—' Well,
I taking some hold on his words that he would tarry seven or eight
days there, I returned those gentlemen to him again, with letters of
invitation to him to come to me : before they came to the place
where they left him, he was gone to his principal house in Tirone,
whither they went to him, and there eftsoons entered into treaty
with him, whom they then found more haught and arrogant than
before. For before, he said he would have his parliament robes
sent him into his own country; and at this time, he cared not, he
said, to be made an Earl, unless he might be better and higher
than an Earl; for I am, saith he, in blood and power better than
the best of them, and I will give place to none of them, but to my
cousin of Kildare, for that he is of my house. You have made a
wise Earl of Macarty More [1]—I keep as good a man as he. And
for the Queen, I confess she is my sovereign Lady, saith he, yet I
never made peace with her but by her own seeking. And whom
would you have me trust, Mr Stucley? I came in to the Earl of
Sussex, upon the safe-conduct of two Earls, and protection under
the great seal, and the first courtesy that he offered me was to put
me in a hand-lock, and to send me into England. And when I
came there upon pardon and safe-conduct, and had done my busi-

---

[1] This peace with Shane was made by the Earl of Kildare and Sir Thomas
Cusack in Sept. 1563. It confirmed Shane in the title of The O'Neill, till
the Queen gave him a more honourable one, and it conceded that it was not
to be taken for a breach of the treaty if Shane refused personally to appear
before the Deputy. On the 20th of October came the Queen's reply. It
offered Shane pardon, command over a certain number of Captains, the title
of Earl, the state and name of O'Neill, and expressed the Queen's detestation
of the attempt of John Smyth to poison him.

ness and would have departed according to the same, the Queen herself told me that indeed safe-conduct I had to come safe and go safe, but she had not told me when; and so held me till I had agreed to such inconveniences against my honour and profit as I would never perform while I live; and that made me make war; and if it were to do again I would do it, for my ancestors were kings of Ulster, and Ulster was theirs, and Ulster is mine, and shall be mine. And for O'Donnell, he shall never come into his country, if I can keep him out of it, nor Bagnall into the Newry, nor the Earl of Kildare into Dundrum, nor Lecale. They are now mine; with this sword I wan them, with this sword I will keep them. This is my answer. Commend me to my gossip the Deputy. God be with you, my masters.

'"Nay," say they, "we brought you letters, and by letters we look for answer." "Well, letters you shall have," saith he; and thereupon caused his man to write, the true copy whereof I send your Lordship, to the end you may see how well his speech and writing agreeth—whereby I found my former suspicion not to be devoid of reason.'

The conversation put by Stucley into the mouth of Shane O'Neill is so singularly like that which dramatic tradition puts into Stucley's own mouth, that it is impossible not to suspect it to have acquired its colour by passing through his brain. The thorough dissimilarity which Sidney intimates that he found between the talk and the letter might have arisen from this cause, as much as from the difference between Shane subtle in the morning and Shane drunk in the afternoon. Sidney, however, was so pleased with Stucley's conduct in the negotiation, that before he finished his letter, he said, 'I pray you let Stucley know that his service is taken in good part,' and from this time perseveringly tried to advance his fortunes.

It was not many days before an opportunity occurred. We have just seen how Shane declared that 'Bagnall should not enter into the Newry.' This refers to Sir Nicholas Bagnall, Marshall of Ireland, who had acquired a title to great estates in the island :—The Castle and Manor of Carlingford and Cowleye, with the fishing: The Castle and Manor of Greencastle and Mourne: The College of the Newry: The Friar-house of Carlingford. (MSS. Ireland, Eliz., Vol. V. 94 i.) Bagnall was by this time tired of Ireland, and therefore bargained to sell his estates and office to Stucley; and both of them repaired to the Deputy to obtain his consent, and his recommendation to the English government to allow the transaction to be completed. Sidney in consequence wrote the following letter to Cecil from Cagrigmaine, where he rested the night after he had left Dublin, on the 7th of March, 1566 (MSS. Ireland) :

'After the dispatch of this bearer, and after I was entered into the journey which now I take, Sir Nicholas Bagnall and Mr Stukeley desired my consent and commendation to a bargain concluded between them, wherein Mr Bagnall had (with conditions of her Majesty's allowance and the Council's) sold his office of Marshall and his whole inheritance in Ireland to Mr Stukeley for the sum of £3000 of that money. The one by the greatness of the sum seemeth to be well satisfied, and the other repenteth not, as he saith, the adventure of his money therefore, in respect to my being Governor. And like as for mine own contentation I ought most to esteem of him that most desireth my company, so when I look farther into the matter I judge Stukeley (having her highness' favour and your good opinions) an apt man both to execute the office and to be a neighbour to O'Neill in the Newry, as one who in time of peace may be a good instrument to continue it, and in war, a lusty soldier to defend his own and his neighbours. And albeit I never had cause to doubt of Stukeley's sufficiency in discretion, saving that his loose dealings for his own commodity was some maim to his credit; yet have I found in his late service with O'Neill such honesty and deep judgment, and such care of the prince's honour and my place, as giveth me a new opinion far different from mine old. And therefore have thought good to desire your helping hand to this his purchase, whereof I hope the more assuredly, being by your commendation of him fully persuaded of your good opinion.'

On the same day Stucley wrote to Cecil from Dublin to recommend his own suit: 'This day I have concluded and gone through with Sir Nicholas Bagnold for all his land which he had in this realm, to me and mine heirs, and with the same have bought his interest of his office of Marshall of this realm: as I have ever found you mine especial good master and friend, even so I do now most humbly desire the continuance of your goodness, that it may please you to be a mediator unto the Queen's most excellent Majesty, that it may please her highness of her clemency to like well of it. Wherein (as I am already bound) so shall you bind me for ever to be at your honour's commandment, as God best knoweth.'

Cecil however wrote to Sidney on the 27th of March: 'The motion made by your private letter for Mr Stucley was here made common in the court with a general misliking for many respects. And her Majesty began one day with me therein with some strange speeches: but, as I answered, I thought you had some consideration that moved you thereto, tending to her Majesty's service more than did plainly appear. I can assure your Lordship whatever answer may be made to you herein by any men's private letters, the appointing of him to a place of that trust is lightly spoken of; wherein I write you plainlier, because I wold not have you abased. And yet for my own part I am fully persuaded that your Lordship seeth many things that move you to think the same should further her Majesty's service.'

Four days afterwards the public letter from the Queen to Sidney was written. It contained her decision on Stucley:—'We find it strange that Thomas Stucley should be used there in any service in such credit as we perceive he is, considering the general discredit wherein he remaineth, not only in our own realm, but also in other countries, for such matters as he hath been charged withal. Whereunto also he yet remaineth by bond with sureties answerable in our Court of Admiralty, according as of late upon supplication of his sureties we wrote to you, that he should return home to answer in our said court.' This common letter was accompanied with a private one from Cecil to Sidney, in which he said:—'I also see her Majesty offended mich with the being of Mr Stucley there, and so she hath written. And I pity his fortune; for there percase he might have begun to turn upward in fortune's wheel, but here I think that he shall not be hable to stir the while." (MSS. Ireland, March 31.)

Sidney replied to Cecil, in a letter of April 17 (Collins, Sidney Papers, I. 10): 'I pity Mr Stucley as you do, and now he repaireth into England. He hoped here to have settled, being well allied to divers noblemen here, and in great towardness to marry the Earl of Worcester's sister.

'If any good come of the intelligence of O'Neill's intendement,

Stucley is to be thanked for it. And for the weight of the office which I recommended him to, only by my particular letters to you, my Lord of Pembroke and my Lord of Leicester, from all which I had before received very favourable letters in his behalf,—such it is, as heretofore (and no longer ago than in my Lord Leonard's Government) the Marshall of his hall was Marshall of the army; and the office was and is of the Deputy's gift. The bargain for the land was made between him and Bagnall before I knew of it: and that being his, I know no man, if the Queen would have peace with O'Neill, that better could please him; nor no man, if her highness would have war, that would more annoy him. And this moved me to consent to it, and yet I neither desire it nor persuade it.'

And so ended Stucley's hopes of being Marshall of Ireland. It is clear from the reference to the Lady Jane (?) Somerset, the Earl of Worcester's[1] sister, that he had by this time lost his wife, and was ready to make another great match. Whether he made it or no I have not discovered, nor whether he took his immediate departure from Ireland. If the Dramatist is right in giving him a share in the defence of Dundalk against Shane O'Neill, he must have remained in Ireland till May 1566. We have no other certain information regarding him till June 1567. He was then again in Ireland, renewing his practices to make himself at once a large landed proprietor, and an officer of the government. Sidney, as before, supported him. This time he purchased from Captain Sir

---

[1] This was William Somerset, ob. 1587. His father, Henry, 2nd earl, had four sons and four daughters by Elizabeth, daughter of Sir Anthony Browne, Kt—William, Thomas, Charles, standard-bearer to the band of pensioners, and Francis, slain at Musselborough field, 1 Ed. VI.

Eleanor married to Sir Geo. Vaughan; Lucy to John Nevil, Lord Latimer, ob. 1577; Anne to Thomas Percy, earl of Northumberland (the rebel); and Jane to Sir Edward Mansel of Morgan, Glamorganshire.

Nicholas Heron all his Irish property, and his office of Seneschall of Wexford. In reply to Sidney's letter, in which the council was recommended to authorize this purchase, Cecil wrote, June 10, 1567, to Sidney, who had sent over his letter by Captain Agard, one of the most efficient English officers then employed in Ireland. 'Mr Agard can report how I, being for my recreation from the court, was directed from the Queen by a messenger to write of two things. The one concerneth her misliking of Mr Stucley to have any office in that country, and especially of Captain Heron, of which matter I had need of more instruction, and so to write larglier.' (MS. Ireland.) Three days later, June 13, he writes further— 'Upon Mr Agard's departure I did make mention of a message sent to me in my absence from the Court by the Queen, particularly concerning the office which Captain Heron holdeth. And in conference with Mr Agard I thought it good to understand her Majesty's pleasure more particularly, and for discharge of my duty to declare my opinion to her Majesty concerning the castle at Laghlin Bridge, and Carlogh, how meet the same was to be in possession of Englishmen, wherein I was able of my knowledge gathered many years past to say more to her Majesty than I think she understood. Nevertheless in fine, she willed me directly to write unto you, that you should have regard how to diminish the charge of those offices which Heron holdeth, and not to bestow the same on any person without her Majesty's knowledge. I have had much ado to compass the treasure now sent, and have for that purpose bestowed my own credit to take up by Sir Thomas Gresham's means £7000 upon the exchequer, so as, when her Majesty should give warrant for that which we had done, she was earnest to have stayed . . . . We are at secret contention with the

French, who shall get the Prince of Scotland. They fish with hooks of gold, and we but with speech. Sir Nicholas Throgmorton is in Scotland.... and whilst Scotland is fully occupied, I wish you to follow the opportunities which God grant your Lordship in Ireland.'

While Elizabeth was thus making huge bones of sending some £7000 over for the general purposes of the government in Ireland, Captain Heron sent in his little bill for the expenses, two posts,—they cannot be called garrisons,—which he had bargained to transfer to Stucley. One was the post at Laghlin; Heron charged for himself three shillings a day, and two shillings for his train: two officers at twelvepence; 20 horsemen at ninepence; 15 harquebusiers at eightpence; 15 archers at sixpence; in all, £739 2s. 6d. a year, or with back wages since the beginning of the reign, £6291 13s. 6d. Similarly the guard at the castle at Carlogh cost £85 3s. 4d. a year, or since the beginning of the reign to the 30th of May, 1567, £720 6s. 0d. Here was almost the exact sum for which Cecil, not being able to screw it out of the Queen, had to pledge his own credit, spent upon two posts which were to be handed over to a notorious spendthrift, without money of his own, but famous for his royalty to men at arms. Elizabeth would not have been Elizabeth if she had permitted it. Even if Stucley had been a minion of hers she would have cashiered him; she might have favoured the man, but she would never have made herself answerable for the money. It reads like an afterthought that, in a letter of a few days later (July 6, 1567), Cecil writes to Sidney that Stucley is supposed to have bought certain hides and skins robbed from the low countries by John Cook, a pirate of Southampton, and by him carried for sale into Ireland. This John Cook was, however, one of Stucley's crew when he sailed from Ireland in 1570.

Notwithstanding all these objections at the Court, Stucley entered upon the functions of Seneschall of Wexford, and also took possession of the property he had bought of Heron. He must have held his office nearly a year before the Council was able to disturb him. His coming fall was not without premonitory symptoms, and he wrote to his uncle Sir Hugh Pawlet to do what he could for him. Sir Hugh therefore wrote a long postscript to a business letter he had to send to Cecil, in which he said : 'As I perceive by letters received of late out of Ireland from my nephew Thomas Stucley, he accounteth himself to be in some disfavour and ill opinion of you and others of the Queen's Council, by slanderous and ill reports made of him; wherein he hath instantly requested me to be mean for him specially to you, that it might please you to take him for the mortified and qualified man that you shall find him to be indeed, and hath been since his being in the place and charge that he hath received there; and that it may likewise please you to credit no reports or informations passed of him to be true, until such time as he shall answer the same upon advertisement of the complaints. Whereof in his behalf I can no less than humbly beseech you of your favourable friendship towards him, as his deserts upon due proof shall require ; taking the more boldness to trouble you herewith, upon the sight of a letter written of late by one of the Queen's Council in Ireland unto my Lord Deputy's secretary, wherein amongst other discourses he affirmeth Thomas Stucley to be sundry ways untruly reported, and doth right well allow and commend his order and doings in this time of his abode in that country.' (MSS. Domestic, June 19, 1568.) But

Pawlet's letter cannot have reached Cecil before the fiat had gone forth. On the 20th of June the Queen wrote to Sidney: 'Whereas also for certain considerations us moving we have thought meet to return Sir Nicholas Heron Kt. to his former charge, which now Thomas Stucley Esq. holdeth, we will that further, as soon as you may, the said Nicholas be placed in the said offices, and continue in our service until we shall otherwise order, as we shall find meet upon the establishing of a President and a Council in Munster, for that we do very well allow of your offer and intention to discharge us of the wages of the soldiers there, now retained in wage, which may be converted towards the entertainment of the said Council.'[1]

Before this letter was written the insecurity of Stucley's title to some of the land he had purchased had otherwise become evident. Sir Peter Carew, a cousin of Stucley's, imagined that by some of his female ancestors he had a right to certain Irish baronies, among the rest to that of Odrone, which Stucley had bought of Heron. So he sent over John Vowel, alias Hooker, a Devonshire lawyer, now best known as the compiler of the later portion of the Irish annals in Holinshed's Chronicles, to investigate his claims. Hooker wrote to Carew, May 26, 1568 (Carew Papers, Lambeth), that the Barony of Odrone was in the tenure of a sect called the Cavanaghs, who were brought to the Queen's peace by Sir Nicholas Heron. Mr Stucley was then supplying his place, dwelling at Loghlin, and keeping them in subjection. 'I am offered,' he continues, 'to have possession of the barony whensoever I will. Loghlin was formerly

---

[1] MSS. Ireland. In vol. 25, no. 11, there is a list of the proposed council, seven members, with six legal assistants. The seven are all Devonshire men, and three, at least, near relations of Stucley.

the house of your ancestors, and by them made a monastery which being dissolved is now in the Queen's hands. Mr Stucley has offered me his house at Dublin, the House at Leighlin, or another which he hath in that neighbourhood, to be at your commandment. If you lie there you shall have all things serving your necessity or pleasure at a far more reasonable hand than at Dublin, where I do find all things to be at double price in respect of our things in England.' 'Truly,' he continues, ' for your barony of Odrone there is no one man in all Ireland of his degree which can do you more pleasure . . . which he will not fail to do, as you shall well perceive at your coming. I am sorry that you had not sent him a letter, which he seemed somewhat to be grieved withal, that he had not been as well considered with one as others were; yet notwithstanding I did by my letters, and then by private conference, excuse the matter, alleging that you resumed the letters from me upon report made that he should be come to London.' Stucley had previously told Hooker 'how much he was bounden to [Carew] in his worst estate; for when all men did speak evil of him, yet you gave good report, and spake in his defence.'

In consequence of this communication Carew embarked at Ilfracombe for Waterford early in August; on his arrival Stucley resorted to him to congratulate him, and provided horses for him and all his company. Carew went first to Leighlin, where he had very liberal and honourable entertainment of Stucley; thither resorted to him sundry of the chief of the Cavanaghs, who then were the occupiers of the Barony; to them he showed that he was their Lord, and that he was come to make claim and recover the same his barony; which speeches were not so hard unto them but they more hardly digested them. By decree of Dec. 17, 1568,

Carew was pronounced right Lord of the Barony of Odrone. Immediately, or not long after, Thomas Stucley was discharged of the custody and garrison of Leighlin, and Carew appointed to the same by a commission from the Lord Deputy, bearing date Feb. 17, 1568-9.[1]

The Queen, as we have seen, had restored Heron to his old offices: but before he could return to take possession he died. Stucley therefore remained in office some time longer, till a successor could be found for him. Cecil ultimately pitched upon a creature of his own, Nicholas White, a lawyer, who had been proposed by Sidney as one of the legal assistants to the Council of Munster. To the disgust of the soldiers in Ireland he was preferred to what hitherto had always been a soldier's post. On the 24th of October (MSS. Ireland) Cecil wrote to Sidney that as he found the Queen earnestly bent to have Stucley removed from his office, and at the same time unwilling to place Nicholas White in commission in Munster, he had moved her to give White Stucley's office, which she readily assented to. Cecil persuaded himself that Sidney would be well content, for otherwise he would never prefer a man without Sidney's allowance. Sidney's reply to this is dated Nov. 14, 1568 (Collins, p. 38): 'My other letters declare my devotion to Thomas Stucley, your poor repentant follower—I am sure from his heart, for otherwise he could not enjoy my good countenance. But since I now see that her Majesty cannot allow of his service, I must be sorry for his undoing, and cease my suit. ... Nevertheless, as I think N. White very able to execute the office of Seneschall of Wexford, being a quiet county where no

---

[1] The Life and Times of Sir Peter Carew, from the original MS. of Vowell, alias Hooker. By John Maclean, 1857, pp. 74-77 and 84.

martial force is used, nor is greatly needful; so if, with his grant the Captaincy of Laghlin, the Cavenaghs, and the leading of soldiers be contained, I cannot counsel that he is fit for that charge. Otherwise I allow of him for his judgment, honesty, and good service.'

We have seen how the Queen had caught at Sidney's project for relieving her of the expenses of the military post at Laghlin. It was not explained how this was to be, till the following letter certified Cecil that his nominee Nicholas White was not to inherit all that Stucley had purchased. On the 23rd of Feb. 1569 (MSS. Ireland) Sir Peter Carew wrote to Cecil that since he had recovered by decree, as well as by common law, the barony of Odrone, Sidney, in his care that the proposed Presidents of Munster might be entertained without charge to the Queen, had been dealing with him for two months past to know whether, if the House at Laghlin were granted to him, he would take the expenses of the garrison upon himself. Carew, thinking Sidney had power to settle this business, consented; whereupon Sidney had cassed the band, and discharged Stucley, and placed Carew in the house. But since that time Sidney had been informed that the Queen had declared that all offices which Stucley had should be delivered to Nicholas White, who thereupon claimed the house of Laghlin and the charge thereof. But before the receipt of these letters Carew had been already placed there; and as all the land round about was his, the house being but bare walls, standing in the middle of his barony, with but little land belonging to it, if he were removed it would be a disgrace to him, a discredit to Sidney, a hazard of unsettling the minds of the fickle people, and finally a wrong, since no stranger could live there without exacting from Carew's tenants. 'I do think therefore that no man in this land, having not the Queen's entertainment, nor yet any commodity there, will either supplant me, or disburden her highness of eight hundred mark for seven nobles (which is the only recompense that I will seek), unless only it be for private malice and despite.'

White arrived in Dublin in March; and was disappointed to find so sorry entertainment. As for the house at Laghlin, Sidney told him, the garrison was already discharged, and a very beneficial offer made by Sir Peter Carew had been recommended. For the constableship of the Castle of Fernes, it had been granted on a long lease to Sir Nicholas Heron, who had sold over his interest therein to a gentleman of this realm, who held the same accordingly. As for the Seneschallship of Wexford, it was worth but £20 Irish a year, without any other allowance, and that Sidney was ready to grant. White also wrote to Cecil (MSS. Ireland, March 10, 1569): 'I perceive Mr Stucley hath both very largely spoken of me before my coming, and also incensed my Lord Deputy grievously against me with no better stuff than that I have been preferred by my Lord of Ormond to his Lordship's deface, and become altogether Ormonds against the Deputy. But since my coming hither he hath not showed *his self* abroad in this city, but is departed hence into the country of Wexford, where men think my Lord hath devised some kind of rule for him. What it is or how much to my hurt, I know not, till time shall disclose both that and the rest; and in the mean I will use patience, and learn by yourself to swallow up these lofty speeches containing more heat than power to hurt.' He then declares that he will yield to the Deputy, and oppose to the envy of the English (to whom he is wholly addict) nothing but the breast-plate of justice.

White's spite against Stucley only grew with time. After three months he wrote again about him (Ireland MSS., June 10, 1569) : 'In my last letter I did somewhat touch what likelihood of evil practices there was in Mr Stucley. And now the same is broken out in more heinous sort than I then suggested, by the accusation of Thomas Masterson, sometime servant to Mr Vicechamberlain, and of one lately placed in the constableship of Fernes in the County of Wexford. These two being sent for to answer a fray happened betwixt them in that County, Masterson, the 7th of this month, in open and vehement manner did charge Stucley at the council-board not only with the matters contained in this paper here enclosed, which is the very copy of that which he subscribed and delivered to the Lord Deputy, but also with putting out of certain lewd persons which are now proclaimed rebels in the County of Wexford, and conspiring with them to levy war against the Queen's Majesty and her subjects.

'Hereupon Stucley is committed to close prison, and the Council deeply debating both for the manner of trial and careful ordering of this cause that so highly toucheth the Queen's highness, her crown and dignity . . . . and to induce the evilness of Stucley's intent there was also disclosed to my Lord . . . . how that about the time of my coming over he made a deed of gift of all his farms and goods to Mr Agard and John Thomas.'

The gravamen, in White's mind, against Stucley, is that he had given what was his own to those whom he chose, instead of waiting to have it all confiscated to the use of one he despised. As for the other charges, though in White's generalities they may sound heavy enough, when we come to know the particulars they turn out to be simply frivolous. The charges were two; first, that he

had used coarse language against the Queen ; secondly, that he had
levied war against her. Here are the particulars. Richard Stafford
and William Hoare were with Stucley at his house at Enniscorthy
on the 6th of June, 1568, when he began to rail and cry out.
They said to him, ' Why are you so offended with the gentlemen of
the County of Wexford? We hear say that Mr Heron will be here
shortly as seneschal, and that the Queen has given him the said
office, and some other part of your living.'[1] Then Stucley said, ' I
care not a f—t for her (hoore) nor yet for her office.' It is clear
that the word in parenthesis might have been addressed to Mr
Hoare, one of Stucley's interlocutors. The rest was slender foundation for an indictment against a soldier. For the other accusation,
it was never pressed against him during his imprisonment, but the
next year the following indictment was drawn up, but never came
to trial : ' Thomas Stucley, late of Inniscorthy in the County of
Wexford, gentleman, Seneschal of the said County, the 27th of
May, 1569, wrongfully came to Inniscorthy, and traiterously
provoked Maurice Kavanagh Duff late of Knockangarrine, Griffin
Kavanagh Mac Morris and Walter Kavanagh, and divers other
malefactors unknown, Irish enemies and proclaimed rebels, to levy
war against the Queen. Whereupon the said traitors came
to Ballynatty in Wexford, and then and there stole thirty kine
of sundry colours each worth 20 shillings, of the goods and
cattles of the said Katern Kavanagh,[2] of Ballynatte widow, one

[1] This is the single charge against Stucley in his indictment for Treason
among the Burghley papers, MSS. Lansdowne, xii., no. 19.

[2] Perhaps this Katherine Kavanagh is the widow referred to by Burghley
and his scribe of 1583. After mentioning Stucley's piracies, for which 'being in
danger of punishment he fled into Ireland,' the paper proceeds: 'where abusing
an honest merchant's wife being a widow, wasted her goods, and having committed some crime against her Majesty whereof he was accused, fled into Spain.'

bay horse worth 20 marks, and one black hackney, worth 5 marks, and two harbergeons each worth 10 marks of the goods of Donogh O'Kynselagh of the same place.' If cattle-driving was to be interpreted as levying war, all England at harvest-tide was in a state of warfare. The disputes about tythes and boundaries were then usually settled by bands of armed men, and the records of the Star-chamber swarm with such cases. A nephew of Stucley's, Hugh Stucley, was in this state of quotennial warfare with his cousin Sir Amyas Pawlet from the 17th to the 22nd of Elizabeth's reign. But whatever weight attaches to the accusation, it is to be remembered that this is the whole case his enemies were able to get up against him, after his flight to Spain, when of course they wished to blacken the character of the renegade as much as they could.[1]

Stucley was kept close prisoner in Dublin Castle for seventeen weeks. Richard Creagh, the Archbishop of Armagh, was there also, with other influential Irishmen. They continued, in spite of all precautions, to communicate with each other. The subject of their communications was this. In March or April of this year the Catholic Clergy and Nobility of Ireland had signed a petition to the King of Spain, which was accompanied by an explanatory paper written by the Archbishop of Armagh, of which the following is a summary:[2]

'There are three things,' said the memorialists, 'which we desire.

---

[1] The information sent over to France by Fenelon in his despatches of July 11 and 27, 1569, concerning Stucley must be false. Fenelon says that Stucley joined Ormond's young brother and captured Cork, but was subsequently himself taken, and brought to London. C. P. Cooper, Recueil des despêches, &c., des Ambassadeurs de France, vol. ii. pp. 81 and 111.

[2] Froude's Simancas Transcripts, vol. B, fol. 109.

'1. To have in the Island the permanent presence of a Catholic Sovereign of the Spanish blood, confirmed by the Holy See.

'2. To live under the joint obedience and protection of the Pope, and the King of Spain.

'3. To be entirely separated and freed from the crown and unstable government of England, and to have no other connection with the English but that of Christian charity.'

The petitioners added to this, that the crown should be offered to Philip's brother, Don John of Austria.

The presentation of this petition and the negotiation of its demands were entrusted to Maurice Gibbon Fitzgibbon, or Reagh, Archbishop of Cashel,[1] a man of whom Mr Myles O'Reilly says very little more than that he was Archbishop of Cashel from 1567 to 1578, and that he has his place in the *Memorials of those who suffered for the Catholic faith in Ireland* in the 16th century. Of this Maurice, and his futile attempt to get possession of his see, Holinshed gives a very uncomplimentary account, which I should not have ventured to believe, unless I had found the main fact confirmed by the Archbishop's own confession. Under the year 1567 Holingshed (or rather Hooker) says: 'About this time one Morice, a runagate priest, having lately been at Rome and there consecrated by the Pope's Bull Archbishop of Cashell, arrived into

---

[1] O'Reilly says that he died about 1578 in exile at Oporto. But he refers to Bruodin as authority for his having died in prison at Cork, May 6, 1578. According to Cardinal Allen (ad persecutores Anglos pro catholicis responsio—in answer to Burghleigh's *Justitia Britannica*, cap. 1) he was executed. The index to Bridgewater's *Concertatio*, rather fuller than the text, says, 'Maurice, Archbishop of Cashel, a man of the greatest integrity and learning, after enduring various exquisite tortures, was at last hanged and subjected to the usual butchery, and so died most happily. With him two other Irish bishops, martyrs, were condemned to death.'

Ireland, and made challenge to the same see: which being denied unto him by the Archbishop which was there placed by her Majesty, the said supposed Bishop suddenly with an Irish skaine wounded the Bishop, and put him in danger of his life.' And under the year 1569 Hooker further says: 'Edmund Butler and his brothers combined themselves with James Fitzmorris O'Desmond, Mac Arty More, Mac Donagh, and the Seneschal of Imokilie and others of Munster, who before (and unwitting the Butlers) had sent the usurped Bishops of Cashel and Emly together with the youngest brother of the Earl of Desmond unto the Pope and the King of Spain for reformation of religion.' After Stucley was withdrawn from Wexford, and was a prisoner in Dublin, James Fitzmorris, who had already besieged Kilkenny, laid Waterford waste, and harried the county of Dublin, turned to Wexford, and at Inniscorthy fair his soldiers 'committed most horrible outrages, lamentable slaughters, filthy rapes,' and then overran Ossory and the Queen's county, spoiling, burning, and murdering; afterwards they combined with the Earl of Clancare, and James Fitzmorris O'Desmond, and 'sent new messengers to the Pope and the King of Spain.'[1] Whether these new messengers were Stucley and his companions, or those who carried the new instructions to the Archbishop of Cashel, dated Tralee, May 4, 1570, there is nothing in Holinshed to show.

This however is certain, that just before he was shut up in Dublin Castle, he had entered into communication with Don Gerau Despes, the Spanish Ambassador at London, and that this communication was maintained during his imprisonment. Stucley had a servant, a Venetian, Alessandro Fideli, who had been with him

[1] See Gonzales, Apuntamientos, &c., in Memorias de la Real Academia de la Historia, vol. vii. p. 349, and Documenti, No. x.

for some twenty years. Fideli had a nephew Cristofero, servant to Ragasoni, an Italian in London; through these a correspondence was begun with the Ambassador, who wrote to Philip II. from London, June 14, 1569:[1] 'Thomas Stucley, an English Captain residing in Ireland, whom, in consequence of his being Catholic, this Queen has deprived of the charge of all the horses she has there, pretends that with his friends he is prepared to give that Island to your Majesty, or another Catholic Prince. And he and some noblemen wish to pass into Spain to beseech you to accept their offer. There is there a Venetian, whom Stucley and the rest trust, and he has here a nephew, a very good man, who is always ready to go to Ireland to treat with the said gentlemen.'

As Stucley was only committed to prison on the 10th of June, it is clear that he began this correspondence previously to that event. And an information dated May 2, 1571, says that 'about two years past, i. e. in May 1569, Stucley sent one Sutton into Spain about this practice.' And in October, 1571, one Richard Smyth confessed that 'William Sutton was the only practiser for Stucley's coming into Spain' (Murdin, p. 185).[2] It is only in his next despatch of July 5 that Don Guerau writes: 'The viceroy, mistrusting Stucley, . . . has imprisoned him' (Ib., fol. 96). How he got out of prison there is no authentic information; the account given by the Archbishop of Cashel is so one-sided and so false in these particulars that can be tested,

[1] Froude's Simancas Transcripts, B, fol. 92.
[2] Murdin, 182, prints a letter to the Duchess of Feria, dated Mechlin, July 3, 1571, 'how Mr Markynfyld here and Mr Stucley with you have been rocked asleep to trust such a fellow as they have done! For look, whatsoever Mr Stucley has imparted to him, be you sure it is in England long since.' This refers to Sutton.

that it cannot be entirely trusted, although Mr Froude, with his characteristic idea that whatever was new (and discovered by him) in old history must also be true, founded his account of Stucley entirely upon it. Part of this account is as follows :—

Stucley 'had hoped to establish his title to the lands in Cork under the Southern Commission and to share with St Leger and Carew in the partition of Munster; but the Queen, hearing reports of murders, robberies, and other outrages committed by him, ordered Sidney to lay hands upon him, and he was locked up in Dublin Castle.

'Implicated as he had been in the spoliation scheme, and concerned also, it seems, in the pillage and destruction of certain religious houses, he had made no friends among the Irish but Shan, and, when Shan was dead, he was regarded with more than the detestation which was commonly bestowed upon Englishmen. Yet understanding Philip's difficulties about Ireland, and feeling that he had no further favour to expect from Elizabeth, he continued while in prison to establish a correspondence with Don Guerau, to pass himself off as a person of great influence among the chiefs, as an ardent Catholic, devoted to the Church, to Mary Stuart, and to Spain, and anxious to play a part beside the noblemen who were working for a revolution in England.

'Having thus opened a way towards his reception in Madrid, he pretended to Sidney that he wished to go in person to his mistress and clear his reputation with her; and Sidney, instead of sending him over under a guard, apparently was contented with his parole. Stucley told him that his defence would require the presence of certain Irish gentlemen, who were willing to accompany him to the Queen. The Deputy permitted him to purchase and fit out a ship at Waterford to transport both them and himself; and when at last he sailed, it was pretended that no one on board suspected his destination. He had seven or eight Celtic cavaliers with him, with their servants and horses, and a miscellaneous crew of adventurers. They had embarked as if for London, and Sidney professed to believe that they were going there; but the story reads like collusion. When clear of the harbour they made for the ocean, landed at Vivero, and sent to Philip to announce their arrival.' Mr Froude finds a confirmation of this story in the fact that the list of the crew shows that Stucley had with him two O'Neills, a Geraldine, a Magennis, a MacPhilip, and another called Murty Paddy. In the Spanish they are called Salbaxes, savages. And also, what he does not tell us, in the English they are all called servants, and in the Spanish horse-grooms, except two, Charles and Philip, who are said to be Irish gentlemen, and savages. On the English list these also figure as Charles Aureley and Phelem, servants. The seven or eight Celtic cavaliers were two at the very utmost.

Stucley was committed to prison on the 10th of June, 1569, and remained there 17 weeks, till the middle of October. Then he was set free on parole, and the Earl of Kildare saw him 'go up and down in the English pale as others did, till such time as he had his pardon.' Of the horses which he took with him, the Earl gave him one and sold him another, 'for when Stucley came forth of Ireland it was thought by all reports that he was coming into England and not departing into Spain' (MSS. Ireland, Dec. 7, 1577. Answers of the Earl of Kildare). He had been free then for months, and had his pardon before he left Ireland, and it is not true that he only went out of prison to depart on parole to England. A paper among the Irish MSS. (May 2, 1571) gives a detailed account of all his doings. On the 1st of February, 1570, his servant

Alessandro Fideli bought for him the ship 'Trinity' of Bridgewater. By an irony of fortune this was one of the ships which Sir Peter Carew had commissioned to search for pirates, and which had arrested Stucley's hulk in Cork harbour. She was herself afterwards arrested by warrant for the death of a man by the capstan in weighing anchor, and sold. On the 13th of March Stucley went to Waterford to prepare her for sea. But between the purchase and the next step recorded in this paper Stucley had gone over to London, and presented himself incognito to Fenelon the French ambassador, and made the following proposals, which Fenelon communicated to the Queen Mother Catharine in a cypher dated Feb. 17, 1570. 'X .... came to me at 10 o'clock at night, to say that if the king pleased to receive him he will willingly pass to his service, with such a good plot in hand, that when the king pleases to put it into action, he will find it very conducive to his greatness; adding many occasions of his discontent, and of that of the principal lords of this realm. Thereupon, not knowing if he came to try me, I answered that I knew not that the king had any other but a very good intention to keep peace with the Queen of England and her realm; but, since all his pretensions and desires could not be known to me, I would not fail to advertise him of what he said, and that he might well imagine his Majesty to have griefs as well as he, from those who governed in this realm; so that he might well accept him, and employ him for their common revenge. On which he said he would return in a little time to know the answer of your Majesty.'

The Queen's reply, dated March 3, 1570, shows that this X was no other than Stucley. 'I have received your cypher containing your opinion of affairs there, and what Stucley came to say to you, likewise your good and prudent answer, in fear that he had been guilefully sent to you by the Queen or her ministers to discover whether there was any ill will against them, and whether you would listen to the offer made to you. It seems to me, that, to keep the said Lady from suspecting, instead of letting him come over here, it will be better for you to keep him in his present good will and affection to do service to the king my Lord and son; and without discovering anything to him on your side, to draw from him all you can, and find out how he can serve you. Nevertheless you will not omit to inform yourself secretly of the means and intelligence he has or may have with the Lords on that side; and I am sure that you can very well judge and know what probability there is in what he has already proposed to you, or may propose, in order to send us your judgment and opinion about it' (Cooper's Despatches, vol. iii. p. 53, and vol. vii. p. 94).

Fenelon does not inform us whether Stucley returned to him. If he did, he must have seen that he could make a better bargain with the Spaniard than with the Frenchman. He therefore returned to Ireland, and on the 13th of March went to Waterford to prepare his ship for sea, and laid in four tons of water, 15 pipes of wheat, and eight pipes of beans. On the 25th he shipped his mariners, and on the 28th 14 horses. Among his mariners were some of the very best English seamen—John More, sometime master of the Saker; Rowland Breton, master of Frobisher's ship; Michael Venety, sometime a master in Hawkins' ship. On the 17th of April he set sail from Waterford, 'and none of his company did understand of his pretence towards Spain, saving one Robert Penn [or Keane, who was dead within a year], pilot of the ship, and Alessandro Fideli.' He landed at Vinero in Galicia the 24th of

April, and on the 25th sent Alessandro Fideli and Reynold Digby, his major domo, to inform Philip of his arrival. They found the king in Seville, who presented them with 200 ducats. They returned to Vinero on the 31st of May, bearing the King's orders that Stucley should remain there; about the same time Stucley, according to Gonzalez, sent Morales de Malla to Philip with very specific information of the state of Ireland, and of the means for invading and occupying it, which Stucley offered to effect without spending a drop of blood.

Mr Froude saw at Simancas the letter which Stucley wrote to Philip on his arrival (Transcripts, B, fol. 142). In it he entreats the King to take possession of Ireland. The land is so fertile, he says, that it will feed all Europe. The fields are covered with cattle; the hills are full of gold and silver, the rivers of salmon. In Cork harbour, if the King pleases, he may have a thousand ships, and build of the timber of the country a thousand gallies. He also assures Philip that the English had not a friend in Ireland, and that in all there were but 1500 of them. Philip, adds Mr Froude, must have thought it strange that so small a body could not be disposed of without him. But it would seem that the last sentence of the letter is wrongly attributed to Stucley; it really occurs in a letter of Antonio de Guaras to Caijas, dated London, June 30, 1570 (Ib., fol. 136), who talks of the alarm in England about the Irish, for their affection to Philip, which arises from their being all Catholics except the English whom the Queen maintains there, who do not amount to 1500 men, distributed in diverse ports, and very few of them experienced in war. While in all Ireland there is no important fortress, and the soil is the best in the world. Under a prince who should keep it in proper subjection and policy it would be a very rich and flourishing kingdom, with very little power in the estates. And the writer refers to Thomas Stucley, who, he understands, is gone out of Ireland to Spain, who can give the King better information.

There must have been negotiations by letter between Stucley and the Spanish Court concerning this Irish project before he was called to Madrid. For while he was still at Vinero, an English resident of the place was directed by the King to attend on him, and we have some record of his conversations with this man. He was named John Dutton. Stucley told him that the King had promised him 20,000 brave soldiers to land in Ireland. 'Where will you land them?' asked Dutton. 'At Waterford,' said Stucley. Then Dutton said, 'If the Queen's ships meet with you they will spoil you.' And Stucley answered, 'I will eat my Christmas pie with the Lord Deputy, for then the Queen's ships will be laid up : and I will pluck the George from his neck, for I will bring the noblest order with me, the order of the Golden Fleece.'[1] Quoth Dutton, 'There are in Ireland brave open harbours and roads.' ' Aye,' quoth Stucley, 'as good as in Christendom.' 'Then,' quoth Dutton, 'the Queen's ships will soon be with you.' 'Tush,' quoth Stucley, 'I will have the Duke of Alva to land 20,000 men in Scotland, and then, with the help of the Catholic noblemen in Flanders and England, we will make the Queen to shake in her chair.' To this period of his sojourn in Vinero we must also probably give the following note. When after many delays the King refused to give him the soldiers to invade Ireland, he asked for three ships to carry on his old trade of privateering against

[1] The golden fleece was to have been offered to Sidney as the reward of his promised adherence to the Spaniards.

Protestants—English, Dutch, or French—and to be permitted to sell his 'wares' in certain of the King's ports, by a license similar to that given by Elizabeth to the Prince of Orange. These ships were granted to him, but within three weeks they were again taken from him.

On the 26th of July, when Stucley was still at Vinero, before he saw Philip, the Archbishop of Cashel wrote to the King to persuade him to seize the opportunity of Stucley's arrival to send the promised aid to the Irish insurgents. He had heard that the English wished to make peace with the King. Forsooth, peace would be very convenient to them, for it would set them free to do all possible damage to the Irish. But the Irish trusted in the King, the more so because 'I have written them many letters to encourage them to resist the English, telling them that you will not fail to send them succours, as I was authorized to do by the Cardinal (Espinoza) and other Lords in your Majesty's name. And our people have many times refused the English offers of an amnesty, relying on these promises. So you cannot (quasi in foro conscientiæ) but send our people some succours, whether for the promises sake made by me in your name, and with great deliberation, seeing I have now been here for a year and three months, or because you are "Catholic King".... And as the Queen of England has secretly helped, and still helps the heretic rebels of France, so you can secretly send succours for us under pretence of sending them to Flanders, when they can, against your will, or on such like pretext, turn aside to Ireland.

'And you have an excellent opportunity for this in the coming of this Englishman Thomas Stucley, who surely has received such wrongs from his countrymen that he will not fail to do them all the harm he can. He is a man of great courage and knowledge of war, in which he has been employed almost his whole life. He thoroughly understands the whole mystery, and knows the fortresses and the ports. He has brought with him, as I hear, the best mariners of all Ireland. The time of year is fitting, for now we have the greatest abundance of corn and cattle; if within three months you do not send some succour, the English will occupy the forts and ports so strongly that all your power will not be able to do them any harm. This I say, because I am advised that the English are making great preparation, and will now attempt to make themselves masters of the country, and to hold it in such subjection that the natives will never hereafter be able to make the least resistance. If they succeed, which God forbid, your Majesty will have the worst turns you ever had. But all this you may prevent if you are beforehand with them, and send a few men to seize the forts and harbours. It must be done quickly' (Froude's Simancas Transcripts, B, fol. 142, &c.).

The Archbishop wrote this letter under the stimulus of a double censure. On the one hand was the Pope, like Samuel, telling him how evil it was that Ireland should seek a king without him; on the other side, the Irish scolding him for not making the procrastinating Philip change his nature, and crying out for a king, as the Israelites cried out for Saul. Under these difficulties the Archbishop at first played the part demanded of him humbly enough. But on second thoughts he fretted more and more that the glory of the action which he had first mooted should be usurped by Stucley. He was a patriot who would save his country if he could, but did not like its being saved by any but himself. This is the opinion that the astute Walsingham formed of him—'he misliked that Stucley should have the glory of the enterprise that they both pretended, and that he first set abroach,' and so was glad to do 'anything that might impeach it.' The two letters which he received from Rome and from Ireland are as follows. The one was from Cardinal Alciati, dated June 9, 1570: 'Out of your letter of March 1 I informed the Pope that the nobles of Ireland had formed the design of delivering themselves to the Catholic King, and, having some time since sent you as their envoy to demand his aid, had recently given you command to offer homage to the King in their name, and to promise that they would do what he ordered. The Pope wonders that such innovations should be attempted without authority; since it is easy to remember that the kingdom of Ireland is a fief of the Church, and therefore cannot be transferred to a new government except by the Pope, who, in his due defence of the Church's right, refuses to write to the King such a letter as you request. But if the King himself shall ask that the fief may be granted to him, I imagine that the Pope will not refuse' (Froude's Transcripts, B, fol. 138).

The letter of the Irish nobles to the Archbishop is given by Gonzales (Documenti, no. x.). It is dated Tralee, May 4, 1570, just after Stucley's departure from Ireland; and though it does not mention a new envoy, it implies that they were not satisfied with their old one. 'It is impossible,' they begin, 'to say how we marvel that in all this time you have not despatched the affairs for which you were sent; this delay has wrought us much evil, for by this time we might have gained many victories over our enemies. We cannot trust the English, whatever securities they offer; between mortal enemies no security is secure. The English have always taken occasion to invade us in time of peace; in which time they are as powerful in Ireland as they are in England. At the time of our writing this we were so wearied with you that we thought of writing to the King to complain of your slowness in the service of your country; but now we ask you to delay no longer in procuring his aid, otherwise we must make peace. We have with us two of the principal of those nobles who lately rose[1] in England, seeking our friendship, and proposing things to which we cannot agree without asking the King, to whom we have sworn fidelity. If by reason of his various wars the King cannot help us, and if, as our friends in the English Council inform us, the Queen wishes to have peace with the King—this is only to deceive him, and to divert his aid from us. The proposal is not for his good, but his harm. We therefore, after deliberation together, depute you to speak to the King, that we may have his brother Don John of Austria for our King. We have written to Don John in this sense. If he accepts, as soon as he sets foot in Ireland we will all be dutiful subjects, and he shall be King not of Ireland only, but of other provinces which we will conquer for him. If we had a King like other nations, no one would dare attack us . . . . but without a King, and divided amongst ourselves, the English rob us daily; and without the King's help we must either be entirely destroyed, or give up great part of our possessions to obtain a disgraceful peace.'

Nothing was done with speed at Philip's Court. Stucley had arrived at Vinero on the 24th of April, and it was the fourth of August before a pursuivant was sent to call him to Madrid, and to present with a thousand ducats. Stucley set out on his progress on the 18th of August. On his arrival the King ordered him to send for his son, and gave him 3000 ducats more, besides the daily expenses

[1] The rebellion of the North in 1569.

of his lodging and diet. It was now September, and the Archbishop of Cashel had ceased to regard Stucley with the same favour as in July. It is not likely that the Archbishop was either so indispensable, or so cold to Stucley, as he afterwards told Walsingham that he had been, but it is quite clear that a jealousy had been set up, which was not alloyed by the royal reception given to Stucley. The Archbishop received a poor pension of 2000 ducats a year from the King; Stucley no sooner appeared at Court, but the King gave him 6000 ducats, and an establishment which cost, as the Archbishop supposed, at least 30 ducats a day more. Stucley too was an Englishman, not an Irishman; a soldier, not a priest, and yet more voluble and plausible than an Irish popular preacher. He invaded the Archbishop's domain, and the Archbishop returned his easy insolence with a thorough and conscientious purpose of revenge. He does not seem to have ventured to say all he meant to say till the eve of his departure from Madrid. But in the mean time he doubtless made his feelings apparent as far as he dared both in words and deeds. Thus on one occasion the Archbishop hid two Irishmen who had fled from Stucley, who thereupon came to him, and finding the men in his chamber, threatened him (MSS. Ireland, May 2, 1571), or, according to the Archbishop's own statement, in consequence of what he had told the Duke of Feria about Stucley, Stucley came and challenged him, and told him, if he were not a Churchman he would be revenged on him for the report he made of him. However it was, the bickerings between the two men were displeasing to some of the court, and the Cardinal president, Rugones, and Secretary Çayas began to dislike Stucley, while the Duke of Feria, Don Antonio di Toledo, the Grand Prior, and the Bishop of Cuença gave him their energetic support.

On his first arrival in court Stucley probably reiterated and enforced the recommendations he had made from Vinero. He asked for a contingent of troops, which was first to be 10,000 men, and then by degrees less, till he declared he would be satisfied with 5000 if he might have Julian Romero to command them. For the approach of the country, he proposed first to seize the Scilly Isles, so as to have a harbour from which he might invade England or Ireland as he pleased. An idea like this would naturally take years to filter through Philip's head. At first Stucley waited about the court and amused the Councillors with his braves and brags. His man Rigsby, who returned to England in August, 1571, purchased his freedom by informing the English Council of his master's talk. The information is probably coloured by the wish of the deserter to make the cause which he deserts as black as may be. One while Stucley would tell the Councillors how the Queen used to beat Secretary Cecil about the ears when he discontented her, and how he used to weep like a child. At another time, when asked why the Queen did not marry, he said she never would marry, for she could not abide a woman with child, who, she said, was worse than a sow. He also said, like Dr Story, that he was no subject to Elizabeth, but sworn servant to the King of Spain; and instructed his men to say to the English in Spain, that as they served the Queen of England, so he obeyed and served the Pope and King Philip. 'As for Elizabeth,' quoth he, 'what hurt I can do her or any of hers I will do it, and I am glad to make her vilely afraid, though yet I hurt her not.' At another time he said he would make the Queen of England to wish herself again in her mother's belly, 'with other things of the Queen and her mother too loathsome to express.' Mr Dennis, a cousin of Stucley's, and like him a refugee at the Spanish Court, replied, 'It is great pity that the wicked race of Henry the Eighth is not rooted out, for then we should have a Catholic country.' 'Well,' quoth Stucley, 'cousin Dennis,[1] I will make her Catholic in spite of her heart, for I will bring the Pope on her neck, and the greatest King in Christendom, and the French King, who I know dare not disobey the Pope, and the good Catholic Queen of Scots, whom she keeps prisoner.' 'Marry,' quoth Dennis, 'cousin Stucley, you say troth, for she is the rightful Queen of England.' 'Yea,' said Stucley, 'I trust to see shortly a hundred thousand pikes and staves couched in the field to fetch her away.' Then Alessandro Fideli interposed—'If you will go to the Pope you shall have men and money enough.' 'Alexander, hold your peace, hold your peace,' quoth Stucley, 'I will talk more with you of that matter,' and then embracing Alexander, he said, 'I will make thee a Lord either in England or Ireland, and to be of as good degree as Cecil.' Then said Digby, his major domo—'Master, do you remember what the Duke of Guise was wont to say?—the fort is well kept that was never assaulted. We Englishmen make ourselves devils before we come to it, and then we be nobody.' 'For my part,' quoth Stucley, 'I hate an Englishman as I hate a dog; for if ever I be betrayed I shall be betrayed by them. But Ireland is the country that I and my child must stick to; for I must live by them and they by me. For there I will build a fair Abbey, and have in it twenty-four friars, and one of them to pray for me every hour of the day and night. And there will I be buried.'

[1] Dennis' grandfather, William of Orleigh, Devon, had married a sister of Stucley's grandfather, Sir Thomas, and a daughter of Sir Nicholas Stucley of Affton. This Mr Dennis was probably either John or William, the sons of Nicholas Dennis of Orleigh.

Another while, thinking in the bitterness of his heart how Nicholas White had been preferred over him in Wexford, he said that he would stay the Queen's frisking and dancing, and would trouble Cecil's fine head once again, to teach her to displace a soldier, and to put in one with a pen and ink-horn at his girdle.

At other times he would talk of his military plans, and say, 'He that will bridle the Queen of England must first take Ireland from her; then Scotland, bordering upon England, will trouble her. I will give a foul push for it when England thinketh least of it.'

When he was asked by Secretary Çayas to give in writing what lands the Queen had taken from him, he is said to have delivered this list. The Castle and Town of Wexford, and the whole County; the Abbey of Inniscorthy, and that country of mosses, and seven or eight farms worth a thousand marks a year. The Castle of Ferel and Kinsale belonging to it, and the house of Lafylond, and the Kavanagh's country, 'which my blinking cousin Sir Peter Carew hath, but at my return into Ireland I will lay him in the black castle of Lafylond with as many irons as he can bear.' The Castle of Carlow and that whole County. The ancient kingdom of Leinster, for which he had paid twenty-two hundred pounds in one day, but which was taken from him because he was a Catholic, and loved and commended the King of Spain. For this, he said, he was in prison seventeen weeks, and like to have lost his life, and hardly escaped.

He was generally called at Court the Duke of Ireland, possibly because Sidney had made him Marshall of Ireland, in the place of Sir Nicholas Bagenall. But he asked the King to make him Duke of Leinster, and his son Marquess; and he would leave him in pledge with the King. He said also that he had built the new Castle in Mc Acre's county.

Stucley's stay at the Court is divided into two periods. One, not of long duration, seems to have been spent at Madrid; it was probably during this time that the conversations more or less truly reported by Rigsby occurred. But it seems that Stucley, either from a true enthusiasm, or from sharing the fashionable feeling of the day, or from calculation that he could so best provide for himself, resolved to spend his involuntary leisure in preparing to enter one of the Spanish orders of religious Knights. Such a proposal would naturally chime in with Philip's disposition, who had already magnificently entertained him at Court, and now took a house for him at a village called Arosso, three leagues from Madrid, where he defrayed his expenses and those of his suit (he had some thirty gentlemen about him), and assigned him as a companion, perhaps to instruct him in his new duties, Don Francesco Merles, of Catalonia, a Knight of the Order of Calatrava. Stucley perhaps made his vows as a Knight of this Order when the King knighted him on the 22nd of January, 1571. It is to this period of his residence at Arosso with Don Francesco that the following letter refers (quoted by Mr Froude, x. 525). It is written to Cecil, by one Oliver King, who had been an officer in the train of the Duke of Guise during the French wars. He was paid off at the peace, and had gone to Spain to take service against the Moors. While at the Spanish Court, 'a certain Duke of Ireland,' he wrote, 'otherwise called master Stucley, being advertised of what I had done against the Prince of Condé, procured that I might speak with him. When I came to him he offered me the greatest courtesy in the world, gave me apparel better than I was used to wear, and entertained me with great and marvellous liberality. In a short time he declared unto me that he with diligence must depart unto his country of Ireland with 10,000 men, in the which army he would have employed me for to have undermined the forts of Dingle, Wexford, and Waterford, with many other castles which were enemies unto this good Duke Stucley. But when I did see all his provision of soldiers, and his intention against my prince and country, I presently desired him of leave, and declared unto him that I came to serve the King, and that I would not, while I had life, bear arms against my natural prince, neither against my country wherein I was born. On the which he called me a villian and a traitor, and caused me to be taken prisoner for a Luteryan in his house. But a certain knight, Don Francesco, which kept him company, did well see every day that I did go to mass, and knocked my breast as well as they; and so he answered for me that I was no Luteryan. And when this good Duke did see that he might not put me to death by the Inquisition, he caused me to come forth in the presence of the knight, and certain captains of his, with all his gentlemen and yeomen, and stripped me unto my shirt, and banished me the town of Madrid, giving me but four hours' respite to depart upon pain of the gallows.'

King thereupon made his way to Pampeluna, and back through the Pyrenees into France. From thence he wrote once more to Cecil to impress upon him the real danger from Stucley's machinations. The Spaniards certainly intended, he said, to make a descent either on Ireland or on England. The Duke's grace Stucley had received the Sacrament and promised to render unto the King of Spain not only the entrance within his Duchy, but also possession of the whole realm of Ireland. The soldiers were amassing from all parts of Spain—Spaniards, Burgundians, Italians, the most part Bezonians, beggarly ill-armed rascals, but their captains old beaten men of war. The King was sparing no cost on the enterprise, and no honours to Stucley, hoping by such means to enlarge his empire (MSS. Spain, Feb. 18, 1572).

This noviciate, or whatever it was, at Arosso seems to have lasted twenty-two weeks. At the end of that time Stucley set out for Rome. He had previously asked for license to resort to the Pope to declare to him the state of Ireland and England, and to procure his help for his enterprise; and the King's answer had been that he should not depart without his own contentation.

These dates are necessary to show how little influence was wrought on the King's mind by the following paper, which came to him from the Archbishop of Cashel soon after the 6th of December, 1570 (Froude's Simancas transcripts, B, fol. 156). It was perhaps addressed to the Cardinal, or to the Nuncio.

'Most illustrious Lord, to fulfil at once my duty to his Majesty and my chiefs, and for discharge of my conscience, it has seemed good to me to inform you of the following facts, that the knowledge of them may better come to his Majesty before I go hence, for it is time for me to go to give account of myself to my chiefs.

'It is some days since there came into Spain a certain Englishman named Thomas Stucley, born (as I am informed) in the county of Devon, a private gentleman whose elder brother and heir of his father (and Thomas' father) is yet living in England as a private gentleman, and so lived the said Thomas long time in England in the service of the Duke of Suffolk, as a retainer of the said Duke, wearing his livery in the manner of that country.

'After the death of the said Duke, having got a ship, how I know not, he went to sea, turned pirate, and robbed all he could. And coming to Ireland to sell what he had robbed, he was taken and carried into England by an Irish gentleman, and thrown into the Tower of London, where he remained some time in very close prison. Afterwards by intercession of his friends, and favour of some noblemen who had known him at the house of the said Duke, he was taken from the Tower and set at liberty. At that time there happened to be in London a merchant surnamed Curtes, Mayor of London (one of the rich men who in years past had held that office), with but one daughter, his heir. Stucley quickly boarded her, and married her without her father's knowledge, and got by her a great inheritance, the whole of which he wasted in a short time after.

'All that wealth being gone he tried once more his luck at sea. He promised the Queen to go and people Florida if she would supply him with ships, promising great advantages to the crown. So having received three ships, and the services of many volunteers who thought to find in that land quantities of gold and silver, and to become presently very rich, he once more went to sea, and forsaking his design on Florida, robbed as before; and so returning to England, was tried for having made so great a failure, and having neither lands nor favour in England, went to Ireland as a private soldier.

'There were once in Ireland two brothers that had a great dispute about certain lands; the elder was favoured by the natives as being true and legal owner; the younger, in order to prevail, betook himself to the Viceroy, offering to hold the lands in the King's name, and to serve the King as his faithful vassal; so that by means of the Viceroy and an English jury the younger brother took the greater part of the lands, and was afterwards turned out of them, like the elder one, because he would not consent with the English in religion. This was in the reign of Edward VI. The Viceroy said that those lands were the King's; and that the King could dispose of them at will, and give them to whom he pleased; the Viceroy therefore by royal authority gave them to a certain English Captain called Heron, who kept possession of them, but not in very peaceful sort; and for this cause the Captain—both for the great trouble in keeping them, and because he wanted to return into England—sold the said lands to the said Thomas Stucley a short time ago, for a very small sum, because the lands were not his own, and he had no power or licence to sell them.

'The Queen being much displeased with the said Thomas for many reasons, because he had not accomplished the project he promised, because he had robbed many and divers English merchants who were daily complaining to the Queen, and also because, as it was said, he had committed certain murders in the said lands, and because he had bought the Queen's lands without her consent or that of the Deputy, ordered the said Deputy to take him. This was presently done, and the said Thomas imprisoned in the city of Dublin so closely that none could speak with him. A little before he was taken, having heard that some of the principal men of Ireland had risen against the Queen, and knowing the ill-will she bore him, seeing he could revenge himself on her no otherwise, he sent to the Spanish ambassador in England praying him that he would conclude with the King to send troops to conquer Ireland, promising him that he should not want favour. This he did, not because he was a Catholic, for it is clear that no one in all Ireland wrought greater ruin in Churches, Monasteries, and Images. And what favour could he give, who was an Englishman, much hated by the English, and much more hated by the Irish, both for the natural and common hatred of all Irishmen for Englishmen, and for the special hatred which all have of him for having bought and held those lands, most Irishmen knowing that neither the Queen nor he has any right to them?

'While he was in prison as aforesaid, he begged leave of the Deputy through some friends to go to England to make his defence; the Deputy agreed, because he thought thus to escape the odium he might incur with some by condemning him to death, however justly. Having obtained the permission, he published that he was going to England, and getting a passport to take with him certain horses which some Irish gentlemen had given him, or which he had bought, certain gentlemen embarked some Irishmen in the ship in which he sailed, both to defend themselves in certain matters of which they were accused, and to beg pardon of the Queen; and others of their own motion who had business in England; all of whom he deceived, and after sailing from the port of Waterford on the plea of going to England, he brought here into Spain, and now they dare not return to England or Ireland, whence seeing themselves without remedy, they are almost desperate, especially for the fear they have of him. For he threatened them, that whoever attempted to go to his own country or elsewhere, should be thrown into prison, and he keeps them all in his ship, of all which things you can easily get information from the said Irishmen, whether those that are here, or those in Galicia, under condition that the said Thomas Stucley shall know nothing of such information, for if he knew, they would not venture to speak the truth for the dread they have of him. And moreover as it is true that the man is and has ever been a private person, it is not credible that the Lords of Ireland would entrust an affair touching them so nearly to the hands of a private Englishman, especially without giving me notice of it;[1] for they sent me here, and know that I am in this Court for love of them; nor can I believe that the chiefs of Ireland would have a private Englishman hold any office in their kingdom, when they so determinately resist the Queen of England, who has often offered them peace with good conditions. So that to me his mission seems a pretence, or without ground, for as far as I have heard he holds no commission from the Lords of Ireland, either to the King, or any one else. This seems confirmed by the coming of a Franciscan Friar with certain despatches for me, whom I had previously sent to Ireland. This Friar was with you in Cordova; neither by his papers did I hear anything of Thomas Stucley, nor could he tell me anything about him, except that there was a report in Ireland that a certain Englishman had gone to sea, as was supposed, to commit piracy, as he had done before. Hence I think his Majesty ought to order enquiries to be made of the said Thomas Stucley, by whose command, and for what cause, he came into Spain. And if he came of his own head it is clear that a private person cannot do much, and that he should not be allowed to depart hence, because he has men and furniture for the sea, and having no country to live in with any certainty, he will go and rob as before, of which the King will give an account to God, being able to prevent him and not doing so.'

[1] Walsingham, however, at Paris had been informed by a man he trusted that 'Stucley had presented an instrument to the King, not only subscribed with the names of the most part of the Irish nobility, but also the names of divers in England of good quality, ready to be at his devotion.' Advice to Cecil from Paris, Feb. 8, 1571. Complete Ambassador, p. 36.

Having thus left his sting in the wound, the Archbishop of Cashel took himself off, if not at once from Spain, at least from the Court—and then, not to Ireland, to render account of himself to his chiefs, but to Paris, in order to betray both Stucley and them to Walsingham, then English Ambassador with Charles IX. The document just given would almost seem to have been concocted from information derived from the English Court, tallying as it does with the letter of Queen Elizabeth to Walsingham, dated Feb. 11, 1571, in which she instructs him to complain to the Spanish Ambassador in Paris about Philip's reception of Elizabeth's rebels. 'We have heard and known it to be true that certain savage rebels being men of no value had fled out of our realm of Ireland into Spain, and to cover their lewdness ... do pretend their departure out of the realm for matter of religion, when indeed they be neither of one nor the other religion, but given to bestiality; and yet they have wit enough to show hypocrisy for their purpose. Since the first arrival of these, we know also that an Englishman, a subject of ours, namely Stucley, not unknown, as we think, for his former prodigal life both in Spain and other places—and notwithstanding great favours showed unto him divers times, upon hope of amendment, and some tokens of his repentance—did this last summer, pretending to come out of Ireland hither, suddenly turn his course into Spain; and as we hear hath light into the company of the aforesaid fugitives and rebels, pretending by his superfluous expenses, which is altogether of other men's goods, to be a person of some quality and estimation, and able to do some great thing in Ireland, whereas indeed he hath not the value of a Marmaduc in land or livelihood; he hath so solicited the King or some about him with vain notions, as it is by him bruited and otherwise with some credit reported unto us (which yet we do not believe) that the King will send a captain of his, such a one as Julio Romero or such like, with a number of soldiers into Ireland, to follow some vain device of those rebels; whereof we cannot but marvel that the King or any of his council, being of experience, can so lightly give any credit to such a companion as Stucley is, which could never live long in any quiet condition at home: of whom we are not disposed to say much because we cannot say any good of him; but may say, it shall be sufficient that his conditions may be only enquired of, and then we doubt not whosoever shall know them will take heed how to adventure anything with him' (Complete Ambassador, p. 40). In obedience to this Walsingham visited Olivarez, the Spanish envoy in Paris, whom he found more solemn (after the Spanish fashion) than wise, and remonstrated with him about Stucley's reception at Madrid. Olivarez replied that the King his master was glad to entertain any gentleman of countenance that offered him service, and to honour him with knighthood. Walsingham then made him acquainted with the course of Stucley's life, as also how little he had to take to, and therefore willed him to consider how unworthy he was of any honour or entertainment in respect of himself, and how much more unworthy in respect of his being a rebel to the ancient ally of the house of Burgundy (Ib. p. 56).

On the 25th of March Walsingham by appointment saw the Archbishop of Cashel; Walsingham already knew a good deal of him and of his doings, but was careful not to say a word about that knowledge; he let him say all that he had to say as if to a sympathizing and believing listener. Having first justified his departure out of Ireland without the Queen's leave because, 'being deprived from his living, and another substituted in his place, whom he confessed to have outraged before his departure, necessity enforced him to seek maintenance some other where,' the Archbishop said that he had left Spain about the latter end of January, and that about September last one Stucley arrived in Spain, who, after his access to Madrid, before he had conference with the King or any great personage, visited the Archbishop, and after protesting how glad he was to see him there, whom he knew to be Catholicly bent, showed him that his intention in repairing to that country was to deal with the King of Spain about reducing Ireland to his government, whereby heresy might be expelled, and true Catholic religion planted. He therefore desired him, as one well acquainted with the Cardinal Espinoza, President of the Council, to deal with him to procure Stucley's access to the King. The Archbishop told Walsingham that his answer was, that he thought the King, in consequence of the amity between him and the Queen, would be loth to deal in the matter; and that he, for his part, misliked such means of planting the Catholic religion; for he would be loth to see his country under any other government than that of Elizabeth and her successors. And upon that the Archbishop refused to bring Stucley to the Cardinal President.

Stucley thereupon, the Archbishop continued, went to the Duke of Feria, who brought him to the King. The King, upon conference had with him, used him very honourably, and appointed him a very fair house, and gave him 6000 ducats, besides a daily allowance for the maintenance of his table, for which he was supposed to spend 30 ducats a day. Two days afterwards the King sent for the Archbishop and asked him whether he knew Stucley? He replied that he had never seen him but in Spain, but he had heard of him as a Pirate, of life dissolute, in expenses prodigal, of no substance, neither a man of any great account in his country, although a gentleman born and descended of a good house. The King then told the Archbishop of Stucley's offer for Ireland, and of his assurance that he had made the Irish nobility ready to receive such forces as the King would send. The Archbishop in reply wished the King not to be so light of belief, because Stucley was not a man of such credit with the Irish nobility as to be able to bring any such matter to pass; for they knew him to be a shifter, who, for the maintenance of his prodigality, sought to abuse all men. The King replied that Stucley's own report of himself was confirmed by his ambassador, who willed him to credit whatsoever he reported.

Not long afterwards, the Archbishop proceeded, the Duke of Feria met him, and asked his opinion of Stucley. He answered that he had made the King acquainted with his opinion, and that he feared the King would be abused by him. The Duke replied that the chances of the enterprise, as shown by Stucley, were so good, that the King ought to embrace it. For besides the Irish nobility he had won a great number of the Queen's garrison to be at his devotion, as well soldiers as captains. To which the Archbishop answered—There will be no great difficulty in the enterprise; but when it comes to the trial it will fall out otherwise. To which the Duke—Well, I perceive you are not willing it should go forward, and therefore you seek to deface this gentleman, whom we honour with the name of Duke of Ireland. The Archbishop said that that was a title unknown in Ireland, and more strange in a man without lands; and the Duke answered that if Stucley might enjoy his own there, it would well maintain that calling: surely, replied the Archbishop, if the rest of his talk prove no truer than this, then shall you see the King much abused by him.

After this, according to the Archbishop, Stucley came and challenged him, and told him, if he were not a man as he was, a man of the Church, he would be revenged on him for the report he made of him. And thereupon the Archbishop departed out of Spain, because he saw great likelihood that the enterprise should go forward, and would be loth, as one descended from the house of Desmond, to be suspected, by his abode there, to be a favourer of the said enterprise, hating nothing more than the name of a traitor.

In the end of his letter Walsingham gives several reasons why he did not believe the Archbishop's protestations of loyalty, although he saw that he hated Stucley. 'I imagine,' he says, 'that he mislikes that Stuckly should have the glory of the enterprise that they both pretended, and that he first set abroach, and therefore would be glad to do anything that might impeach the same' (Complete Ambassador, p. 58, seqq.). Walsingham granted one more interview to the Archbishop, who then told him that his only reason for leaving Spain was to obtain license to return into his country with the Queen's favour, and to eschew the name of traitor; also that it was more than time that the Queen sent some one to Spain about the matter, 'both for that the Queen's Majesty hath many traitors in Ireland of the Irishmen and English soldiers there; and also because the King of Spain doth what he can to win the French King's brother to his side.' The Archbishop added that Stucley had sent to Morlaix a Spaniard to spy out and discredit James Fitzmorris who was there. Walsingham took measures similar to those with which the Archbishop was so familiar, and surrounded him with Irishmen who professed to be his friends, but who were to do all they could to bring him into discredit with the Duke of

Guise (Ib., p. 74). He did not return into Ireland; but from France he went into Flanders, and there tried to make the Duke of Alva aid the Irish by invading England.[1] On the 12th of August, 1573, Pope Gregory XIII. wrote to Alva in favour of the Irish, recommended to the Duke by his venerable brother the Bishop of Cashel;[2] but Alva was probably warned from Madrid concerning the character of this venerable man. In 1574 Dr Nicholas Sanders warned Philip against Lord Morley, who had rendered himself suspicious by his familiarity with the Archbishop of Cashel, and Thomas Jennis, in Belgium, and with the English Ambassador in Paris (Froude, Simancas Transcripts, B. 332).

After receiving his knighthood, Stucley remained some months in Spain, with continually smaller chances of obtaining ships and men for Ireland. For in truth Philip was then deeply engaged in the league against the Turk, of which his brother Don John of Austria was generalissimo, and towards which he contributed, besides, the lion's share of expenses, 83 ships and many thousand men. But Stucley's failure was attributed in England not to the other claims upon Philip, but to the King's discovery of his 'lewdness and insufficiency.'[3] On the second of May Sir William Fitzwilliams wrote to Cecil that he had sent to have it placarded in Dublin, that

---

[1] Walsingham had been warned of this as early as the 8th of Feb. There was a design on Ireland, which, though the King of France was not privy to it, was greatly promoted by the Duke of Guise; and the Papal Nuncio was offering the Duke of Anjou 100,000 francs if he would join in it; the promoters professed that its execution would not be difficult, and that Ireland once theirs, the winning of England would be an easy step (Complete Ambassador, p. 36).

[2] He must have been in the interim prisoner in Scotland. Dom. Eliz. 1572, vol. 88, no. 29, June 26. Hogan details to Leicester the 'treasonable dealings in Spain of Maurice, Archbishop of Cashel, now prisoner in Scotland.'

[3] Cecil to Walsingham, June 5, 1571 (Complete Ambassador).

Stucley was departed Spain, and had been put out of pension (MSS. Ireland). According to another information of May 13, it would appear that the design of the Irish invasion was not finally abandoned till about April 25, when Stucley went to Vinero, and discharged most of the men whom he had brought with him from Ireland, being fully determined to repair to Rome to the Pope, and for that intent returned again to the Court to take his leave, but in no such estimation as he was at his first coming (MSS. Ireland). Thus the fear which had fluttered the Court of Elizabeth for some months was for the time allayed. There was nervousness enough at Dublin; but it was little in comparison to that of the more experienced heads at London, to whom Nicholas White wrote from Ireland, with his old grudge—'As for Stucley we judge more malice in him than power to do any hurt here; nor can be persuaded that any wise prince would adventure so great an enterprise upon so slender a warrant, and so ill a quarrel. Nevertheless we will with all carefulness observe the contents of her Majesty's letters, and provide for the worst' (MSS. Ireland, April 9, 1571).

Stucley had, however, as we have seen, been for a long time talking of his going to the Pope, but Philip could not make up his mind to dismiss him. A warrant was given by Philip to him[1] a week after he was knighted (Jan. 30, 1571), certifying that Thomas Stucley, Knight of England, had come out of England to the town and port of Vinero, in a ship in the which he brought his son and others his servants, and after staying there some days, had

[1] A copy is in the Cotton manuscripts (Galba. vi. pt. i. no. 3), among the papers given to Daniel Rogers, sent as envoy to the Duke Casimir, in 1577, to represent, inter alia, the way in which English fugitives and rebels had been maintained by Philip.

come with royal licence to the Court, and now was returning with the same licence, leaving his son with the King, and taking with him his ship and people. 'And because, as well before now as in the time that he hath here remained, we have known the Christianity, virtue, and goodness and other good qualities of the man, and the desire that he hath to serve us, and that all things wherein hitherto he hath been dealt withal he hath well performed :' Therefore, proceeds the document, 'it is our will that he is to receive good treatment, and purchase of provisions at reasonable rates, in all ports whither he shall come. Stucley did not act upon this till the 6th of March, when he went to Vinero, and made known that the King's pleasure was to receive him and his household servants into the royal service, and that he should now remove his household and servants to those parts convenient for the King's service. He therefore requests that three of his men, Nicholas Abbot, James Marchant, and Thomas Jaquet, shall receive the entertainment provided for in the warrant. It looks as if this was the time that he dismissed his other servants, and sold his ship to Robert Boene, of Vigo' (MSS. Ireland, May 2, 1571). Even his old servant Digby was dismissed, after his twenty years' service, and in March, 1572, found himself a prisoner in the Gatehouse in London (MSS. Domestic, March 6, 1572). Murdin (p. 185) gives an account of Stucley at this time—February, 1571. He was engaged with Englefield in Flanders and the Duchess of Feria in Spain, in settling the choice of an heir-apparent for the English throne, viz. the King of Scots. It was through Englefield's representations that Stucley was stayed in Spain longer than he otherwise would have been, as a man very necessary to be used in some military service by land or by sea. He did at last obtain his warrant to go to Rome, but not till Sir Henry Cobham [1] had started on a mission from Elizabeth to Philip, to represent to him among other things, that he must order the English rebels out of Flanders, and abandon Stucley, who had been received and caressed at his Court, before she would enter on the question of the restoration of captured goods and vessels. Stucley accordingly departed towards Rome about the end of April, and was splendidly received by Pope Pius V. Probably he took warm recommendations from Philip; but whether he owed his special honours to any suspicion of a semi-royal birth, or to his being a knight of Calatrava, or a famous English captain, I know not. At Rome, Laderchi tells us, he was much closeted with the Pope in consultation for the restoration of religion, and at length he generously undertook the exploit, which, he says, will be told in its place (Annales Eccle., tom. xxiv. p. 246, no. xlv.). Laderchi never returns to this matter, but the exploit he meant was doubtless that which Jerome Catena mentions, and which Camden, Rapin, and the English historians generally relate after him—namely, the offer to conquer Ireland with 3000 men, and to burn the ships in the Thames, with a detachment of two ships and two armed Zebras under one of his pilots.

But it is not likely that this exploit was intended to take place immediately. Ridolfi's negotiations with the English malcontents, the Scottish patriots, and the Duke of Alva, were still going on. The Duke of Norfolk was not sent back to the Tower till the fifth of September, and before that time the plot can scarcely be said to have been ripe. But just then the Pope was straining every nerve to add ship to ship and man to man for the fleet of the league

---

[1] Cobham's instructions are dated March 20. He was in Madrid in May and June; Philip's letter to Elizabeth which he took back was dated June 30.

against the Turk. And when we find that Stucley served in that fleet we can only suppose that he was directed by the Pope first to perform that service, and afterwards to hold himself in readiness to conquer Ireland.

Whether Stucley was in one of the Pope's vessels, or in one of the Spanish contingent, I cannot tell. A rumour reached Ireland in the middle of February, 1572, that Stucley had returned from Rome to the Spanish Court about five months before, in the middle of September, and had been seen there with his son. But he must have embarked again immediately, for he was present and acquitted himself like a man at the battle of Lepanto on the 7th of October. Many English volunteers fought there, and ten were killed. Robert Hogan, in an information to Cecil, gives the names of four of them—Mr George Neville, Mr Claborne,[1] who was a valiant soldier in very good estimation, Mr Brooke, and Walter Beamont (MSS. Dom. March 6, 1572). At the battle, says one Nicholas Rice, Irish Merchant, Stucley was captain of three gallies under Don John.[2] On the 13th of April, 1572, some merchants landed at Galway, who reported that Thomas Stucley, by means of his manly deeds done in the Levant Seas in company of Don John of Austria, was lately reconciled to King Philip, and now with him in great estimation and credit[3] (MSS. Ireland, Ap. 12, 1572). The same report

---

[1] A person of the same name, perhaps a brother of this Claborne, accompanied Stucley in his expedition in 1578.

[2] MSS. Ireland, vol. 36, no. 29, May, 1572.

[3] For the rejoicings in London at the receipt of the news of Lepanto, see *Correspondance diplomatique de Fénélon*, iv. p. 281 and p. 285, and compare the following two publications: 1. 'Letters sent from Venice, Anno 1571, containing the certain and true news of the most noble victory of the Christians over the army of the great Turk ; and the names of the Lords and Gentlemen of Christians slain in the same battle. Translated out of the French

had been brought a fortnight before by Walter French, merchant of Galway. 'Stucley is returned unto the Court at Madrid from Don John, with whom he was in his last skirmish against the Turk.'

But before Stucley had returned to Madrid the English plot had collapsed, and his Irish enterprise had lost its appositeness and relevancy. Philip, we are told by Catena (Vita de Pio V. Roma. 1587, p. 118), lamented this failure to Cardinal Alessandrino, the Pope's nephew, who with a splendid train left Rome on the 30th of June, and arrived at Madrid on the 29th of September. He said, 'Never was there a plot more excellent or better ordered than this, and never was there seen greater union or constancy among the conspirators, for it was all the while never discovered on their part, and it was a plot very easy to execute, because with the sudden passage, requiring only a day and night, of three thousand harquebusiers out of Flanders, who were to land at the appointed time in a certain place near London, where both in the Tower, and in the guard at Court, there was perfect understanding, and people all prepared, the fact would have been performed before the French heard of it,—the Queen of Scots set free, and established Queen of England as legitimate heir, and the Catholic religion restored. Especially as there was a certainty that Thomas Stucley, an English

copy printed at Paris by Guillem de Niverd with the Kings privelege. Imprinted at London by Henrie Bynneman, and are to be sold in Paules Churchyard by Anthony Kitson,' n. d. 5 leaves, 12mo. b. l.

2. 'The whole discourse of the victorie that it pleased God to give to the Christians against the Turks, and what loss happened to the Christians in the said conflict. Englished by a French copy printed at Paris by Fleuri Prevost, priveleged by the King. Imprinted at London by Henry Bynneman. And are to be sold in Paules Churchyard by Anthony Kitson,' n. d. 5 leaves, 12mo. b. l.

gentleman, with the conduct he had held in Ireland, would in a few weeks, with some armed ships granted him by the King of Spain, and with three thousand men he would take over, make the whole Island turn to the devotion of the Catholics : besides sending with two ships and two armed Zebras one of his pilots to burn all the naval establishments in the Thames.'

Philip did not at all exhaust the ramifications of this plot. He had been deluded into a correspondence with Sir John Hawkins, who promised him, on conditions, to enter his service with sixteen ships, 1585 men, and 420 guns, with the object of re-establishing the Catholic religion in England, destroying the tyranny of Elizabeth, liberating the Queen of Scots, and setting her on the English throne. He insisted on having a pardon signed by Philip for all his piracies; all these papers he duly submitted to the Queen's counsellors, and thus proved to demonstration that Philip's only aversion to pirates was when they were not in his service.

But these disappointments did not alter the King's kindness to Stucley. If it had ever cooled, which is a report that comes to us only on the authority of the agents of the English government, it was now again as warm as ever. The Irish merchants reported that his allowance was now 1000 ducats a week, which John Grafton, the intelligencer at Galway, thought must be a mistake for 1000 ducats a month; the success against the Turks also excited the Spaniards to 'use more cruelty and earnestness in matters of religion than they were accustomed.' English and Irish denizens were imprisoned for a while, and their goods and ships stayed, and a great armada was being prepared which was said to be intended to pass the seas under the leading of Stucley, either against the Moors or against Ireland, to which Island the Spaniards boasted they would come when they had done with the Turk. This was at the end of 1571 and in the early part of 1572. Stucley came to the Court at Seville on the 2nd of March, 1572 ; whether sent for or of himself was not known to Lee, Burghley's informant (MSS. Dom. Addenda, March 12, 1572). The King received him with his old kindness, and Stucley in return undertook with 20 ships to keep the narrow seas against the Queen's navies. But he demanded that the ships should be altered to his fancy. 'He has already taught the Spaniards,' says Lee, 'to frame their ships after our manner, which they are persuaded will annoy us greatly in a short time, and it is reported that he will be made Admiral or Vice-admiral of the whole' (MSS. Dom. Addenda, May 7, 1572).

On the first of May, 1572, Pius V. died ; and with him died the force by which the league against the Turks had come to be, and was held together. Philip was left to be the chief personage of the league, and his cold procrastination addled the victory of Lepanto, as it had formerly addled that of St Quentin. During 1572, while the Turks were weak, he ordered his fleet not to proceed to the East, but kept it at Messina, where Don John joined it only in October, and then with the intention of sailing back into Spain. This year therefore there was nothing to take Stucley to sea, except in case Philip might order Don John to sail towards Flanders, to aid the English and Irish malcontents. Accordingly the few glimpses we have of him show that he was still about the Court, suggesting his plans to Philip, or recommended to him by Englefield for a mission into France. In the middle of April a treaty was made between Elizabeth and Charles IX. at Blois.[1] In June

[1] Thuanus, iii. 97. Letter of Elizabeth to Philip about Stucley, March 20, 1572, and Philip's reply, June 4, 1572, are in the National Library at Paris, MSS., Coll. Dupuy, vol. 462, p. 109.

Francis Montmorency, Paul de Foix, and la Mothe-Fénélon went over to England to receive Elizabeth's ratification. Dr Nicholas Sanders, who was continually sending advices to the English at Philip's Court, about this time had composed an elaborate address to him on the necessity of the Conquest of England; in this address he enclosed the following brief note in Spanish :—

'They say that the Duke of Montmorency goes presently to England. The negotiation is pretended to be for Alençon, but the intention is to compass the destruction of the Queen of Scots, because the present rulers of France, England, and Scotland are agreed in preventing the union of the two latter countries, whose union the Catholics of England, and they of the house of Spain and Burgundy, alone have reason to desire. For when that Queen is despatched, there is an end to the amity and ancient league between Spain and England. Which pretence, though his Majesty will not believe it, he and his successors will feel when it is too late to remedy, as he now feels it in the affairs of Flanders, which he was just as little willing to believe when he was advised in time.'

To this paper the following notes are affixed in Philip's handwriting : 'As I was going to Mass, Stucley gave me this paper, and he gave me this other note, saying that it was from Sanders, and because I did not know where to put them or leave them, I told him to give them to Santogo, and so he did, and I have read them, and cannot tell why they are in Spanish and not sealed, when the others came in Latin and sealed. And in passing Stucley said to me that I should order that heretic to make haste hence. I believe he spoke of the Milord who talked to me the other day. Let his paper and these be put before the council, and let it consider what is fitting in regard to them. This of Sanders' came waxed and sealed with this envelope. Stucley told me that Englefield had sent him this paper' (Froude's Simancas Transcripts, B. fol. 279). Perhaps Englefield's paper is that at fol. 275 verso. Its date is June, 1572. The subject of it is the Pope's wish for a league between France and Spain to restore religion in England, and a suggestion that the best means of bringing it to pass would be that King Philip should send Stucley as his agent into France. In fact, Stucley had already been to Paris early in the year. Strype (Ann. II. i. p. 65, 66) gives an abstract of a letter dated March 23, 1572, which says that at Paris there were Egremond Ratcliffe, and Jenny who came out of Spain, and Chamberlain, who after conference with the King of Spain's secretary repaired to the Duke of Alva. Stucley was there also, but now is returned to Spain in company with J. Doria.

The year 1572 therefore seems to have been comparatively a quiet one for Stucley. So was 1573, so far as we may judge by the absence of all alarm in England or Ireland concerning his designs. The English exiles at the Spanish Court were now quite tired of the wonderful delays of Philip. A couple of years before Englefield had written to the Duchess of Feria about the 'Spanish consultations,' which 'dwell and busy themselves so long in deliberations, till all help and recovery be in effect desperate.' Lorenzo Priuli four years later reported of Philip, ' he rarely speaks with his ministers, but lives in retirement, and conducts everything by writing. He is always either writing or reading. Every minute detail passes under his hand. But as he cannot suffice for everything, matters are so delayed, that everything is done too late, and negotiations with him are insufferable. His industry is cause of the greatest confusion.'

In the vain hope of putting an end to this system the chiefs of the English exiles, the Countess of Northumberland, Leonard Dacres, Christopher Neville, and Francis Englefield, wrote to the Cardinal of Como from Brussels June 29, 1573, to tell him their opinion that some English exile should be deputed by the Pope as agent of the English at Philip's Court in order to 'rouse to earnestness the torpid mind of the prince, and to answer by the force of reasoning the scruples which his timid mind always offers to his sloth.' For this purpose, they said, no one is so fit as Dr Nicholas Sanders, if not the sole, yet the singular honour and safeguard of our nation. So they ask for his appointment by the Pope, for letters from the Cardinals to the King in his favour, and for the payment by the Pope at least of his expenses to Spain' (Theiner, i. 187). Sanders was a great believer in Stucley, but he does not seem to have entered into his functions at Philip's Court early enough in 1573 to have hatched any plans for the soldier's employment. Stucley, on the other hand, was probably preparing for another campaign against the Turk under Don John. For the league was again active this year, till it was suddenly broken up by the secession of Venice, which made a separate peace with Constantinople, in March; the Spanish preparations were therefore turned against Africa, and probably Stucley accompanied Don John in his bloodless but short-lived conquest of Tunis.

But in the next year the activity of Dr Sanders put forth buds and blossoms, if not fruits. Theiner (i. 310) could have supplied us with interesting documents for the period; but he prefers giving us his own meagre abstract. Philip, he says, 'this year entered into the enterprise of making war against England, deposing Elizabeth, liberating Mary, and declaring her the legitimate Queen:

he communicated his design to the Pope and the King of France, that they might each aid him, according to his kind, in despatching the affair. He had great hopes that they would soon re-establish the Catholic religion in England. To this end he also tried to persuade the Pope to decree by his own authority that Elizabeth, already deprived of the English crown by public sentence of the Church, had forfeited her other realm of Ireland ; which sentence was not to be published before Philip and the French King had invaded England. But the very wise Pontiff altogether rejected this counsel as very full of peril.' This, as we have seen, was the very plan for which Stucley went to Paris in March, 1572, and was to have been sent again in June that year, but which was crossed by the league between Elizabeth and Charles IX. The amity then warmed into life had since grown cool, and the same instruments were ready to reawaken the same dormant league which that amity had eclipsed. In Mr Froude's Simancas transcripts there are long papers by Dr Sanders, which probably represent but a small part of the activity of that teeming brain and flowing pen. There is a long paper (B. fol. 373) addressed to Philip, on the necessity of conquering England as a means of subduing Holland, with a list of the causes which were to make the conquest very easy, and of the factions and divisions which would prevent any common action of the English. There is another paper (B. fol. 331) in which Sanders gives an account of the activity in the English dockyards. All these ships, he says, are meant against the King. The Hollanders, Rochellers, and such like will have free use of all the ports of England to prepare their enterprises, they will seize the narrow seas, and will let no occasion of mischief escape them. Either, therefore, you will require a mighty fleet to resist so many and so well found ships, or you must obtain secure harbours at least on one, if not on both sides, or you must go another way about, which will be more gainful and less perilous. You must invade and take possession of England. Stucley, he concludes, will manage it, for he is well known to, and much liked by, the English sea-captains.

Philip in the mean time sent one of his own experienced men of war, Diego Ortiz, to make a detailed survey of the Irish coasts, and to report on the capacity and strength of the Irish harbours. He also was more industrious or more lucky than usual in his efforts to buy over to his interest some of the chief persons in England. Among the numerous lords and gentlemen, says Gonzales (p. 388), who voluntarily offered themselves to the service of Philip out of hatred to Elizabeth, was Sir Henry Sidney, Viceroy of Ireland and President of Wales. He proposed to enter the service of Spain with 6000 Englishmen, giving as security for his good faith his own son, heir of the Earldoms of Berwick and Leicester, and godson of King Philip. Whether Sidney's offer was a piece of the same kind of buffoonery as that of Hawkins had been, or an endeavour to patch up his ruined fortune with Spanish gold, or a real piece of treason, has not been cleared up.

Philip also was preparing a great fleet, and alarming reports of its destination were continually reaching the English government. On the 25th of April the Deputy wrote to the Council from Dublin with information of the Mayor of Waterford about the preparation of a fleet in Andalusia of Spaniards, Portuguese, and Flemings, and about Stucley's threats that he was coming over. Another report was brought by a ship from Cadiz that Stucley with his men, and a fleet of a hundred sail, was coming to the parts about Waterford.

This was just at the time and place of the Earl of Desmond's rising. On the 2nd of June the Deputy wrote again about the Desmond rebellion, with further information about the preparation of ships and troops in Spain and Portugal, and about an English galley-slave to whom Stucley had written to know if he had been on the coast of Ireland. The experienced mariners whom he had taken with him in 1570 had by this time been dispersed, and he had to search for fresh pilots. But whatever were Philip's designs against England, he was perpetually thwarted by the quarrels of the English and Irish fugitives, on whose information and aid his enterprises depended. In February, 1574, the Archbishop of Cashel came to Brussels and was made much of by Requesens; he was joined by Lord Morley and his brother Dr Parker, Lord Westmoreland, Norton and his son, and divers priests from Louvain. But Englefield kept aloof, because of his own quarrel with Westmoreland, and Stucley's with the Archbishop. Stucley's friends wrote to him that the Archbishop was alluring all the English noblemen to him. He therefore contrived through the Duchess of Feria to send 500 crowns to Westmoreland, which converted him; the Earl thereupon asked for six months' pension to go to Rome to the Jubilee, intending to go by Spain to see the Duchess and Stucley. The cause of Morley and his brother's enmity to Stucley was Stucley's misuse of Egremond Ratcliffe, who wrote to Burghley this year, 'my very enemies will bear witness what injuries I have suffered in Spain for defending the Queen against Stucley and others, and what a number malice me because I seek my pardon.' On the other hand, the quarrel between Stucley and the Archbishop was that each wanted for himself and his friends the sole conduct of the Irish enterprise. Stucley therefore wanted to discredit the Archbishop, and Lord

Morley and Westmoreland wished to discredit Stucley (MS. Dom. Addenda, Sept. 3, 1574). By July the alarm seems to have subsided, and Henry Acworth writes to the Deputy that the citizens are much beholden to Stucley for the trouble and expense he has put them to. But he had put Philip to still greater expenses. Among Burghley's papers in the British Museum (MS. Lansdowne xviii. no. 80) is a list drawn up by one Littleton of the English pensioners on Philip's purse; in it occurs this entry. 'The King hath given to Thomas Stucley at times from his first coming into Spain in an. 1570 to this time of August 1574, and for keeping his house at Madrid at the Kings charge for six months at 500 pieces of plate per day, which amounts in the whole sum to 27,576 ducats. The King doth give to Thomas Stucley for his pension by the year 600 ducats, and to William Stucley 400 ducats.'

According to Dr Parker, Lord Morley's brother, Stucley had lost credit again towards the end of the year, being 'ordered to stay in a village, and not come to the Court of Spain' (Dom. MSS. Addenda, Oct. 24, 1574). In the early part of the year, April 20, 1574, Lord Morley had opened his mouth widely against Stucley. He said that he had come to Spain, not to ask the King for money, but to tell him of the treasons of the Duchess of Feria, Stucley, and others, whom he would accuse of capital matters. He declared that Sir Thomas Stucley was a knave and a villain, and challenged him to fight in Algiers, if he might not in Spain. That Sir Thomas was the Duchess' champion, like Gnatho in Terence on a stage-play, and that he was not a Catholic, but a deceiver of princes. The bitter in the cup of Morley evidently was that the Duchess would only procure a pension of 50 crowns a month for him, which he thought proceeded from her spite to the houses of Norfolk and Arundel.

He accordingly wrote to Elizabeth to tell her what traitors the Duchess and Stucley were, and the next year (Oct. 31, 1575) he wrote to Burghley, assuring him that if he had followed other courses he might have been worth £20,000, and have had more credit than such rascals as Stucley and other disloyal subjects (MSS. Dom. Addenda, Oct. 31, 1575, and vol. xxiv. no. 103).

Early in the next year (Jan. 4, 1575) Elizabeth wrote from Hampton Court to Philip, requiring him in virtue of existing treaties, and for the sake of the good harmony which ought to exist between the two crowns, to expel from his dominions a company of 25 rebels, whose names she gave; and after this list she added another list of 'fugitives or rebels who are co-adjutors with the others, and foment rebellion with letters and messages: they are, Francis Englefield, Kt, Thomas Stucley, Ralph Liggons, Francis Payte, Hugh Owen' (Gonzales, p. 395). From this it appears that in January, 1575, Stucley was neither in Spain nor in Flanders; he was probably either in Rome or in France. The author of the play tells us that Stucley was sent by Philip to represent him at Rome on occasion of the Jubilee. Such an incident would not be impossible. Philip had before this employed Sir Richard Shelley, the English Prior of Malta, as his Ambassador to Sebastian of Portugal, and some of the Sherleys were afterwards employed on similar missions. Moreover on occasion of the Jubilee, which began on Christmas Eve, Dec. 24, 1575, in the 4th year of Gregory XIII., the princes, as Theiner tells us, whom the Pope had invited, being hindered by the troubles of the time, were only present by their ambassadors. This, however, would not account for Stucley's presence in Rome a year previously. We know that he was there in October, when he wrote the following letter to

Mistress Julyan. Who the lady was, and what were his relations to her, I have not discovered. If, as may be suspected, Stucley was contemplating another marriage, he either never was, or had ceased to be, of the order of Calatrava, which, I believe, tolerated no second marriage (Lansdowne MSS. xx. no. 44).

'To my very good friend Mrs Julyan.

'My good Mrs Julyan: I have received your gentle letter by this bearer, whom I offered all courtesy for your sake; whereas you required me to deliver him iii or iv score crowns for your use, he would not have it for that as he told me he had not any occasion to use it. Trust me whensoever it shall please you to command, if it be for ten thousand crowns, you may boldly employ me, for I will as willingly disburse it to pleasure you as I would give one point. By proof you shall best know the desire I have to serve you and give you content, whensoever it shall please you to use me; now I refer it to yourself to command me, for I am and ever will be ready (with God's grace) to obey you. I thank you for the ij dozen of poynts which you sent me; I received them as thankfully coming from you as if it had been so many dyamantes.

'I send you by this bearer half-a-dozen of pictures wrought upon taffyta. What estate I am in I refer to be told you by this bearer, which is and ever shall be to honour and serve you: pray for me as I will do for you; I commend me most lovingly unto your self, and us both unto God, who of his goodness send us a joyful meeting. From Rome, the 24 of October 1575.

'Yours faithfully and most assuredly,
'THOMAS STUCLEY.'

Stucley seems to have had at this time great wealth at command.

The 'pictures wrought upon taffata' show that certain privileges and indulgences which have generally been assigned to the year 1578 must have already been granted to him at this time. In Strype's Annals, vol. ii. pt ii. p. 191, will be found a copy of Indulgences granted to Stucley's crucifixes. Strype suggests, without proof, that 'he was to sell them, and to make his gain of them, as it seems.' The indulgences were granted to persons who prayed before these pictures, which were crucifixes painted on silk 'for the Church, the exaltation of the Catholic faith, the preservation and delivery of Mary Queen of Scotland, the reducing England, Scotland, and Ireland to the Catholic religion, and the extirpation of heretics.' Special indulgences were granted to the bearers of these pictures 'in going to any conflict or feat of arms against the enemies of the faith,' or dying in battle. Anthony Munday in his 'report of the execution of traitors' (reprint of Shakespeare Society, p. 121) says that he put this question to Kirby, the priest, at his execution in 1582. 'Did not you in your chamber deliver to me certain silk pictures, which you told me, at Stucley's being there, were hallowed by the Pope, and what indulgencies were allowed them? One of them, which was a crucifix, you gave me, the other you willed me deliver to your friends at Rheims and in England. And because they were so few (as indeed I think they were no more but five) you gave me two Julies to go into the city to buy more, which I did; and having brought them to you, three or four of the fairest you took from me, promising to get them hallowed at the next benediction. The other indeed you gave me, and I took them with me.' Dod also says that he had seen a copy of these indulgences. As Munday had returned to England from Rome in 1577, the grant must have been either in 1575 or 1576. Perhaps Stucley had a monopoly of the sale of silk crucifixes like those which had been distributed just before the battle of Lepanto.

In another book of Munday's, *The English Roman Life*, 1582, there is also a mention of Stucley. He saw at Rome, he says, 'Stucley and three more Popish gentlemen in great credit with the Pope .... These three other gentlemen came from the North of England, and were to go forward with Stucley in the enterprise, and to have the Pope's army committed to their conduct, and so to overrun England, and to make kings and dukes and earls at their pleasure.' It seems that already, in 1575, the English exiles had transferred their hopes from Philip to the Pope.

Stucley, however, was in Spain for part of this year, and there quarrelled with Egremond Ratcliffe, as he had quarrelled the year before with Lord Morley. Ratcliffe wrote to Burghley that his very enemies would bear witness what injuries he had suffered in Spain for defending the Queen against Stucley and others, and what a number maliced him because he sought his pardon (MSS. Domestic, Addenda). At Rome, Stucley seems to have been a magnet to draw round him those who thought they could use him; amongst others, a nephew J. S. (perhaps John Stucley, eldest son of Sir Lewis) wished to go there; and the following characteristic letter from Stucley's old major domo, Renold Digby, to another of his discarded servants, who had followed him from Ireland into Spain, and had been cashiered in March, 1571, relates to him. We have seen that Digby was prisoner in the Gatehouse at Westminster in March, 1572, when Hogan suggested to Cecil to examine him; it was doubtless then that he first 'declared his master's villainy,' and afterwards went on to 'spread him and all his doings to the best.' It is to be remarked that the sketch of Stucley's life given in this letter is followed literally in the joint work of Burghley and his scribe in 1583. The Lord Treasurer knew better, but it suited his purpose to give currency to the serving man's calumnies, rather than to reveal matters in which his share had not been very reputable. The following is Renold Digby's letter:—

'Friend Lettleston, I have me commended unto you, thanking you for your gentleness in my absence. You shall be sure to command me to my power as one friend to another. As touching J. S. which you wrote to me that is going for Rome, he shall hardly scape this way, and be sure that and I may once either hear or see him I doubt not but to use the matter that he shall not come to Rome this year, and that (as)sure yourself of. I have howsed the matter so that and he have put over any money by exchange either to Englishman or Italian here I will know of it; or if he lie within forty myle of Antwerp I will know of him, if he pass not through France he shall have much to do to scape my hand. The traitor his uncle hath caused letters to be written here against me to the Commendadore, and hath written against me himself that I was a spy for the Queen's Mty in Spain, and hath two of his Apostles here which solicit his matters in secret, which is one Anthony Naylor and Cotton, but I will do well enough with them and him for all his Italian devices. I would I had him here, but I have declared his villainy, first in K. Edwards time and second to the French K. and then to the Emperor, and fourth how traitorously he hath dealt with her Mty who was his good lady and mistres inventing how he might by devices abuse the K. of Spain to set him and her Mty together by the ears. I have and will spread him and all his doings to the best. I have some partakers to further his doings. Here is one Humphrey Gene and whom he and Naylor put into the inquisition in Spain which lay there a year and a quarter in the holy house at Toledo. I doubt not by Gods help between him and me but to make him run by moonshine as I did make him at Madrill. Some of his friends hath had the gallows here; and they look not the better to themselves they may chance want some of their limbs to carry them to Rome. This traitor Naylor who fled his country for treason against her Mty, and Cotton, rail against you and say you betrayed the good Knight Sir Thomas Stucley, and that you and I did undo him in Spain. I marvell this traitor Naylor is not banished among the rest, who is practising every day with the Hamiltons and Cotton. Also you might do very well to let my L. Treasurer understand of these fellows, for they have great practices in their head with the hamell towns. I pray you let me hear by the next post further of J. S. to the uttermost you can learn. I would be loth he should scape me. Mannell would come but he hath ix^{li} to receive for his wages which he would fain handle. He is promised for every day, but you know the Spaniards drywenye. Here is no likelihood of peace; the xxiith of this month it will fall out peace or wars, but here is great preparation for wars both for sea and land. I refer the likelihood to you, and thus I commit you to God, who send us well to meet. From Andwarpe the 17th of June, 1575.'

If Stucley was in Rome for the Jubilee, he saw there his old chief Don John of Austria, who at the end of February started thence on pilgrimage to Loretto, to fulfil a vow he had made before the battle of Lepanto (Theiner, ii. 259). Later in the year Stucley made a similar pilgrimage. In the spring he was at Madrid with Dr, afterwards Cardinal Allen, negotiating for the deliverance of

Mary Queen of Scots, and for the reduction of Ireland. From Madrid the negotiators went to Rome, bearing letters from Dr Sanders in favour of Englefield and Allen. Stucley was as well known as Sanders in Rome, but he thought it worth while to procure letters in his favour from the Bishop of Meath to the Cardinal of Como; in this letter James Fitzmorris was coupled with him. It is dated May 5, 1576, and is as follows:—'As it is certain that all good things come from God, we must believe that it is he who has moved the hearts of the noble and valiant soldiers James Fitzmorris and Thomas Stucley, not only to brave the danger of death for the restoration of the Catholic religion in Ireland, but to make a long journey to his Holiness, to whom the kingdom of Ireland is known by right to belong, to the end that by his authority and power the heretics and schismatics may be driven out and the Irish people restored to the Catholic faith and religion.'. The Bishop goes on to ask for some provision to be made for him in Brittany, as he had grown too old to endure the heat of Spain; while 'Brittany, as being near Ireland, is more convenient; I can take advantage of the intercourse between the two countries, at least to exhort my flock by letter; and how noisome it is to a stranger every month to have to wring his pension out of the hands of laymen I leave to your own judgment.' The Bishop of Ross, says Theiner, carried on similar negotiations at the Court at Paris.

The negotiators at Rome were not satisfied with the expedition of that Court. Here is a portion of a letter of Sir Francis Englefield, at Rome, June 2, 1576, to Mr Cotton, one of Stucley's 'apostles,' who was I think at Paris. The letter is written, not, as was common in those days, between politicians, in terms of merchandise, but in literary language, as if Cotton had written a book, the propositions of which he wished to submit to the Roman authorities. The book was of course the plot and the articles of the enterprise in hand. 'If you be well informed of my state here, you may be the more securely assured that here wanteth nothing on my part to give to your deserts that which is due unto them. But if you be wrongly borne in hand that I can here do that which I cannot, then may you perhaps ween amiss of me, that I use not the endeavour I might. And surely when I compare this mich that reason yieldeth to your demands with the little hope that appeareth here of answerable performance, believe me it grieveth me to write at all unto you. For mine own part all that I can do is to commend you. And without flattery I say it, I cannot therein do so mich as 1 am persuaded you deserve. The translating, correcting, and supplying of some small defects asketh the help of them that can do more than I. And the proposing to persons requisite doth require the like, all which I have not letted to further and advance to the uttermost. If it take not the effect it deserveth, accuse not me—for truly I do all I may—nor condemn not those others that would do better if they could. There is an old proverb in England that no cloth is so well fulled as that which is of the fuller's own making. I am constrained to leave these matters and papers of yours in other friends hands and sollicitation, because the heat will not permit me to tarry. Yea rather I feel that I have tarried long already. Fear not them to whom I have committed it, I mean for their good will and assuredness. Sir Thomas [Stucley] is gone to Loreto some days past, and will not return till some weeks more be past. If you have cause to write any further of these matters, direct open letters to Mr Dr Lewis who hath here best acquaintance and most hability to prefer and commend whatsoever shall occur as it deserveth. And therefore with him I leave all your informations, with such charge and request as I can make to perform that which is begun, and to pursue to some end that which I have often proposed and commended. And in time I verily believe some better fruit shall follow than the blossoms do give hope of. The temperance you use in asking no money cannot but advance the spiritual petitions. Marry, because the plot is new, rare, and without precedent—of fresh memory I mean—it requireth therefore a greater travail, a more frequent conference, and a more mature and exact penning than perhaps you think for, specially to satisfy this authority, which conceive less and understand little of these matters which to you and us appear facile and plain. If yourself were here to find and feel how little is conceived of large informations, how little believed of manifest experiences, and how quickly forgotten is all that was inculked with great labour, you would not only wonder and marvel thereat, but conceive also more despair than I ween we do.'

It is clear that the minds of people at Rome were exercised concerning the division of the expected spoil. The different proportions accruing to the French, the Spaniards, and the English exiles were all to be settled beforehand, and were a source of great difficulty. 'There is no one inpediment greater than how to know a difference between the goods of a Catholic and an heretic. Likewise between him that is no heretic but in appearance for fear, and an heretic indeed. And thirdly how to give your company a place and privileges requisite without others prejudice that are in possession. And the greatest difficulty of all is that these folks which were never troubled with the sickness of the Western seas cannot be made to feel nor smell what manner of pain it is, much less how to temper the remedy for it. Give not over for all this, but proceed as you may in maintaining yourself and your company, as the time will suffer you ' (MSS. Domestic, June 2, 1576). Another letter of nearly the same date from the Countess of Northumberland, probably at Brussels, also contains some references to Stucley: 'Touching the matter between *Lord Morley* and *Stucley* I meddle not withal, but suppose the same will be taken up and ended without either's prejudice, and so I let it cease for the time. *Stucley* they say is gone to Loreto, whereof divers give sundry constructions. From *Englefield* I hear very seldom, and have not received any letters but once since his being in the place whereas he is, but I understand that he hath moved for divers, amongst them specially for *Cotton*, but there all things went so straitly as there was little hope of comfort or speed; yet by the end of this month or a little within the next I trust *Cotton* shall receive better contentment. Englefield is so troubled with the catarrh, which by the air there doth so increase to the weakening and impair of his *health* (?), that he must be forced to leave *Rome* (?) sooner than he determined and go to the mountains.' (MSS. Domestic, June 9, 1576. The words in Italics are in cypher.)

To pass for a moment to another subject. The author of the following drama would have us believe that Philip pushed on Sebastian to the Moorish expedition, which was fatal to him and Stucley. Though it was sometimes so reported, yet those who knew anything, knew better. It was in this year that Sebastian, King of Portugal, met his uncle Philip II. at the Monastery at Guadalupe, persuaded thereto, says the author of a Spanish newsletter in the Record office, by some of his counsel, 'who seeing him very much disposed to make wars again in Barbary himself in person, which none of his own Counsel could dissuade him from, they thought they could not use a better mean than to procure the meeting of the uncle and nephew, that the King of Spain by his authority might dissuade him from that so chargeable and dangerous an enterprise.'

In January the following year, 1577, Walsingham heard a report, which he sent to Sidney, that Stucley had come to Lisbon, and was keeping himself close, as if in preparation for his Irish expedition. But it was not the case. He left Rome early in the year to go with Don John into Flanders. On his way he passed through Florence, where also Henry, Sir John Cheke's eldest son, then chanced to be, and to be in some danger, 'means being used to entrap him.' Cheke 'was advised of this by a certain English gentleman, who coming into the company of one Stucley from Genoa to Sienna, gave him warning to seek some other place, and to look carefully to himself, as one greatly noted by some of his countrymen, who had spoken such words in his hearing, he said, as he might not declare unto him the particulars' (Strype, Life of Sir John Cheke, p. 143). Strype's narrative is quite unintelligible, but he seems to hint that Stucley was the person who had spoken the words that Cheke was warned of. From Italy Stucley went into Flanders; on the 19th of February Dr Wilson, the ambassador at Brussels, writes to Walsingham : 'The rebels swarm about Don John, being come unto him of late the lewd Earl (of Westmoreland), Stucley the Romanist, and Jeny that was at Milan, besides the whole rabble of the rest.' Wilson had written to the States to have them banished ; and the Bishop of Liege had promised him that they should have no sojourn in his dominions. He asks the Queen to write to Don John, and press him to banish them. 'Great pity it is,' says he, 'that such lewd persons should be suffered to rest anywhere.' At this time the ambassador was anxious to disturb the pacification of Ghent, which had been accepted by Don John on the 17th of February. Wilson thought it certain, that as soon as he had peace with the Prince of Orange, he would at once go to war with England. It was of great importance therefore that he should procure some severe measures against the fugitives. On this subject he wrote again to the Queen, Feb. 25, telling her that he had given to the Duke of Arschott the names of these rebels, and prayed him to deal so with Don John that they might not be cherished as they are, being always about his person, as though they were of counsel with him: but rather that they should be executed as they had deserved, or else delivered to the ambassador to be sent into England. Is it not enough to have them banished? asked the Duke. No, said Wilson, for they all have been once banished, and being returned contemptuously should be executed forthwith, according to the intercourse of 1495 betwixt Henry VII. of England and Philip Duke of Burgundy, and confirmed by the Emperor Charles, and King Philip II. Wilson then proceeds to complain that Hamilton, a Scot, has been sent to the Prince of Orange, and that Standen has been enlarged out of prison at the instance of the Queen of Scots, who, he suggests, should not have liberty to write such requests.[1]

From Flanders Stucley probably went to Rome, and in October was said to be returning to Flanders again. On the 6th of October Woodshaw wrote to Burghley from Brussels: 'Divers of her Majesty's enemies are coming here from France, Burgundy, Savoy, Spain, &c., both Spaniards and Scots, especially the two Hamiltons, Stucley, Norton and his son, &c.' (MSS. Dom. Addenda). At

[1] MSS. Flanders.

the same time advices sent from Lisbon about the movements of James Fitzmorris add: 'It is reported of a truth that Stucley is here; he is kept close in the Spanish ambassador's house' (MSS. Spain, Oct. 13, 1577).

James Fitzgerald Fitzmorris O'Desmond was at this time in Lisbon ready to go over into Ireland; he had been so often promised Spanish aid, that he had in turn deeply engaged himself to his friends at home, and now saw no way of saving his truth but to return naked to die among them. The following letters of his are in Theiner. The first is to Gaspar de Quiroga, Archbishop of Toledo, to whom Philip had committed the superintendence of the Irish affairs; it is dated Oct. 30, 1577 (Theiner, ii. 338): 'I received your letter of the 23rd of September in October. You require me no longer to delay my voyage to Ireland. The cause of my delay was your former letter. Since I received the last I have besought the ambassador and king to find me a ship; till yesterday, without success. Then, however, I made a bargain with the mariners, which binds us to depart hence within nine days. Then we shall proceed in the name of the Lord. . . . . I beseech you to arrange with the King of Spain to send aid after us into Ireland, and that speedily, at any rate before February, and before I and mine are quite worn out and impoverished. After we have gone hence we will communicate with Bishop Cornelius of Leighlin, who while he was journeying home before us, was stripped by pirates of Rochelle. He is quite faithful to us, and to him we commit all our secrets, and especially our negotiations with you about the aid to be sent to us. If he comes with the supplies, he will be able to give the needful directions how to effect a landing in Ireland, and to open speedy communications with us.'

On the 9th of November he wrote again to the Cardinal of
Como (Theiner, p. 339): 'I came to Lisbon, that I might sail to
Ireland, where I should have been long since if the Nuncio at
Madrid had not delayed me, thinking to procure me some help.
But in his last letter he tells me to expect nothing. I therefore
start immediately for Ireland, without arms, without ships, without
men, in the name of our Lord Jesus Christ, relying on the Pope's
authority, and trusting much in your prayers to obtain victory
against the enemies of the Church. I have waited till now for
help, and now that I have got none all my friends who were
anxiously looking for me have become lukewarm and discouraged;
and my enemies will be all the more confident, when they see me
come without arms or help. Therefore I ask your Eminence, in
whom I trust, to hasten the promised supplies after me to Ireland,
and to solicit the Catholic King to send help, who has promised so
much to the Bishop of Mayo.'

There is a letter from Dr Sanders at Madrid to Sir Francis
Englefield at Rome dated Nov. 30, 1577, which refers to the
succours to be sent after Fitzgerald, and which apparently suggests
Stucley as the proper man to conduct them (MSS. Cotton,
Caligula, C. iii. 501). After saying that the Pope had given Sir
James (Fitzgerald) his name and authority, and that Philip had
contributed 3000 crowns, Sanders shows how an army might be
got together, however small. The Pope would give 2000 men,
and 'if we stand upon more, the whole fault is in us. . . . *Non in
multitudine exercitus victoria.* . . . if that be true (and how can
God's word be false) as good 2000 (when we can get no more) as
a greater army, specially when God giveth them by his Vicar.'
Then he says that he knows that the Pope intends to adventure his

2000 men on his own account, and that he utterly despairs of the King of Spain. Finding the English afraid to attack England with so small a force, the Pope applies himself to Ireland. Sanders conjectures that he will keep the business in his own hands, and thinks in his conscience that it is well he does so, 'for sure it is, Ireland may be taken.' Herein, says he, I dare not name—(here follows a cypher, which perhaps means Stucley) till I know your mind, but I myself intend to go. 'How happy shall the realm be that may be governed by the Pope, and how easily will the poor people be brought thereto, will or nill the nobles that seek a king, by flattering whom they may increase their state as they imagine, where indeed they are most of all spoiled and undone by kings, if they will mark it. For what noble house continueth long?'

The Pope's keeping Ireland to himself was perhaps connected with the proposal for making his illegitimate son Giacomo Buoncompagno the King of Ireland. Philip had already discovered that this young man was the weak side of Gregory XIII., and had offered him a 'provision' (not 'pension') of 6000 ducats. The Pope at first would not let him receive it, but at last allowed him to do so with the addition of the grade of general of the men at arms in the state of Milan. 'Whence it appears,' says Tiepolo (Alberi Series ii. vol. 4, p. 230), 'that he is pleased with these demonstrations of the king;' and he was as well pleased with the subsequent demonstrations of Fitzmorris and Stucley, who offered the same young man the crown of Ireland. Sanders had previously written to Dr Allen that Philip was as fearful of war as a child of fire; and that all their trust must be in the Pope, not in the king (MSS. Dom., Nov. 6, 1577). But for all this he ceased not to urge the King to action. Among Mr Froude's Simancas transcripts there is Dr Sanders' paper of reasons for invading Ireland, presented to the King Dec. 16, 1577 (Froude, C. fol. 23). His conclusion is, Let English and Irish Catholics go over every second or third month from some port in Italy with one or two ships and stores, and at least 15,000 or 20,000 ducats, which will be of great effect with so poor a people as the Irish. It is, he says, of great importance that some English should go, because the English Catholics will communicate with them. These dropping and dribbling little invasions had no chance; the spies who wrote to Burghley about them assured him that there was no great harm in the French ship of 80 tons which Fitzmorris had freighted at Lisbon. But Stucley's presence gave more uneasiness. 'It is said that Stucley came here before Fitzmorris, and has gone with him in his ship; but others say he is secretly in the ambassador's house' (MSS. Dom. Addenda, Dec. 9, 1577).

But Stucley had hit upon a notable plan for preventing these weak detachments from being overpowered. He knew that besides the royal navy the Queen used upon occasion to equip other ships; therefore he proposed to freight as many English vessels as possible by Flemings, Frenchmen, Spaniards, and Italians, and to send them upon long voyages with or without cargo; in the mean time he would attack the royal navy, then very weak, and try to burn the ships in the several harbours where they lay. This would open the way for him into Ireland, where he did not question but the native Irish would join him; and after the expulsion of the English he was to cause the Pope's son to be proclaimed King (Rapin, vol. ii. p. 109; and Baker's Chronicle, p. 354). Sir Amyas Paulet, Stucley's first cousin, was ambassador to France in 1577. His letters during that year are silent about his cousin's designs, but contain much about Fitzmorris and La Roche, and the project of uniting France, Spain, and Rome against England. La Roche, like Stucley in 1563, pretended that his preparations were for Florida, but the ambassador had good information that he had intelligence both with Fitzmorris and the Earl of Westmoreland, and that he was bound for Ireland. La Roche, however, did not give the ambassador much anxiety, because he was 'a gusard, and a man of no habylitie to bear the charge of any great enterprise.' This same man had previously, in 1570, caused an alarm of a French attack upon Ireland; then he was a tool of the Duke of Guise, though his project was not without the privity of the King.

But the Pope had another enterprise in hand besides this attack on Ireland. Of all the princes of Europe there was one whose enthusiasm seemed to make him the model of a ruler such as Rome desired. Sebastian of Portugal was as devout as a monk, most punctual at mass, and attending to it with the greatest reverence; saying the long office every day, confessing and communicating at all the principal feasts, and often at other times; so chaste moreover as to seem a woman-hater, and to cause his physicians to suspect him to be unfit for marriage; governing by the counsel of his confessor and of the monks around him, who seem to have encouraged him to make himself an ideal knight, chaste and strong, inuring himself to danger in the hunting-field, and using his people to no other end but as men to be trained to fight against the infidel, or to labour to find the sinews for such wars. One Pope, Pius V., had once given him good advice, and urged him to marry Margaret of Valois. The Cardinal Allessandro had even made him promise to do so in 1570; but the counsel of his confessor had prevailed over reasons of state, and the Pope in this respect had given place to the monk. On all other occasions the Popes had always urged him on in his enthusiasm. Sebastian, on his side, had shown himself not a little selfish and wilful; he had refused to join the common league against the Turk, apparently because he wished to have the undivided glory of some great exploit against the Moor. But this love for his own glory does not seem to have made any unfavourable impression. He was the darling of the Roman court, and Gregory XIII. even went so far as to send him one of the sacred arrows with which his namesake Sebastian had been martyred. Cupid's keenest shaft could not torment the heart of a lover more than this arrow inflamed the enthusiasm of Sebastian. An exploit against the infidel became the sole end of his existence and the aim of his thoughts, and to this all the duties of a King and all the happiness and prosperity of his subjects were sacrificed. Some of his nobles, who understood a little political economy, thinking to wean him of this Quixotic project, procured an interview between him and his cold-blooded uncle Philip II. at Guadalupe in 1576. There Sebastian explained what a grand opportunity he had in Morocco, where a legitimate King had turned out a usurper, and this usurper Mahamet had appealed to Sebastian to right him. In Sebastian's eyes there was no right or wrong between Christians and infidels; their divisions were the Christians' opportunity, who had simply to look to their own advantage, not to those questions of right which between Christians would be the chief pivots of the decision. Philip, who unknown to Sebastian was in alliance with Mahamet's rival Muley-Moluck, naturally did what he could to dissuade his nephew from his project, and in the advice he gave, he unwittingly exposed his reasons for his own extraordinary slackness in carrying out the designs of the English and Irish refugees against

Elizabeth. 'You must not trust Mahamet,' he said, 'for faith is never to be given to the sayings of those who are driven from their dominions and seek to recover them; for their desire to regain what they have lost is so great, that they give easy credit to many false suggestions, and add many falsehoods from their own imaginations, so that between what they believe and what they say they believe, they stuff those princes to whom they apply for help so full of hope, that they make them either go to great expense for nothing, or else engage them in an enterprise which ruins them.' (Cicarello, vita de Gregorio XIII., apud Platina, vite de' Pontefici.) Philip, however, did promise aid to Sebastian on two conditions; first that his expedition should come off in 1577, next that the Spanish forces were not required to defend Italy from the Turk. Sebastian was too crazy to feel the coolness of his reception, but departed quite satisfied with the results of the interview. He set himself with all his energies to be in readiness to sail to Africa in the prescribed year. In July, 1577, Gregory XIII. granted him the revenues of three Portuguese bishoprics towards his charges, and wrote to the Viceroy of Naples to impress all ships touching there, and force them to hire themselves at a moderate rate to the King, who was preparing to war against the enemies of Christ (Theiner, ii. 332). On the 9th of November there came a sign from heaven which is mentioned both in the ballad and the play : 'there appeared in the Zodiac, in the sign of Libra, near unto the station of Mars, the goodliest and greatest comet that hath been seen in many ages; the which, happening in the progress of this war, amazed many .... and forasmuch as the ancient captains with their divines did interpret it to good, nor for that they believed it, but to encourage their soldiers; the Portugal likewise, taking it for a favour, said that this comet spake unto the King, saying *accometa, let him assail him;* not having any such belief, but for flattery, fearing more the King's choler by reason of his rough inclination than the heavens. But his exertions were in vain; the year passed, and the expedition, in spite of the most tyrannous exercise of the royal prerogative in Portugal, could not be got ready. Philip therefore was now free from his promises. But this important defection daunted neither the King nor the Pope, who neither of them had the least idea of the required proportion of means to ends, but considered that the blessing of the Church would make up for any defects. At the end of January, 1578, Gregory wrote to the Catholic princes of Italy exhorting them to assist Sebastian with men and money, with a free passage for his soldiers, and with provisions at reasonable rates, because his enterprise was solely for the glory of God, and the dignity and increase of the Catholic religion (Theiner, ii. 420).

While all these preparations were going on at Lisbon, there was a similar movement going on in the Papal states for the expedition to Ireland. O'Sullevan tells us how James Geraldine, after speaking with Philip in Spain, passed thence through France to Rome, where he found Cornelius O'Melrian and Thomas Stucley, who were asking the Pope for aid against the English in the name of the Irish. Sanders was there also, the honour of the English nation, who had just written his book on the English schism. The preface to this book, in which the writer made his well-known charge[1] against Henry VIII. and Anne Boleyn, provoked a reply

---

[1] Anna enim concubinarum Henrici adhuc viventium alterius quidem soror alterius filia erat; quinetiam ipsiusmet Henrici propria filia non sine multis indiciis habebatur.

from Sir Richard Shelley; this reply is said not to have been misliked by the Pope and Cardinals, and only to have displeased the French Cardinal of Sens, the Bishop of Ross, and Dr Lewis, Archdeacon of Cambray and Referendary to the Pope, afterwards Bishop of Cassano, who were Stucley's counsellors, and active in soliciting Gregory XIII. in behalf of him and his projects. (Strype, Ann. iii. 1, p. 191. Sanders, De Origine et Progressu Schismatis Anglicani, Rishton, 1610, Pref.) Gregory gave Shelley warm letters of recommendation in April this year to Philip and Sebastian, the latter of whom he reminded that Shelley had once been Philip's Ambassador to the Court of Lisbon (Theiner, ii. p. 436). While at Rome Stucley and Shelley acted in concert as inquisitors into the lives of the English who happened to come there. 'In Rome,' says one Robert Barrett (MSS. Domestic, Jan. 1580), 'I was had before Mr Stucley, one Mr Shelly who calleth himself Lord Prior of England, and an old man called Goldwell [Bishop of St Asaph], before whom I was sharply examined, and had been put to some great trouble had not a French gentleman called M. de la Grand of Arles . . . . spoken very friendly for me to Stucley and the rest.'

The memorial presented to the Pope by Fitzmorris and Stucley is among the Fugger MSS. in the library at Vienna.[1] Ranke gives some account of its contents. It represented to the Pope that there was no nation more strictly and immoveably Catholic than the Irish, but that it was tyrannously ill-used and plundered by the English government, kept diligently in discord and barbarism, and coerced in its religion. Hence it was ready for war at a moment's notice; there was wanted only a small force to second it; five

[1] Discorso sopra il regno d'Irlanda, e della gente che bisogneria per conquistarlo, fatto a Gregorio XIII.

thousand men[1] would suffice for its conquest, for there was no fortress there that could hold out above four days. Gregory was persuaded without difficulty. He gave Stucley 40,000 scudi to furnish himself with vessels and men, and paid also for a small body of soldiers who were to join him upon the French coast. Philip had no inclination for overt war, but was glad enough to see Elizabeth provided with business at home. He also contributed 20,000 scudi towards the enterprise, and persuaded Leonard Dacres, Charles Goade, and other English gentlemen then at Madrid, together with the Bishop of Leighlin, to join in the expedition.[2]

At this time, proceeds O'Sullevan, sundry companies of bandits were giving great trouble in Italy, by their night attacks on villages, and their robberies of travellers. James Geraldine, who joined Stucley in begging for aid for the well-nigh spent church in Ireland, at last obtained a general pardon for all these bandits on condition that they would go with him to Ireland. So what with them, what with other recruits, he collected about a thousand soldiers, over whom the Pope set Ercole Pisano and other Roman Knights as captains, and embarked at Civita Vecchia with Bishop Cornelius and Doctor Sanders. Fitzmorris, according to the examination of Friar O'Haie (Carew papers, August 17, 1580), was chief of the two—Stucley and himself—with the Pope; though it does not appear that the Pope conferred any such sounding titles on Fitzmorris as those which he gave Stucley. However that was,

---

[1] Hence probably, because 5000 men were asked, Cicarello in his Life of Gregory XIII. says that 5000 were raised, and placed under the guidance of an Englishman, who had promised, by his knowledge of the places, to capture by a *coup de main* certain cities, and so to open a ready way to the conquest of that kingdom. Apud Platina, ut sup.

[2] The Nuncio Sega, *relazione compendiosa* MS. in the Berlin library.

O'Sullevan tells us that Fitzmorris ordered Stucley to proceed to Lisbon, and there wait for him, while he went to fetch his wife whom he had left in France (Philip O'Sullevan, Historiæ Catholicæ Iberniæ compendium. Lib. iv. c. xv.). These preparations were being made in February, 1578, at which time Killegrew wrote to Davison that armaments by land and sea were progressing both in France and Spain, and that Stucley and Sir James Fitzmorris had ships and 1500 men to make some rebellion in Ireland (Dom. MSS. Addenda, Feb. 22, 1578). The following letter from Parsons at Rome to Campion at Prague (Nov. 28, 1578) gives some details of the departure from Rome (Simpson's Life of Campion, p. 91):

'You shall understand that Sir Thomas Stewkly, who was made here Marquis before his departure, is now dead in Africa with the King of Portugal; the particulars of his death I have not received. He took here away with him at midnight out of their beds all the Irishmen in Rome, and one English gentleman named Mr Minors, nephew to Cardinal Pole, who had good entertainment here of the Pope before,—that is to say, twenty crowns in gold a month. This Mynhurst, with one Sedgrave, an Irishman, which once had been of our company, Sir Thomas, being on the sea, upon what cause I know not, would have hang'd them, and being prohibited to do it by the earnest request of certain Italian captains that went with him, he deferred the work until he came to Portugal; and there arriving, condemned both of them to the gallies for term of life, and so led them slaves with him into Africa; but since his death they are delivered by the new King of Portugal, which is the Cardinal: and this much Minors hath written hither himself. And other provision that went with Sir Thomas, all is dispersed; and so this enterprise is come to nothing.'

On the 4th of April Stucley arrived at Cadiz,[1] where he gave the following passport to some English and Irish merchants whom he seems to have brought with him from Rome. It shows us what titles he had received of the Pope.

'I Thomas Stucley Knight, Baron of Ross and Idron, Viscount of the Morough and Kenshlagh, Earl of Wexford and Catherlough, Marquess of Leinster, General of our most holy father Pope Gregory XIII., make ample and infallible certification that Bennet Veglan, Gregory Silvester, and David Mortin, Englishmen, who were imprisoned in Rome by the Holy Inquisition, of whom the Pope made me Godfather, and whom he permitted me to deliver and set free, are good men and of good condition; that they are setting forth from this present Port of Cadiz, desiring to go to their own homes and country; and that they have besought me to give them the present passport, whereby I command each and every person to give them free passage in the name of God, to aid and assist them with alms, that they may pass safe and sound to their homes. In faith of the above we have ordered the present to be written by our secretary, confirmed by our own hand, sealed with our usual seal, and countersigned by the hand of our said secretary; given in the Port of Cadiz, in the Ship called St John Baptist, this tenth of April, 1578. By command of his Excellency' (MSS. Ireland, June 21, 1578). The date of this shows the falsehood of Parsons' assertion (Andreas Philopater, Elizabethæ reg : edictum, 1592, no. 103) that when Stucley and James Fitzgerald asked help for Ireland from Philip, the King thought himself bound by his religion to give none; and for this cause Stucley, with the few troops he had received from the Pope on his voyage from Italy, was not allowed to

[1] MSS. Ireland, May 31, 1578.

enter any Spanish port, but passed on to Portugal and landed at Lisbon. Evidently he went into Cadiz, where he is said to have stayed till May 14, and then proceeded to Lisbon, where he had agreed to meet Fitzmorris. Before May 28 Stucley arrived at Lisbon. His ship, the San Juan of Genoa, was a large one of 800 tons, carrying about 700 soldiers, as Stucley himself gave out. Pillen, who gave information about them to the English government (MSS. Dom. Addenda, April, 1578), saw them and thought they amounted to about that number. Sebastian, hearing of their arrival, and having for want of funds failed to obtain the Italian soldiers he expected out of Tuscany, desired to see them, with an intent to retain them, and use them in the war of Afric; and having caused them to disembark, and to lodge at Oeiras near to the mouth of the Tagus, he went one day to view them; and although there were no chief men, yet did he admire their order, their speedy discharge of their harquebuzes, their disposition to handle the pike, and their strict obedience; and having had some conference with Stucley, he persuaded him to promise to go with him into Afric. The Catholic King, for that he would not show himself a party, would not contradict it. The Pope was so far off that before the news could come unto him Sebastian gave them impress, and they remained for his service.[1]

Pillen says that when they were mustered before Sebastian he liked them well, for that there were eighty who were very expert soldiers. Stucley, he says, was called by no other name than Marquess,[2] and he brought with him one Irish bishop and three or

[1] Jeronymo de' Franchi Conestaggio. The historie of the uniting of the Kingdom of Portugal to the crown of Castille. English Translation, published by Edward Blount, 1600, p. 27.
[2] So he is called by the Spanish and Portuguese historians as Hieronymo

four priests. For a fortnight after his arrival he kept on board, and there entertained resorters, but afterwards a house was prepared for him in Lisbon. When he first came he humbled himself to have kissed the King's hand, but he would not suffer it, but embraced him, and took the letters which Stucley had brought from the Pope. At Lisbon Stucley rode about with a page before and another behind him, in the degree of a Marquess. The Spaniards with him called him His Excellence. He told Pillen that the King of Spain had proffered him great titles of honour, which he had refused; but that the title which the Pope gave him of Marquess of Leinster and Baron or Earl of Washford he could not refuse. He declared also that though it was said in England that he was going to Ireland, he was not appointed thereto; that he knew Ireland as well as the best, and that there was nothing to be got there but hunger and lice. 'They say (said he) that I am a traitor to her Majesty. 'Tis they are traitors that say so. I will ever accept her as my Queen. It is true there is in England my cruel enemy Cecil the Treasurer, whom I care not for. I have had 1000 ducats of the Pope, and I have 1000 ducats a month, and am to serve the King of Portugal in Africa against the Moors.'

This speech of Stucley's gives some small ground for supposing that one of the arguments by which Sebastian turned him from his Irish enterprise was the traitorousness of the attempt. But whatever arguments were used, the thing that determined him seems to

de Mendoza, Jornada de Africa, p. 13, 'seicentos Italianos aquē regia o Marques Tomas Sternvile.' Mariana also calls him Sternvilio. Turquet, (Grimston's Translation, 1612, p. 1199) calls him a 'Licentious Englishman who not long before had gotten from the Pope the title of Marquess of Ireland.' Antonio de Herrera, Cinco libros de la historia de Portugal, 1591, also calls him Esternulio.

have been this, as Friar O'Haye deposed. Stucley's intent was to
come into Ireland, but he changed that pretence because the King
of Portugal had promised him aid (Carew Papers, 17 Aug., 1580).
With this agrees Philip O'Sullevan, who says that Sebastian promised Stucley, after the war in Africa was over, either to accompany
him in person to Ireland, or at any rate to send with him more
ample forces than those he had, which he as well as Pillen saw to
be totally insufficient. Pillen says that he saw no likelihood of
Stucley's invading Ireland, as he had neither power nor shipping,—
the San Juan had been broken up,—except the navy which Sebastian was preparing was meant for him, and not against the Moors,
as was given out. The Italian soldiers, on the other hand, seem to
have thought that the conquest of Ireland would be an easy matter.
Friar O'Haie heard them say that Fitzmorris and Stucley were
going to divide the land of Ireland between them, except O'Desmond's lands, which they would not touch, because they were assured to have help from him.

This assurance of the Earl of Desmond's help was not an
entirely safe one. The Queen wrote to him to keep him in allegiance on the 5th of June, and though he did not answer till the
30th of September,' when the alarm was dissipated (Ireland MSS.
Sept. 30, 1578), yet Sir William Drury had previously assured the
Earl of Leicester that he had found Desmond attentive to show his
loyalty and service upon the bruited foreign invasion by Stucley
pretended. Desmond repaired to Limerick, and brake with the
mayor to be in readiness to resist those attempts, promising that he
and his forces would join him. He apprehended also certain malefactors; and he came to Dublin of his own accord to show himself
to the Lord Deputy Sidney before his departure (Carew Papers,

Aug. 25, 1578). But whatever may have been Desmond's private intentions, there is no doubt that the English government were in great alarm about the projected invasion. On the 31st of May the Privy Council wrote to the Lord Deputy that the Queen had sent ships to cruise during the summer, and had ordered levies of 1000 Welshmen, and 1000 men of Somerset and Dorset, Devon and Cornwall, with stores of victuals. Cork, Waterford, Kinsale, and other places were to be fortified, and as many troops as could be spared were to be transported from the English Pale into Munster, to withstand the 'pretended invasion.' The Deputy also wrote special letters to all the port towns, and to most of the noblemen and gentlemen of account in the south and west of Ireland, instructing them how to provide against any sudden attack.

Whether Stucley would have succeeded better than the wretched San Giuseppe, who landed with some few hundreds of Italians at Smerwick in 1580, and took the fort there, but was speedily cut to pieces by Lord Grey and his soldiers, never came to the proof. Stucley preferred going with Sebastian to Africa, rather than to lead his forlorn hope into Ireland. And yet to his soldiers' eyes the Portuguese army must have offered anything but security of victory. There were 3000 Germans sent by the Prince of Orange who were well disciplined; also a few Spanish veterans. But Philip took care there should not be many of these; the stipulated year had gone by, and now he would have nothing to do with the enterprise; and he put out a severe proclamation, forbidding any of his subjects to cross over to Africa. This, says Mariana (vol. iv. p. 310, Ed. Haga, 1733), was with the intention of deterring Sebastian from his purpose. Stucley's Italians were also good soldiers; but for the Portuguese—'the gentlemen instead of scouring their arms guarded their habits; for corselets they provided doublets of silk and gold; they were charged with sugar and conserves instead of water and biscuit; the vessels of silver, and the tents lined with silk and satin, were without number: every gentleman went furnished like a king, and the poor soldiers died for hunger.' There was a day fixed for their departure, but it was not observed. So the King 'going one morning in great troop to the Cathedral Church with the standard he meant to carry into Afric, he caused it to be hallowed with great pomp, and so returning (many believing he would have returned to the palace), he went directly to the galley wherein he would pass, to hasten the rest, saying that he would presently depart. And although this were the 17th of June, 1578, yet did he stay eight days in the Port, and never disembarked, preparing the rest of the soldiers who were no sooner ready than the day after midsummer,' when he at last set sail with his motley fleet, and more motley crew, leaving his realm 'emptied of money, naked of nobility, without heirs, and in the hands of ill-affected governors' (Conestaggio, ubi sup.).

Philip had already done much to divert his nephew from his ill-starred enterprise. He had written him many letters, and had caused the Duke of Alva to write to him. Alva had refused to see him, for he had learned by what had passed at Guadalupe and by Sebastian's letters that he was resolved, and that it would be impossible to make him change his resolution. Alva therefore said that having been discreet in his youth, he would not in his declining age make himself author of the ruin of a king and kingdom. But all these things were done in Philip's usual undecided way, and were by many people taken in ill part. They said that Philip's demonstrations were but counterfeit, and that he really wished

Sebastian should go. For whatever the event, it would be Spain that should gain. If Sebastian took any coast towns, Philip as their nearest neighbour would be the most advantaged. If Sebastian perished, Philip would be left heir to his kingdom. The truth, however, was that Philip was in confederacy with Muley Moluck, and therefore could not send troops against him. But he invited Sebastian to rendezvous in Cadiz bay, and thither he sent the Duke of Medina Celi to make a last effort to divert him. The Duke received the King with great magnificence, and entertained him with bull-fights, and such other sports as the desert coast allowed. But though this diversion contributed much to the demoralization of his army, neither it, nor the entreaties of the Duke, could turn the King from his purpose.

The way in which the African expedition was conducted, with its tragical end, and important consequences for European politics, is a matter fully treated of in histories;[1] but the historians give no account of Stucley beyond saying that his Italians, with the Germans, were in the centre, and bore the brunt of the battle, till they were overwhelmed by the flying Portuguese troopers under the Duke of Aveiro, who, encouraged by a premature success, had ventured too far into the enemies' lines. Stucley seems to have been killed early in the day, and not, as balladers and dramatists agree in representing his case, killed at the end of the day out of revenge by his mutinous soldiers. His English admirers, partly it appears on the authority of his letters, tell something about him. Westcote (View of Devon, p. 271) gives this account:—He was persuaded to serve Sebastian, 'yea rather, according to his own speech and letters, to assist him in this action ; wherein he failed nothing to

---

[1] See, for instance, Thuanus, lib. LXV. c. ix.—xvi.

perform the part both of a skilful leader and valiant soldier, and, as it was vulgarly reported, had the Council of war approved, and the King followed his advice, and foreborne the fight for that day, the victory had been clearly his: but otherwise persuaded by his inexperienced nobles, young and full of courage, who also taxed Stucley of cowardice for giving procrastinating counsel; to whom he replied, "Out of your inexperience and ignorance in the stratagems of war you deem me a coward; yet this advice would prove safe and victorious, and your great haste be your overthrow: yet proceed, and when you come to action you will look after me, and shall apparently see that Englishmen are no cowards." All which he verified in his proceedings, and died nobly. And so Alcazarquiber, called commonly Alcazar, was made famous, the fourth of August, 1578, for three kings in re and one in spe there slain that day.'

Philip O'Sullevan tells us that the Italians who escaped the slaughter of Alcazar returned to Spain, whither James Fitzmorris had come from France. With them, and some Spaniards given him by Philip, he made up his forces to 800 men (O'Sullevan, ubi supra). Another information tells us in March, 1579, that Stucley's well-appointed ship, with two Irish bishops and three hundred soldiers, was at Lisbon (MS. Ireland). As Stucley's ship had been broken up, this was probably the ship which Friar O'Haie declared that Sanders had bought, for which he was ordered by the King to depart his dominions (Carew Papers, Aug. 17, 1580). Philip seems to have continued his favour to Stucley's son, whom we hear of at the court of Spain 'in 1584 (MSS. Ireland, Aug. 21, 1584), and a Stutley who was dead before August, 1591.[1] But

[1] Deposition of John Semple, Aug. 13, 1591 (Domestic MSS.). 'Of

the favour given to Stucley seems to have been continued by Philip's successors to still another generation of his name and family. James Wadsworth, who returned to England in 1630 and related his continental experiences in *The English Spanish Pilgrim*, says (p. 67) : 'As for English fugitives in Italy there are very few. At Milan there resideth Sir Thomas Stucley, who hath 100 crowns a month pension from the King of Spain. This Stucley is a grand traitor and enemy to his country, and were it not for the Duke of Feria, who entertaineth him at his own table, he might long since have rode back to Madrid on an ass as he came.'[1]

Burghley's account of Stucley finishes thus : 'Of this man might be written whole volumes to paint out the life of a man in the highest degree of vain-glory, prodigality, falsehood, and vile and filthy conversation of life, and altogether without faith, conscience, or religion. And yet this man was he whom the rebels aforenamed (the Earl of Westmoreland, Norton, Leonard Dacres, and Markenfield) and all other fugitives being conversant at Rome did hang all their hope upon, to have their malicious purposes performed to the ruin of the Queen their sovereign and their native country. But the end hereof so fell out by God's ordinance as by this traitor neither her Majesty nor her subjects received any damage; neither yet

Englishmen in Spain there are Sir Willian Stucley . . . Captain Cripps, entertained in the gallies with 50 crowns [a month], and Robert Parsons a Jesuit. Also Mr Stutley, since dead, Mr Copley, Mr Parsley, secretary to the Duchess of Feria, &c.' Two persons of the family appear in a list of the alumni of the then English College at Rome, in Father Parsons' handwriting, now at Stonyhurst. No. 9, Thomas Stucleyus, Devoniensis, ætat. 25, admissus an. 1593. No. 16, Augustinus Stucleyus, Devon. ætat. 18, admissus Feb. 1593. These two Stucleys were afterwards at Valladolid.

[1] This may be the Sir Thomas Stucley mentioned in a letter of Dudley Carleton to John Chamberlain, May 2, 1606. 'Sir T. S. is in Town : he has bought a manor of Lord Lisle.'

could any person in England or Ireland become owner of one foot of land by his death. Neither of Dukedoms, Marquisates, or Lordships was it possible for her Majesty to benefit any person with the forfeitures thereof. But if his death did profit any, it was to the King of Spain and the Popes, by determination of their pensions, although it was credibly reported that the King of Spain, by advice of some of his wise counsellors, had discharged him of all pensions and entertainments and gave him passage to Rome.'

Burghley's account of Stucley's two companions, Sanders and Fitzmorris, deserves to be added: 'This companion [Stucley] also to further his designs matched himself, or rather took to attend upon him, a scholar of England, a doctor of divinity by his title, a fugitive and a vain-glorious person, who with his grand vain Capitain should also go as a legate from the Pope into Ireland, as after the death of Stucley he did, carrying a banner of the Pope's, and some money, with a company of captains and soldiers, most Italians, who for the greater part were put to the sword by the Queen's forces in Ireland: and Sanders the pretended legate escaping the sword, wandering in the wild Irish, died of a pestilent fever in the fields, being stricken with madness before his death.

'A third man is to be remembered to mark the better the displeasure of Almighty God against rebels, and his favour towards the just right and cause of her Majesty. One James, a gentleman of Ireland, commonly called James Fitzmorris, because his father's name was Morrice, who was a fourth son of the grandfather of the Earl of Desmond, now Earl. This James Fitzmorris by reason of the multitude of children that were and are living was in no likelihood of possibility to come to the Earldom by a great number of persons, except he would have been a murderer as his father was, who killed his own brother's son (being called also James Fitzmorris) because he was of the elder house, before him. This James Fitzmorris of whom mention is made as a third person to be an actor in Ireland came also into Spain and to Rome, entitling himself as next heir to the Earldom of Desmond, whereas there were living a number of children of five lines before him, but yet falling into company with the Duke Stucley he was by his preferment both in Spain and at Rome titled to be the next heir to that Earldom. Betwixt this James Fitzmorris and Stucley there was the difference, that though Stucley would be a Duke and had no land, yet the other had some right in blood to be a Desmond. And after our rebels and fugitives at Rome had made a full reckoning of triumph and victory by these three persons, James of Desmond, knowing the falsehood of Stucley, and disdaining him, being no more than a private lewd gentleman, and far unmeet to be a general in any army, and specially to have any superiority in Ireland where James should have charge, he so fell out with the Duke Stucley as neither Sanders nor any of the other rebels or fugitives could any ways reconcile them to join in the action; and so James and Sanders took the charge upon them, and Stucley mutinying in Portugal against the Italian captains that were sent by the Pope, for that they would not permit him to have the treasure at his commandment, which was levied of the clergy by the Pope's authority towards the war, he stayed at that time going into Ireland, and went into Barbary with the King of Portugal's army, where he was slain : and James Fitzmorris entering into rebellion in Ireland was slain also in the field by a young nobleman, a good subject, and a kinsman of his own, called Tybbald Burgh ; a just reward for his treason, and a due punishment for the murder committed by his father Morris upon his brother's son, called also James Fitzmorris.'

Among the Spanish papers in the Record Office is one of Nov. —, 1580, containing the Spanish Ambassador's reply to the Queen's speech of July 10.

. . . . Touching Ireland, he told her Majesty two years since of 22,000 crowns sent with Stucley, afterwards employed with James Fitzmorris. Her Majesty told him of certain Spaniards landed in Ireland, and that they should be brought hither. He hath heard nothing, nor thinketh that Julio [the informer] was a Spaniard. . . . If the Pope do attempt anything he is to answer it. His master has nothing to do with it. In that he is in league with him, he cannot deny him passage. Finally, there are no more Spaniards in Ireland than English in the Low Countries.

I have no positive proof that the following biographical drama belonged to the Lord Chamberlain's men; still less that Shakspere ever wrote on the subject. Yet it is clear that it belongs to the same political school as the *Alarm for London*, and that many of its scenes satisfy Chettle's description of the purport of Melicert's songs nearly as well as that play. Besides, the introduction of Alva and Sancho Davila, who, as in the *Alarm*, is called Sancto Danila or even Danulo, as the representatives of Spanish policy, appears to prove that it must have been acted by the same company. Moreover, it was manifestly intended by the last corrector to be a biographical play, exhibiting in five acts five distinct pictures of the hero's life, in different age and circumstances, just like the plays of Sir Thomas More, Thomas Lord Cromwell, and Pericles. I do not know of any other biographical plays in this form, which seems to be a speciality of the dramas brought out by the Lord Chamberlain's company, and is quite in accordance with Jaques' famous comparison of the seven ages of man to seven acts of a play in *As you like it*. The drama, I say, was intended to be of this form. But it has come down to us in a very imperfect state. The three first acts are finished parts of a whole which was to exhibit five distinct pictures of Stucley's career—in England, Ireland, Spain, Rome, and Africa. Up to Stucley's departure from Spain towards Rome the play is carefully finished. After that all is confusion. A chorus is introduced to make up for the want of dramatic evolution. It informs us that Stucley's Roman adventures found a place in the play, and that he was

——by the Pope created, *as you have heard*
Marquess of Ireland.

But the audience has never heard anything of the kind. Instead of the scenes in Rome, we are taken to the court of Don Sebastian at Lisbon, and learn all about the preparations for his expedition to Africa. This part is evidently taken from some play on the subject of Don Antonio. It is well known that after the slaughter of Sebastian at the battle of Alcazar in August, 1578, his uncle the Cardinal succeeded to the crown, and after a brief reign left it a prey to pretenders. The most powerful of them, Philip II. of Spain, seized it. But Queen Elizabeth favoured Antonio, whose claims were barred by his bastardy. The fragment which does duty for the 4th act of the play was once a part of a drama intended to recommend to the English the claims of Antonio to the crown. And so Sebastian is made to give to him

For your princely self
Your right unto the crown of Portingall

> As first and nearest of our royal blood
> That, should we fail, the next in our succession
> Tis you and yours to sit upon our throne;
> Which is our pleasure to be published.

A great deal of the fifth act is also taken from the same play, and what was so taken was so carelessly fitted in, that after the battle the chorus invites the audience (sig. L 3)

> Sit now and see unto our story's end
> All those mishaps that this poor prince attend.

But not a word more is said of him, or of his captivity among the Moors, and his marvellous escape.

With these fragments of a play upon *Don Antonio*, there are interwoven, in the fifth act, fragments of another play upon the *battle of Alcazar*, or *Stucley*, or the Moor Mahamet and his wife Callipolis. These fragments are in a more archaic style, like that of Peele or Greene, and somewhat in Cambyses' vein. The persons also are the same as in Peele's *battle of Alcazar*, the poetry of which was ridiculed both by Shakspere and Ben Jonson.

But amidst these fragments there are a few interpolations by the writer of the three first acts, who seems to have grown weary of his original plan, and after finishing three acts to have botched up the rest with the first matter that came to hand. These interpolations consist of a few short speeches, the council scene, p. 257, and the conclusion. The fragments of *Antonio* comprise the scene at the court of Lisbon, beginning at p. 244, and ending with the chorus, p. 248. The latter part of this chorus is, however, interpolated and altered by the writer of the three first acts. To the same play belongs the scene of Antonio disguised, p. 262, with the subsequent chorus.

The fragments from the archaic play of Peele or Greene are comprised in the Callipolis scenes, p. 250, &c. But even the writer of the three first acts seems to have had a precursor in his labours, to whom we owe the prose scene under the walls of Dundalk, p. 192 to p. 194. This is clearly the first scene of the second act, as originally designed. The last writer, however, rewrote it, and turned it into verse. Thus in this play there are traces of four different hands, one of whom, the last, is a writer of great diffuseness indeed but some power, whose characterization of his hero is gradually evolved in spite of his wilderness of words to a considerable degree of force and distinctness.

How this confusion might arise we are enabled to understand by the MS. of the play of *Sir Thomas More* in the Harleian collection of the British Museum (No. 7368). That play was originally the composition of one writer; the manuscript was submitted to criticism, and various portions were ordered to be rewritten; more than one dramatist fulfilled this task; and one, whom I imagine to have been the manager and factotum of the company, namely Shakspere himself, rewrote some scenes, generally keeping pretty close to the original (which is preserved with the alterations), but making wonderful improvements upon it. Finally, the stitcher or binder did his part and confounded the previous confusion by misplacing several of the scenes, and preserving fragments which have no proper place in the play as finally altered. If the MS. from which *Stucley* was printed was anything like this, the confusion of the two last acts is not at all to be wondered at.

The author of the corrected drama was satisfied with forming a very vivid conception of Stucley's character, and troubled himself scarcely at all to know anything of his history, beyond what was contained in ballads and plays. This came to pass, not because he undervalued historical truth,—for he must have taken considerable pains to get up his Irish history in the second act,—but because he had no sources of information for the true life of his hero. Stucley had rapidly become a mythical personage. His career had been too subordinate to secure the attention of the annalist and historian, and the memory of his soldier-like qualities, his valour and royalty to men at arms, had created a history for him. And at the time when the controversy between the partisans of the soldier under the banner of Essex and the partisans of the civilian under that of the Cecils divided men's minds, and when at the same time the question of peace with Spain and that of the proper treatment for Ireland were occupying attention, Stucley was a useful and popular figure to be used by the political dramatist. For all these reasons I couple this play with the *Alarm for London*, and I attribute the final alterations in it to the same presiding direction.

As to the authorities which the writer followed, they must have been meagre enough, or he would have kept nearer to historical truth. He cannot have had much besides ballads and tradition for Stucley's English, Irish, and Spanish adventures. Of his career in France and Flanders, and his voyage to Florida, the dramatist seems to have known nothing, though the voyage had been made the subject of more than one ballad. We cannot tell how much he knew of his hero's Roman life, for that part of the play is lost. The close of his life in Africa was better known, for the report of the battle of Alcazar had awaked an echo in the English press. On the 19th of February, 1579, two ballads were licensed to Edward White, the second of which was 'a brief rehearsal of the bloody battle in Barbary.' The interest it excited was enough to make the author of a reply published this year to Stephen Gosson's *School of Abuse* to entitle his defence of the stage, music, and dancing, 'Strange news out of Afric.'[1] On the 24th of March, 1579, 'The Barbary news of the battle there' was registered to John Charlewood. It is probably the prose tract, still extant, *A dolorous discourse of a most terrible and bloody battle fought in Barbary the fourth day of August last past*, 1578. *Wherein were slain, two kings, (but as most men say) three, beside many other famous personages: with a great number of captains and other soldiers that were slain on both sides. Whereunto is also added a note of the names of divers that were taken prisoners at the same time. Imprinted at London by John Charlwood and Thomas Man*. In spite of the long title, the information contained in this short tract is very meagre. It contains no allusion to Stucley.

There are four copies of the following ballad in the Roxburgh collection in the British Museum. There is nothing to show the date of its first composition. It was probably founded upon the play of *Stucley*, which was also partially followed by our dramatist.

1 In the West of England—Born there was I understand
    A famous gallant was he in his days—
    By birth a wealthy clothiers son—deeds of wonders hath he done
    To purchase him a long and lasting praise.

2 If I should tell his story—pride was all his glory
    And *lusty Stucley* he was called in court

---

[1] Some idea of this book may be gleaned from Gosson's *Ephemerides of Phialo*, extracts of which are given in Arber's reprint of Gosson, p. 62.

He served a bishop in the West—and did accompany the best
  Maintaining of himself in gallant sort.

3 Being thus esteemed—and everywhere well deem'd
  He gain'd the favour of a London dame
  Daughter to an alderman—Curtis she was call'd then
  To whom a suitor gallantly he came.

4 When she his person spied—he could not be denied
  So brave a gentleman he was to see;
  She was quickly made his wife—in weal or woe to lead her life
  Her father willing thereto did agree.

5 Thus in state and pleasure—full many days they measure
  Till cruel death with his regardless spite
  Bore old Curtis to his grave—a thing which Stucley wished to have
  That he might revel then in gold so bright.

6 He was no sooner tomb'd—but Stucley he presum'd
  To spend a hundred pound a day in waste.
  The greatest gallants in the land—had Stucleys purse at their command
  Thus merrily the time away he past.

7 Taverns and ordinaries—were his chiefest braveries
  Golden angels there flew up and down
  Riots were his best delight—with stately feasting day and night
  In court and city thus he won renown.

8 Thus wasting lands and living—by this lawless giving
  At length he sold the pavement of the yard

Which covered was with blocks of tin—old Curtis left the same
   to him
Which he consumed lately as you've heard.

9 At this his wife sore grieved—desiring to be relieved
       Make much of me dear husband she did say
   I'll make more of thee (said he)—then any one shall, verily
       I'll sell thy clothes, and so I'll go my way.

10 Cruelly thus hard-hearted—away from her he parted
       And travelled into Italy with speed
    There he flourish'd many a day—in his silks and rich array
       And did the pleasures of a lady feed.

11 It was the ladys pleasure—to give him gold and treasure
       For to maintain him in great pomp and fame
    At last came news assuredly—of a fought battle in Barbary
       And he would valiantly go see the same.

12 Many a noble gallant—sold both land and talent
       To follow Stucley in this famous fight
    Whereas three kings in person would—advent'rously with
       courage bold
    Within this battle show themselves in fight.

13 Stucley and his followers all—of the King of Portugal
       Had entertainment like to gentlemen
    The King affected Stucley so—that he his secrets all did know
       And bore his royal standard now and then.

14 Upon this day of honour—each man did show his banner
       Morocco and the King of Barbary

Portugal and all his train—bravely glittering on the plain
    And gave the outset there most valiantly.

15 The canons they rebounded—thund'ring guns resounded
    Kill kill then was the soldiers cry
    Mangled men lay on the ground—and with blood the earth was drown'd
    The sun likewise was darkened in the sky.

16 Heaven was so displeas'd—and would not be appeas'd
    But tokens of Gods heavy wrath did show
    That he was angry at this war—he sent a fearful blazing star
    Whereby the kings might their misfortunes know.

17 Bloody was the slaughter—or rather cursed murder
    Where six-score thousand fighting men were slain
    Three kings within this battle died—with forty dukes and earls beside,
    The like will never more be fought again.

18 With woeful arms infolding—Stucley stood beholding
    This cursed sacrifice of men that day.
    He sighing said, I woeful wight—against my conscience here to fight
    Have brought my followers all unto decay.

19 Being thus sore vexed—and with grief oppressed
    Those brave Italians that did sell their lands
    With Stucley for to venture forth—and hazard life for little worth
    Upon him all did lay their murd'ring hands.

20 Unto death thus wounded—his heart with sorrow sounded
    And to them so he made his heavy moan

Thus have I left my country dear—to be thus vilely murder'd here
E'en in this place whereas I am not known?

21 My wife I have much wrong'd—and what to her belong'd
I vainly spent in idle course of life
What I have had is past I see—and bringeth nought but grief to me
Therefore grant me pardon gentle wife.

22 Life I see consumeth—and death I see presumeth
To change this life of mine into a new
Yet this my greatest comfort brings—I lived and died in love of kings
And so brave Stucley bids the world adieu.

23 Stucleys life thus ended—was after death befriended
And like a soldier buried gallantly
Where now there stands upon the grave—a stately temple builded brave
With golden turrets piercing to the sky.

The tune of this old ballad is 'King Henry's going to Boulogne.' Another ballad relates to Stucley's pretended voyage to Florida in 1562. It was evidently written just before he set sail, and anticipated nothing but a prosperous termination to his venture.

A Commendation of the adventerus viage of the wurthy captain, M. Thomas Stutely Esquyer and others towards the land called Terra Florida.

If fortunes force procure   The valiant noble heart
In travail pain and dangers great   In wars to have his part

If loss of goods ensue   Through valiant enterprise
Or for slackness, or the foresight   Of diligent advice
Yet of his worthy praise   I cannot speak to miche
Who ventreth both his goods and life   His country to enrich
The worldly wise do muse   And also do envay
At noble hearts when that their wealths   Do fall unto decay
As now of late I knew   And saw the evidence
Of one whose part it was to shew   The like experience
A noble heart indeed   And worthy great renown
Whose fortune was not to remain   In city nor in town
A young Eneas bold   With heart and courage stout
Whose enterprise was only pight   Strange things to bring about
And though that all men seem'd   His doings to deride
Yet this his fact he would not leave   Nor throw it so aside
But still he doth procure   With bolden'd heart and mind
That thing which erst he had assay'd   By travail now to find
Into a land unknown   To win him worthy fame
As exequies and memory   Of his most noble name
Which if it fall to his lot   With fortunes helping hand
He may well make a laughing-stock   Of them which him withstand
Some term it Stolida   And Sordida it name
And to be plain they do it mock   As at a foolish game
If reasons sense be cause   Of this forespoken talk
Or fayned folly be the ground   Why mens tongues thus do walk
Then might it seem to me   The Frenches labour lost
Their careful pain and travail eke   That they therein have cost

The chronicles also   Which only seem as true
And writ by them that of that place   Before did take the view
The Spaniards eke do shew   And verify the same
To be described as a thing   Deserving such a name
The Portingales do say   The crowacles be just
And all that travelled have that coast   The same confess it must
Of that in times before   Through talks men have refrain'd
Which for the love of travail sore   Their hearts have long been pain'd
Columbus, as I read,   The space of many years
Was counted as unwise also,   As in writers appears
His earnest suit denied   Yet in the final end
His words and deeds did seem at length   On reason to depend
The like assay in hand   He did at last procure
Whose life and lucky viages   Good fortune did assure
At thend in savety home   At length he did return
And quenched all their mocking hearts   Which erst did seem to burn
For fire of force must needs   Declare his burning heat
Though for a time in smothering smoke   It seems itself to beat
So talk of tongues may not   By smothering through be tame
But bursting out at length will turn   Into a fiery flame
And then the malice gone   The fire falleth down
And quenched quite, as by this man,   Which was of great renown.

Now, Stuteley, hoice thy sail   Thy wished land to find
And never do regard vain talk   For words they are but wind
And in reproof of all   I will not once refrain
With prayer for to wish that thou   Maist safely come again
And that some fruit at length   By travail thou mayst find
With riches for to satisfy   Thy manly modest mind.

       Finis Qd . Robert . Seall

 Imprinted at London at the long shop adjoining unto Saint Mildreds Church in the Pultrie by John Allde.

Westcote, in his 'View of Devonshire,' preserves a fragment of another 'ditty made by him or of him,' which must have related the disastrous end of his Florida expedition:

> Have over the waters to Florida
> Farewell good London now
> Through long delays on land and seas
> I'm brought, I cannot tell how.
>
> In Plymouth town, in a threadbare gown
> And money never a deal
> Hey trixi trim, go trixi trim
> And will not a wallet do well?

For other poetical references to Stucley see Dyce's introduction to Peele's *Battle of Alcazar*. In that play Stucley is one of the persons of the drama, and he is made to give an account of himself in his last dying speech:

> Hark, friends, and with the story of my life
> Let me beguile the torment of my death.
> In Englands London, Lordlings, was I born

On that brave bridge, the bar that thwarts the Thames.
My golden days, my younger careless years
Were when I touch'd the height of Fortunes wheel,
And liv'd in affluence of wealth and ease.
Thus in my country carried long aloft
A discontented humour drave me thence
To cross the seas to Ireland, then to Spain.
There had I welcome, and right royal pay
Of Philip, whom some call the Catholic king :
There did Tom Stucley glitter all in gold
Mounted upon his gennet white as snow
Shining as Phœbus in King Philips court :
There like a lord famous Don Stucley lived,
For so they call'd me in the court of Spain,
Till for a blow I gave a Bishops man
A strife gan rise between his lord and me
For which we both were banish'd by the King.
From thence to Rome rides Stucley all aflaunt ;
Received with royal welcomes of the Pope ;
There was I graced by Gregory the Great
That then created me Marquess of Ireland.
Short be my tale, because my life is short.
The coast of Italy & Rome I left :
Then was I made lieutenant general
Of those small forces that for Ireland went
And with my companies embarked at Ostia.
My sails I spread, and with these men of war
In fatal hour at Lisbon we arrived.
From thence to this, to this hard exigent

Was Stucley driv'n, to fight or else to die,
Dar'd to the field, that never could endure
To hear God Mars his drum but he must march.
Ah sweet Sebastian, hadst thou been well advised
Thou might'st have managed arms successfully!
But from our cradles we were markèd all
And destinate to die in Afric here.
Stucley, the story of thy life is told;
Here breathe thy last, and bid thy friends farewell:
And if thy country's kindness be so much
Then let thy country kindly ring thy knell.
Now go, & in that bed of honour die
Where brave Sebastian's breathless corse doth lie.
Here endeth Fortune's rule and bitter rage;
Here ends Tom Stucley's pilgrimage. [*Dies*.

As in the preceding ballad and the following play, Peele makes Stucley die at the hands of his own Italian soldiers.

Besides the *Battle of Alcazar*, another play on the subject of Stucley is supposed to have once existed, on the strength of some lines which Peele addressed to the Earl of Essex, Norris and Drake, on their expedition to Cadiz in 1589:

> Bid Theatres and proud tragedians
> Bid Mahomet, Scipio, and mighty Tamburlain
> King Charlemagne, Tom Stucley, and the rest
> Adieu. To arms! &c.

Dyce considers that the drama thus alluded to was a different one from that now reprinted, which he is disposed to identify with the *Stewtley* first acted by the Lord Admiral's company 11th

Dec., 1596 (Henslowe's Diary, p. 83). But I consider that this play belonged to the Lord Chamberlain's men, and that Henslowe and the Lord Admiral's company had nothing to do with it. As for its date, a play in which the death of Sebastian is shown, without a hint of the story of his not really dying, can scarcely be later than 1598, when the news of the appearance of a claimant of Sebastian's personality and throne began to make a stir in England. 'A book called strange news of the return of Don Sebastian' was registered at Stationers' Hall, Feb. 3, 1598. June 28, 1599, Chamberlain wrote to Carleton 'The fable of Don Sebastian is still much talked of.' In 1601 Anthony Munday published a narrative of the reappearance of the lost King, with the title 'the strangest adventure that ever happened.' In May of the same year Decker and Chettle finished a play for Henslowe's company, 'Sebastian King of Portugal.'

In connection with the following play, I have to mention the second part of Deloney's *Gentle craft*, a collection of tales tending to the glory of shoemakers. This probably appeared shortly after the publication of the first part in 1598. Like Decker and Wilson's play of the *Shoemaker's holiday*, Deloney's book bears clear signs of a political purpose in exact contradiction to the aim of the following drama, or of the *Alarm for London*.

The last-named play is meant to show the inferiority of a burgher militia to professional soldiers in war. Deloney and Decker, on the other hand, undertook to flatter the citizens who already counted the four prentices of London above all the nine worthies, and to soothe the tradesmen of London into the belief that their extemporized bands were as good as, or better than, the regular troops, led by the most famous noblemen or captains who made war their profession. One of the tales in Deloney's book relates the successive combats of Captains Stucley and Strangwidge with Peachy the shoemaker of Fleet Street and his forty men, two and two together, and the defeat of the Captains in every encounter, till they were fain to get their friends at Court to patch up a peace. The mode in which the question is treated from both points of view shows that both series of stories and dramas belong to a time when the civil and military elements were pleading for precedence at the national bar, the one advocating age and wisdom in council, and industry and obedience in the nation; the other crying out for youthful counsels, a dashing policy, a military organization, and an offensive war. The one was the party of the Cecils, the other that of the Earl of Essex.

When Dyce published his edition of Peele's works, he could give very little more information about Stucley than was afforded by Fuller. Since then Mr Froude has brought from Simancas transcripts of many papers which refer to him; and the publication of the Calendars of our own Records have made many documents available which could hardly have been known to Mr Dyce. Even yet there is much to be learned about Stucley, which will probably not be known till Mr Brewer has completed his survey of the reign of Henry VIII., and M. Friedmann has calendared the Simancas records up to 1578. Even then there will still be curious particulars to be gleaned concerning him from the records of the Vatican, or the papers preserved in the various Papal families, which probably contain some notice of his negotiations with Pius V., and of the steps by which he rose in the favour of Gregory XIII., till that Pope created him Marquess, Earl, and Baron, with Irish titles, and made him his generalissimo. I have taken some trouble in examining the sources which are at present open, and from them I have compiled the foregoing memoir of Stucley, which seems to be a fitting introduction to the play of which he is the hero.

Anthony a Wood, in a kind of postscript to his notice of Sir Lewis Stucley, has a brief notice of Thomas, and adds, 'I have by me a little book printed in an English character, entitled *The famous History of Stout Stucley: or, his valiant Life and Death.* At the end of which is a ballad on him, to the tune of K. Henry's going to Bulloin; the beginning of which is this:

> In England in the West
> Where Phœbus takes his rest
> There lusty Stucley he was born;
> By birth he was a clothiers son,
> Deeds of wonder he hath done,
> Which with lasting praise his name adorn—&c.'

This must be the most civilized edition of the ballad given above; I have no notion where the book is to be seen. Bliss gives no reference to any copy in the Bodleian.

THE FAMOUS HISTORY OF THE

Life and Death of Captain Thomas Stukeley,

WITH HIS

MARRIAGE TO ALDERMAN CURTEIS' DAUGHTER,
AND VALIANT ENDING OF HIS LIFE AT THE BATTLE OF ALCAZAR.
AS IT HATH BEEN ACTED.

Printed for Thomas Pavyer, and are to be sold at his shop at the entrance into the Exchange, 1605.

DRAMATIS PERSONÆ.

SIR THOMAS CURTIS, *Alderman of London.*
LADY CURTIS, *his wife.*
[ANNE] CURTIS, *his daughter.*
VERNON.
CAPTAIN THOMAS STUCLEY.
OLD STUCLEY, *his father.*
MASTER NEWTON, *a citizen.*
Tom Stucley's page.
ARTHUR CROSS, *a Mercer.*
JOHN SPRING, *or* SPARING, *a Vintner.*
WILLIAM SHARP, *a Cutler.*
THOMAS BLUNT, *or* THUMP, *a Buckler-maker.*
[1] CAPTAIN HERBERT.
HAMDON, } *friends of Vernon.*
RIDLEY, }
Cashier to Sir Thomas Curtis.
GEORGE HAZARD, *tennis-keeper.*
HENRY CRACKE, *fencer.*
JEFFREY BLURT, *Bailiff of Finsbury.*
Lieutenant, Ensign, Ancient Drummer, Soldiers.

[SHAN] O'NEILL, }
O'HANLON, } *Irishmen.*
NEILL MACKENER, }
GAINSFORD,

Herbert's page.
ALEXANDER OGE, } *Scots.*
GILLIAN BUSK, }

HERNANDO, *Governor of Cadiz.*
His Wife.
Provost, servants, and attendants.
King PHILIP II. *of Spain.*
The Duke d'ALVA.
SANCHO DAVILA.
BOTELLO, *Portuguese Ambassador to Philip.*
MARSHALL VALDES, *a messenger.*
Master of English ship.
ADELANTADO.
Officers.
HERNANDO, *a courtier.*
SEBASTIAN, *King of Portugal.*
ANTONIO.
CARDINAL, *Sebastian's uncle.*

Chorus.

MULY MAHOMET.
CALLIPOLIS, *his wife.*
HAMET.
ABD EL MELEK.
The Duke d'AVEIRO.
Portuguese, Moorish, and Italian soldiers.

---

[1] Holinshed, p. 334, describes the valiant service of Capt. Geo. Hervie against O'Neil. Perhaps Herbert is meant for Hervie.

𝔏ife and 𝔇eath of 𝔈aptain 𝔗homas 𝔖tukeley.

Curtis. Proceed, son Vernon, on with your discourse.

Vernon. Sir Thomas Curtis spare that name of son
I must confess I should have been your son
And had thereto your wifes and your consent.

Cur. And had, son Vernon? Aye, and so have still
Bones a Dod man, if I be a knight
Sir Thomas Curtis and an alderman
They that say deny[1] my daughter is not yours: [*Roundly off.*
By yea and nay I think them not my friends.
Passion of me man! not my daughter yours? 10
What say you wife?

Wife. Husband, what should I say?
Is it not known through London? do not our friends
Daily expect the marriage of our child
To Master Vernon here? and ask ye me
'What say you wife'?
      Why heard ye not his words

Cur. 'He must confess he should have been our son

---

[1] say, deny. The existence of these two words in the text proves that the play was printed from the author's manuscript. He first wrote—'They that say my daughter is not yours,' and then for the metre substituted 'deny' for 'say.' The printer put in both words. Ann Curtis who married Thomas Stucley was granddaughter to Sir Thomas Curtis.

And thereto *had* both your consent and mine'?
Have you denied him since? Passion of me
Bess and son both, these speeches make me muse—
Not have our daughter! 20

Wife. Husband, husband, perhaps his mind is changed
Or our girls portion is not great enough
And therefore now he seeks to break it off.

Cur. Sits the wind there wife? ha, think ye so?
By yea and nay then, wife, he deals not well.
Come roundly, roundly, come, what is the matter?
Passion of me, break off, and for no cause? ha?

Ver. Sir Thomas, patience [1] but yourself awhile
And you shall see that mere necessity
Breaks off our match.

Cur.   On then a' God's name. 30

Ver. I doubt not but by marriage of your child
You seek such comforts as the sacred state
Yields you as parents, us as children? [2]

Cur. What else son Vernon?

[*Ver.*] And those high blessings noway are attained
But by the mutual sympathising love
That, as combining hands, so should the hearts
Of either party, else it cannot be.

Cur. All this is true son Vernon.

Ver. Now then, Sir Thomas, you cannot expect 40
These comforts by our match [3] on neither part
If you give me her hand and not her heart.
The one I know you may, compulsively:

---

[1] patience, a verb. [2] children, a trisyllable. [3] Ed. matches.

The other never but unwillingly.

Cur. Bones of dod man, how ? what have we here?
' Her hand and not her heart.' Nell, come hither Nell,
Passion of me wench, how comes this to pass
We 'point ye one, you love another, ha ?

Wife. May this be so, maid ? ha, why speak ye not ?

Ver. Madam, and good Sir Thomas, be not rough   50
With your fair daughter; what her bashfulness
Conceals from you, favour[1] me to disclose.
See ye this gentleman here, Master Stukeley ?

Cur. Oh Master Stukeley, a courteous gentleman;
What of him ?

Ver.   He is the substance of my shadowed love
I but a cypher in respect of him.
You give me your consent, but he gains hers:
You wed me to her hand, he hath her heart.
Oh what a wrong in you were this to her
Being your child, and hope of after joy !   60
Oh what a wrong in me were this to him
Being my friend, my dear esteemed friend,
To rob her of her hearts best happiness,
Him of the good his gracious fortune gives,
If I should hinder him, or you keep her
From this right match, which reason doth prefer.

Cur. Bones a dod Nell, how ? love Master Stukeley ?

Wife. A handsome proper man. But how now daughter,
Must maids be choosers ?

Stuk. Madam, and kind Sir Thomas, look on me   70

[1] favour me, *i.e.* suffer me.   Ital. *favorisce.*

Not with disdainful looks, or base contempt.
I am a gentleman, and well deriv'd
Equal, I may say, in all true respects,
With higher fortune than I aim at now.
But since your daughters virtues and firm love
In each of us hath made resolved choice;
Since my dear friend to me hath yielded up
What right he might prefer to your fair child
In true regard of our so mutual love:
So you yourselves make perfect those fair hopes   80
That by contracted marriage you expect,
Where either party resteth fully pleased.

   Hel. Upon my knees dear parents I entreat it;
And count it not in me immodesty
To love the man whom heaven appointed for me.
Your choice I must commend, but mine much more
Bearing the seal of firm affection.
His virtues in the public worlds repute
Deserveth one more worthy than myself:
Since Master Vernon then prefers his friend   90
Before himself, and in so just a case,
Let me intreat that reason may take place.

   Ver. To further it, thus frankly I begin.
Here, dear Tom Stukeley, all the right I have
In fair Nell Curtis[1] I resign to thee
Be but her parents pleased as well as I
God give you joy as man and wife, say I.

---

[1] Cf. 'Two Gentlemen of Verona,' V. iv., 83—'All that was mine in Silvia I give thee.' The lady's name was Anne, not Nell.

Stuk. What says Sir Thomas ? shall I call him father?
And Madam, you my mother?

Cur. Soft and fair sir.
Come hither wife ; Stukeley's a gallant man, 100
And one here in our city much belov'd.

Wife. Nay husband, both in court and country too :
A gentleman well born, and as I hear
His fathers heir[1] ; the match were not amiss
Since Nell is so affected to him ; and beside
You see that Master Vernon leaves her quite.

Cur. Passion of me wife, but I heard last day
He's very wild, a quarreller, a fighter
Aye, and I doubt a spend-good too.

Wife. That is but youthfulness ; marriage will tame him ; 110
Young gentlemen will run their course awhile
And yet be ne'er the worse.

Cur. Say ye so wife ?
Well, son Vernon (should have been) and Master Stukeley,
Come, we will dine together, and talk more
Concerning this new motion. Well Nell, well
You cannot choose a man, not you ! by yea and nay
I grow in good opinion of him : come no more ado
We will to dinner, and be merry too.

Stuk. I feel thee coming, fortune ! If it prove
Blest be the wooing speeds so soon of love. [*Exeunt.* 120

---

[1] Thomas Stucley was a younger son of Sir Hugh Stucley of Affton, Devonshire, and not his heir.

Enter MASTER STUKELEY *and* MASTER NEWTON, *a citizen.*

Old Stuklie. Be'r Lady, we have sitten well my host:
Tis one o'clock, my watch says: what says your clock?

Newt. Much thereabout sir. Is 't your pleasure we
Prepare your lodging?

Old Stuk. What else sir? nay I will not change mine host.
Good Master Newton I'll be bold with you,
Mine old friend and acquaintance and companion—
Whoever else be here, I must be one;
You shall not drive me from you, that you shall not.

Newt. My very worshipful and loving friend   130
Master Stukeley, you're right welcome to my house
And be as bold here as you were at home.
Will you abroad so soon sir after dinner?

Old Stuk. Yes sir about a little businesses.

Newt. Beshrew me sir, you have come far to day
I pray you rest yourself this afternoon
Your bed shall be made ready if you please
And take tomorrow for your businesses.

Old Stuk. O sir I thank you, but it shall not need
I thank God sir, I am as fresh and lusty   140
As when I set this morning from mine Inn—
Tut, forty miles; 'tis nothing before noon,
Now, in mid April, and the ways so fair.

Newt. I'm younger than yourself by twenty years
And be'r Lady would not undertake it.

Old Stuk. Ho twenty years ago! I have ridden from
This town to my house and ne'er draw bit.
But Master Newton those days and I be parted.

Well sir I'll to the Temple [1] to see my son.
When saw you that unthrifty boy, Tom Stukley? 150
   Newt. He was not here since you were last in Town
But th' other day I saw him come up Fleet-street
With the Lord Windsor and Lord Aburganny
An Irish Lord or two in company—
I promise you he is a gallant man.
   Old Stuk. I had as lief you'd seen him in the Temple walk
Conferring with some learned Counsellor
Or at the moot upon a case in law.
   Newt. Sir so you may I doubt not on occasion.
   Old Stuk. I promise you I doubt it Master Newton : 160
I hear some things that pleaseth me but a little.
It is not my allowance serves the turn
To maintain company with noblemen.
   Newt. Why sir, it shows he bears a gallant mind
I' faith he is a gallant sprightly youth
Of a fine mettle and an active spirit.
   Old Stuk. God make him honest sir, and give him grace.
   Newt. My wife expects your company at supper.
   Old Stuk. Yes sir, God willing.
   Newt. And if your son be at leisure, I pray you bring him. 170
   Old Stuk. I thank you sir
I hear his courage very much commended,
But too licentious—that is all I fear.
But that he doth accommodate [2] with the best,

---

[1] Stucley was never a student of the Temple.

[2] accommodate.—Cf. Bardolph on this word, H. 4, B. III. 2. 71 sqq., and Bobadil, *Every man in his humour*, I. iv.

In that he shows himself a gentleman;
And, though perhaps he shall not know so much,
I do not much mislike that humour in him.
A gentleman of blood and quality
To sort himself amongst the noblest spirits
Shows the true sparks of honourable worth   180
And rightly shows in this he is mine own.
For when I was of young Tom Stukeley's years
And of the Inns of Court, as he is now,
I would be conversant still with the best,
The bravest spirits that were about the town—
But soft this is his chamber as I take it.   [*He knocks.*

Enter the page.

  Page. Who calls there?
Gods me, my masters father! Now my master
He's at the Tabling-house[1] too! What the devil
Makes this old crack-breech here now? How the pox   190
Stumbled he hither? God save your worship.
  Old Stuk. How now boy? Where's your master?
  Page. He is not come from dinner sir.
  Old Stuk. How not from dinner? 'tis past dinner time
I' th' hall an hour ago. Hark ye sirrah tell me true,
Is he in commonds, tell me not a lie now?
  Page [*aside*]. What shall I do? I'm in a pitiful case.
A pox on him for an old Scand-pouch: if he take me with a lie now,
By this flesh and blood, he'll whip me most perniciously:
If I should say he is in commonds and he prove it not so,   200

[1] Tabling-house, gambling-house?

By this light he'll pepper me.   Faith, I'll tell truth.

Old Stuk. Sirrah, why speak you not

Page. I think he be not in commonds, sir.

Old Stuk. Where dines he?

Page. At Palmers ordinary.

Old Stuk. Your master is an ordinary student!

Page. Indeed sir he studies very extraordinarily.

Old Stuk. And you the rope-ripe ordinarily.

I sent him money to provide him books.   209

Page. See see, the devil ought my master a shame and now he has paid him; he had ne'er so much grace as to buy him a key to his study door; if he have e'er a book there, but old hacked swords, as foxes, bilboes and horn-buckles, I am an infidel. I cannot tell what to do.   I'll devise some 'scuse.

Old Stuk. Sirrah hear ye me, give me the key of his study.

Page. Sir, he ever carries it about him.

Old Stuk. How? let me see, methinks the door stands open.

Page. A plague on 't, he hath found it.   I was not ware.
Sir, belike he'd thought he had locked it, and turned
The key too short.   220

[*Aside*] Now we shall see this old cutter play his part,
For in faith he's furnished with all kinds of weapons.

Old Stuk. What, be these my sons books?   I promise you
A study richly furnished.   Well said Tom Stukeley

[*Laying out all his tools.*

Here gallows-clapper, here.   Be these your master's books?
For Littleton, Stamford and Brooke
Here's long-sword, short-sword and buckler;
But all's for the bar; yet I had meant to have my son

A Barrister, not a Barrater: but I see he means not
To trouble the law; I pray God the law 230
Trouble not him! Sirrah Halter-sack![1]

Page. Sir?

Old Stuk. Where is this towardly youth your master?
This Lawyer, this lawyer, I would fain see him,
His learned mastership, where is he?

Page. It will not be long before he comes sir.

[OLD STUKELEY *goes again to the study.*

If he be not curst in 's mother's belly
He'll keep him out of the way: I would I were
With him too; for I shall have a baiting worse than a hanging.

Old Stuk. If he have so much as a candstick[2] I am a traitor,
But an old hilt of a broken sword to set his light in. 241
Not a standish as I am a man, but the bottom
Of a Temple pot, with a little old sarsnet in it.
Here's a fellow like to prove a lawyer, if sword and buckler hold.

Enter STUKELEY *at the further end of the stage.*

Stuk. Boy, has Dick Blackstone sent home my new buckler? rogue, why stirs thou not?

Page. What a gaping keep you! a pox on 't my old master is here; you'll ha't i' faith.

Stuk. How long has he been here rogue?

Page. This two hours.

Stuk. Zounds, he has been taking an inventory of my household stuff: all my bravery lies about the floor. 250

---

[1] Halter-sack, *i. e.* slip-string   [2] Candstick, *i. e.* candlestick.

Old Stuk. O thou graceless boy, how dost thou bestow thy time?

Stuk. Your blessing good father! [*He kneels down.*

Old Stuk. O thou blessed boy! thou vild lewd unthrift!

Stuk. How does my mother Sir, and all in Hampshire?[1]

Old Stuk. The worse to hear of thy demeanour here.

Stuk. I am glad to hear of their good health. God continue it.

Old Stuk. Thou graceless rake-hell, and is all my cost
This five years[2] space here for thy maintenance
Spent in this sort, thou lewd misordered villain?

Stuk. Sir, I am glad to see you look so well, 260
I promise you it joys me at the heart.
Boy bring the chair, and let my father sit,
And if old Master Provye be within
I'll call him sir to bear you company.

Old Stuk. Aye, aye, thou carest not how thou stop'st my mouth
So that thou hear'st not of thy villany.
It is no marvel though you write so oft
For several sums to furnish you with books!
Believe me sir, your study's richly furnisht.

Stuk. This villain boy ne'er dresses up the chamber: 270
I pray thee put these things out of the way.

Old Stuk. I would I could cast thee out of the way
And so I should not see my shameless son—
Be these the books, sir, that you look upon?

---

[1] Hampshire. Devonshire was the County of the Stucley family.

[2] five years. As the average age of students entering the Inns of Court was about 18, Stucley is supposed to be 23. In reality he was about 40 when he married.

Stuk. Father, this is as right a Fox[1] as e'er you saw
And's been as soundly tried as any blade in England.
   Old Stuk. I trust you'll make me account sir of my money.
   [*Stuk.*] Indeed Sir, he does rascand[2] very fast i' th' hilts
And is a little crooked at the point.
   Old Stuk. Tom Stukeley, what a shame is this for thee,   280
To see so many of thy countrymen,
Of whom the world did ne'er expect thy hopes,
So forward and so towardly to the law,
And thou, whose infancies did flatter me
With expectation of so many goods,
To prove a very changeling, and to follow
These ruffianly and vild disordered courses.
   Stuck. Nay hark you father, I pray you be content,
I've done my goodwill, but it will not do.
John a Nokes and John a Style and I cannot cotton.   290
O, this law-French is worse than butter'd-mackerell
Full o' bones, full o' bones. It sticks here; 't will not down.
Aurum potabile will not get it down,
My Grandfather bestowed as much of you
As you have done of me; but of my conscience
You were as I am, a true man to the house,
You took nothing away with you.
   Old Stuk. O had thy grandsire been as kind to me
As I have been to thee, thou vild lewd unthrift

---

[1] a fox. A sword with a fox engraved on the blade.

[2] rascand, to shake, to be loose in the hilt. A.S. ræscian, to shake, vibrare, unless perchance it is a misprint for reascend, 'the curve at the hilt is too sharp.'

I had done well.   300

 Stuk. Nay, so you do, God be thank'd. But heark you father
There is a nearer way to the wood¹ than all this;
A nearer cut than scratching for things out
Of a standish all a mans life, which I have
Found out, and if you 'll stick to me, I doubt not
But you shall think I have bestowed my time well
And this it is. I am in possibility
To marry Alderman Curtises daughter
Now father if you will open the bag of your affection
And speak but a few good words for me to the old Alderman 310
She's mine, horse and foot.²

 Old Stuk. But with what colour can I speak for thee
Being so lewd and prodigal a spendthrift?
A common quarreller, with shame I speak it
That I dare scarcely own thee with my credit?

 Stuk. Peace good father: no more of that; stick to me once
If you will but tickle the old fellow in the ear, look you,
With a certain word, called a Jointure—
Ha that same Jointure, and a proper man
Withal, as I am, will draw you on a wench,   320
As a squirril's skin will draw on a Spanish shoe.³

 Old Stuk. Now afore God, Tom Stukeley,
Thy riots are so notorious in the city
As I am much afraid the Alderman
Will not be wrought to yield unto the match.

---

¹ a nearer way to the wood, now we say 'out of the wood.'
² horse and foot. *Dekker*, Vol. ii., p. 214—he 'is overthrown horse and foot.'   ³ This figure of the shoeing horn is common in old ballads, &c.

Stuk. Aye father, this is certain : but all that's nothing ;
I have the wench's good will, and he must yield
Spite of his heart : she 's worth forty thousand pound
O father this is the right Philosophers stone !
True multiplication ! I have found it. 330
 Old Stuk. Well Sirrah, come, and go with me to supper
Whither I'll send for a friend or two of mine
And take their better counsels in the matter.
 Stuk. I pray you let it be so : Sirrah boy
Lock the door and bring my sword.
 Page. I will sir. [*Exeunt.*

Enter at one door CROSS *the Mercer, at another* SPRING *the Vintner.*

 Cross. I ne'er heard such a murmur of a marriage ;
Yet for my life I cannot meet a man
That soundly can report the certainty.
 Spring. I cannot meet a man in any place
But still he hath this marriage in his mouth 340
This day, says one ; tomorrow, says another ;
Another says, 'tis past, and he was there ;
Another tells me that upon his knowledge
It is not yet this three days at the least.
I think the world is set a madding, I.
 Cross. What Master Spring the Vintner ? I pray God sir, your smell be as good as your taste.
 Spring. Master Cross the Mercer, is 't even so ? you have something in the wind. I believe you have been brought to the book as well as your neighbours. Upon my life he comes upon the

same business that I do, and perhaps he can tell me how the world goes here. Well met Master Cross. 351

Cross. What Master Spring, whither away?

Spring. I was about to ask you as much.
Come, I know you are hearkening to Alderman Curtis here.

Cross. O, you would fain have some company; I feel you.
Go to, Tom Stukeley shall have the wench,
And helter-skelter, the Aldermans bags shall pay for all.

Spring. Art thou a true prophet?

Cross. I was adreamt to night that he paid me all in double pistolets.[1]

Spring. I would I had mine in plain testerns. 360

Cross. Tut, beggarly payment, hang it—

Enter SHARP *the Butler, and* BLUNT *the Buckler maker.*

What, more of the same covey, all birds of a feather.

Spring. Sharp the cutler of Fleet-Street methinks,
And Blunt of the Strand the Buckler-maker.

Cross. Have at him at Blunt and Sharp, for sword and buckler; we are for him.

Sharp. Well met Master Spring.

Spring. So are you Master Sharp.

Cross. What Master Blunt, shall we lie at Ward?

[*Putting out his hand.*

Blunt. I pray God we may sir, to save ourselves by this marriage.

---

[1] (B$_2$ verso) I was adreamt (I dreamed). Cf. H6A. 1, 1, 126. All the whole army stood *agazed* on him. Lr. II. 3. 6. [I] am bethought to take the basest shape (*i. e.* I think, or mean).

Spring. Stay, here comes Tom Stukeley and Jack Harbart. 370

Enter STUKELEY *and* HARBART *in their hose and doublets.*

Cross. What's the matter?
Stuk. To speak it publicly in such a presence—
'He hath undone his daughter by the marriage,'—
You are a most disgraceful idiot
The greatest injury e'er cross't my spirit
Could not have drawn so base a wrong from me.
Harb. I spake it but in mirth; but since your snuff
Is so soon lighted, let it quench again.
Are you so tetchy Stukeley, with a pox?
   Stuk. You are a slave thus to abuse me Harbert. 380
   Harb. You are a vain fool Stukeley so to call me.
   Stuk. Enforce me not I prithee at this time.
   Harb. Enforce you? 's blood, you will not be enforced.
   Stuk. Harbert, your blood's too hot.
   Harb. You have brought me into the air to cool it then.
   Stuk. Thou hast almost tempted me beyond my strength.
   Harb. If I wist[1] that I'd be your evil spirit.
   Cross. Here's sword and buckler, by me—Call for clubs!
   Spring. So we may beat out the brains of our business.
   Sharp. We come in an ill time. 390
   Blunt. So I fear.
   Cross. How now Sharp, is your edge taken off?
   Sharp. I am blunted with my neighbour in faith.
   Stuk. Thou cam'st on purpose Harbert to disgrace me.

---

[1] *wisht.* Ed.

Harb. Sirrah, your mothers son lies in his throat.

Stuk. I pray thee stand not thus.

Harb. To under-prop your choler, lest it fall.

Stuk. Thou hast found a time to triumph on my courage
When I am gyved: durst thou else have said
Thus much?

Harb.   When will ye be unfettered?   400

Stuk. Whereere I meet you next, I'll have you by the ears.

Harb. Stukeley you shall not; I'll keep you from my ears
By the length of my rapier.

Stuk.   Say no more.

Enter CURTIS, *Mother, Bride, and the rest.*

Bride. Where is my husband, where is Master Stukeley?
Alas my heart! upon my wedding to fall out thus!

Mother. For Gods love, good son Stukeley and Master Harbert
Pacify yourself.

Curtis. Fie Tom fie! Bones a Dod, man, what coil is here?

Stuk. What mean you sir? why rise you from the table?
We rise for nothing but to talk a little.—   409
[*Aside*] Harbert look to it; by this blessed day I'll be with
  you.

Harb. I would the day were come
But you take day still with your creditors.

Spring. I do not like that.

Cross. What dost thou mean?

Spring. That he should take longer day with his creditors.

Mother. For Gods love, good son Stukeley, be content.

Curt. Gods blest, Captain Harbert, Bones of Dod man, be content.

Harb. We are good friends with all my heart—
The dining room Sir growing somewhat hot
We stept out hither but to take the air. 420

Bride. I pray thee good sweet-heart be not so angry
And Captain Harbert, let me tell you this
Knowing the disposition of your friend
You might have spared the speeches that you used.

Harb. If they have any way displeased you
I'm very sorry.
But let him take them how he will, I care not.

Stuk. Harbert, I'll make you eat your words

Curt. Gods me blest; lets to dinner again, all's well, all's well.
Come, come, come. 430

Mother. Come Master Harbert, you shall be my prisoner
Daughter take you your husband by the hand
And let us in to dinner. [*Exit.*

Cross. Here's a wedding indeed. I perceive by this
That we come in ill season for our money.

Spring. I would I had my debt before Harbert and he meet.

Sharp. Why so Master Spring?

Spring. Because
If they two meet, I fear one of them pays for 't:
They're two tall gentlemen as England yields. 439

Blunt. Well, let's away for this, and come tomorrow the sooner.

Cross. Content. [*Exeunt.*

Enter VERNON, *with* HAMDON *and* RIDLEY, *two of his friends.*

Ham. If not at our requests, yet gentle friend
For your own safety, change your former mind,
Have you not wealth? why should you leave the land?
   Rid. Are you not here of credit in the city?
Why should you then betray your forward hopes
Upon a wilful and uncertain humour?
   Ver. I know that my estate is sound and good,
As on the one side strengthened with rich friends,
And on the other well established   450
By the assistance of a private stock:
Yet what is this, or all external pomp
That otherwise is incident to men
If the mind want that comfort it should have?
Believe me gentlemen, it is as musick
To men in prison, or as dainty meat
Brought to a sick man, whose afflicting pain
Hath neither left him appetite nor taste.
   Ham. How springs this discontent? wherein lies
This gall of conscience that disturbs you so?   460
   Rid. We are your friends; show us your inward grief,
And we will either find a remedy,
Or, sharing every one a part of it,
So lessen it, and it shall lose his force.
   Ham. Is it for sorrow you forsook your Bride
And gave your interest to another man?
   Rid. You hit the nail upon the head: 'tis that

And nothing else that breeds this discontent.

Ver. Be not deceived; 1 did it by advice
Nor do I any way repent me of it.   470
She loved not me, albeit I honoured her,
And such a match, what were it but to join
Fire and water? Marriage is no toy
To be desired where there is dislike;
And therefore, weighing his deserts with mine
Her love to him, and his to her again
I rather chose to benefit my friend
Whereby two might be pleased, than greedily
Assuming what I might, displease all three.   479

Ham. What then hath wean'd you from your country's love?

Ver. Nor that, nor anything—I know not what!
Yet whilst I breathe this native air of mine
Methinks I suck in poison to my heart;
And whilst I tread upon this English earth
It is as if I set my careless feet
Upon a bank, where underneath is hid
A bed of crawling serpents. Any place
But only here, methinks, would make me happy,
Say 'twere the meanest cottage in the world:
But here I am accurst, and here I live   490
As one deprived both of soul and sense.
Which strange conceit, from whence it should proceed
I cannot utter, other than from this
That I am fired with a desire to travel
And see the fashions state and qualities
Of other countries: Therefore if you love me

Offer no further to resist in me
The settled resolution of my mind.

Rid. Yet since you needs will leave us and the realm
Go not to Ireland: the country's rude   500
And full of tumult and rebellious strife.
Rather make choice of Italy or France.[1]

Ver. My word is past unto a gentleman
With whom I will not break; and here he comes.

Enter HARBERT, *and another Captain.*

Harb. Sir as I told you, even at dinner time
His fury was so great as he must needs
Rise from the table to confer with me
About my speeches which I did maintain;
And sure if place had served we there had fought.

Cap. I would I could devise to make you friends   510
The rather for I hear he is appointed
To have a charge in this our Irish expedition.

Harb. It is no matter. Harbert fears him not;
I make as little reckoning of my blood
As he of his; and will at any time,
Or when he dares, meet him upon that quarrel.

Ver. Captain well met!

Harb. Master Vernon we stay for you,
Our horses half an hour ago were ready

---

[1] It seems by these lines that at the time the play was written Italy and France were quiet, and Ireland in one of its rebellions. This would suit 1598.

And we had back't them, but we lack't your company. 520

Ver. Some conference with these gentlemen my friends
Made me neglect mine hour: but when you please
I now am ready to attend on you.

Harb. It is well done, we will away forthwith.
Saint Albans, though the day were further spent,
We may well reach to bed to night.

Ver. Kind friends, I now must bid ye both farewell

Ham. Nay we will see you mounted ere we part. [*Exeunt.*

Enter CURTIS *and his Casher.*

Cur. Sirrah, what men are those that stay without?

Cash. Some that would speak with Master Stukley, Sir. 530

Cur. Know'st thou what their business is, or whence they come?

Cash. Tradesmen they are, and of the City sir
But what their business is I cannot tell.

Cur. Upon my life some creditors of his,
That, hearing of his matching with my daughter,
Come to demand some money which he owes them.
It is even so. They know he hath received
His marriage money: they perceive he's flush [1]
And mean to share with him ere all be gone.
I'll see the sequel. Here he comes himself 540
And with him (O the body of me)
Half the tradesmen in the town, I think.

---

[1] flush, lusty; flush of cash, abounding in money.

Enter STUKELEY *with bags of money. After him thronging* ARTHUR CROSS *the Mercer*, JOHN SPARING *the Vint.*, WILLIAM SHARP, THO. THUMP, GEO. HAZARD, *tennis-keeper*, HENRY CRACKE *the Fencer, and* JEFFERY BLURT, *Bailiff of Finsbury: with written notes in their hands.*

Stuk. Now ye slaves: a man can no sooner step
Into a little wealth but presently
You'll have the scent of him, you'll visit him.
Here's bills enough: had I now as many
Shot and pikes, I would with a valiant band
Of mine own subjects march among the Irish.
But let me see. Deliver your petition. [CROSS *delivers his bill.*
I'll prove an honest man a' the Chancery.   550
 Cur. Little law, I fear, and lesser conscience.
 Stuk. The gross sum of your debt sir?
 Cross. Two hundred pound.
 Stuk. For what?
 Cross. For silks and velvets sir.
 Stuk. Your name?
 Cross. Arthur Cross the Mercer.
 Stuk. Well master Cross, the first syllable of your name might have spared you this labour: but all's one: there's your money.
 Cur. Two hundred pounds? so there's an end of that
I will be sworne I got it not so soon.   560
 Stuk. Your title to my purse?
 Spar. Thirty pounds Sir.
 Stuk. For what?

Spar. For tavern suppers and for quarts of wine.

Stuk. Oh at the Grey-hound in Fleet Street?

Spar. Aye sir, the same.

Stuk. Your name is Sparing?

Spar. John Sparing Sir, the Vintner.

Cur. You spared him not when you did score so much

Stuk. There Master Sparing, would I were your scholar 570
That I might learn to spare as well as you.   [*Exit* SPARING.

Curt. That will ne'er be until it be too late.

Stuk. Now sir to you.

Sharp. Your servant sir. William Sharp for bilboes, foxes, and Toledo blades.

Stuk. What?

Sharp. Forty marks.

Stuk. You cut somewhat deep Master Sharp; but there's a preservative for a green wound.

Cur. Beshrew me but a wounds me: what preservative have I for that?

Stuk. Of whence are you?

Thu. Thomas Thump Sir the Buckler maker of S. Giles. 580

Stuk. The sum thereunto belonging?

Thu. Fifteen pounds sir for broad lined bucklers, beside steel pikes.

Cur. Body of me, half the money would arm five tall fellows for the wars.

Stuk. Thump, I will not answer you with the like violence, for if I should, the broadest buckler that e'er you made would not defend you from being bankerout.

Thu. I thank your worship.   [*Exit* THUMP.

Stuk. Are you sick of the yellows too?

Haz. Not so sick sir but I hope to have a childs part by your last will and testament.

Cur. There's a knave.   He thinks, after they are paid   590
He means to go and hang himself.
Whats his legacy?

Stuk. For tennis balls when the French Ambassador was here, thirteen pound.   Was it so much?

Haz. Just so much, with the fouling of fair linen when you were hot.

Cur. Fair linen? hoy day! your fair linen wipes him of a good deal of money.

Stuk. George Hazard, I take it that's your name?

Haz. My name is so sir.

Stuk. George, you have hit the hazard.   [*Gives him money.*

Cur. It was a hazard whether he would have it or no
But for my money.   600

Stuk. What else?

Crack. I hope sir your worship hath not forgot Harry Crack the fencer for forfeits and vennyes given upon a wager at the ninth button of your doublet, thirty crowns.

Cur. Crack his crown and that makes one and thirty.

Stuk. Well Crack I have no way to defend your thrust but by this downright blow.   [*Gives him money.*

Crack. I take it double sir an' 't please you.

Stuk. Let it suffice.   You're valiant, and my choler past.
More clients yet?   Your name?

Blu. Geffery Blurt sir Bailif of Finsbury.   610
For frays and bloodshed in the Theatre fields, five marks.

Cur. Body of me, ne'er a surgeon in this town would have ask'd more.

Stuk. Blurt, I have no reason to pay the whole.

Blu. Why so an' 't please you?

Stuk. Jack Dudley and I were halves in that action. Take part of him.

Blurt. Alas Sir, he's in Finsbury Jail for hurting a man behind the windmills last Saturday.

Stuk. Why then belike you have good pawn for your money?

Blu. I would we had sir. 618

Stuk. Well I see your dogged natures. A good sword and buckler man is of no reckoning amongst ye. But let the Sheriff think, when he hath lost Jack Dudley, he loseth twenty mark a year as good fee-simple as e'er a Baron in England holds. Theres your amerciaments. And give Jack Dudley this from me to pay his fees. [*Exit* BLURT.

Blu. I thank ye sir.

Cur. I would he had broke his pate e'er he went, in earnest
Of a new reckoning: ah son, son, thou hast deceived my opinion,
My daughter cast away, and I have
Bequeathed my money to a prodigal.

Stuk. Father why so? shall I not pay my debts? 630

Cur. Not with my money son, not with my money.

Stuk. It is mine own, and Stukley of his own
Will be as frank as shall the Emperor.
I scorn this trash, betrayer of mens souls;
I'll spurn it with my foot; and with my hand
Rain showers[1] of plenty on this barren land.

---

[1] Ed. shewers.

Were it my fortune could exceed the clouds
Yet would I bear a mind surmounting that.
Father you have enough for your, and for your store
When mine is gone you must provide me more.   [*Exit.*   640
    Cur. Is it even so? The captain's words are true:
He is a spendthrift. But I'll keep him short
He gets not a denier more than he hath.

Enter LADY CURTIS *and* OLD STUKELEY.

    Lady. Husband, you are sent for in all the haste
To the Guild-hall, about the Soldiers
That are to be dispatched for Ireland.
    Cur. I may be sent for wife whither I will
And tis no matter greatly where I go.[1]
    Lady. Why so I pray?
    Cur.   Would you e'er have thought
That Taverns, Fencers, Bailiffs, and such like   65
Should by the fruits of my late sitting up
And early rising, have maintained their state?
    Old Stuk. What mean ye brother Curtis?
    Cur. Ah brother Stukley
My meaning, had you been but here e'en now
You might have scanned without my utterance.
Here was Item upon Item, such a crew
As ne'er I saw one man indebted to.

[1] Cf. Macbeth V. v., line 41.

Enter STUKLEY'S *Lieutenant, Ensign, Drum and Soldiers.*

Lieu. Here stay we soldiers till the hour be come
Our Captain did appoint to meet with us,   660
The valiant Stukley: we shall have a guide
There's not a better in the regiment.
It is not one will say unto his men
' Give you assault upon the enemy ',
[But] ' follow me ' : and so himself will be
The foremost man that shall begin the fight.
Nor will he nicely creep into the town
When we are lodged within the dampish field
But voluntarily partake your toil
And of his private purse relieve your wants.   670

Ens. Lieutenant, he's a gallant gentleman
We know it well, and he that is not willing
To venture life with him, I would for my part
He might end his days worser than the pestilence.[1]

Lieut. Nay if you look but on his mind [2]
Much more occasion shall ye find to love him
He's liberal, and goes not to the wars
To make a gain of his poor soldiers spoil,
But spoil the foe to make his soldiers gain—
And here he comes; stand all in good array.   680

---

[1] The pestilence possibly refers to one raging at the time.
[2] Cf. Shakespeare, Son. 69—' They look into the beauty of thy mind.'

Enter STUKLEY *and his wife.*

Stuk. I prithee wife importune me no more :
Might tears persuade, or words prevail with me
Thy tears and words e'er this had won me straight[1]
But 'tis not thou, nor any power but his
That has that power to take away my life
That can abridge my purpose.   I will go.
   Wife. Shall then my joys have an end e'er they begin?
And shall the term of three days being wife
For ever after cause a widowhood?
We scarce are joined together, and must part!   690
We scarce are warm within our nuptial bed
And you forsake me, there to freeze alone.
Oh do not so an' if you ever loved!
Or if you never loved, yet in regard
Of my affection, leave me not so soon.
   Stuk. Good Lord, that thou wilt still importune me!
Have I not said I undertake this task
Only to make thee great?
   Wife.   But I desire
To be no more than what I am already
So by your absence I be made no less.   700
   Stuk. But that contents not me.   It is not chambering
Now I have beauty to be dallying with,
Nor pampering of myself with belly-cheer
Now I have got a little worldly pelf,

---

[1] Ed. state.

That is the end or levels of my thought.
I must have honour; honour is the thing
Stukley doth thirst for, and to climb the mount
Where she is seated, gold shall be my footstool.
 Wife. But there are many dangers by the way
And hasty climbers quickly catch a fall.   710
 Stuk. He soonest loseth that despairs to win
But I have no such prejudicial fear
If there be any shall outlive the brunt
Of raging war, or purchase dignity
I am persuaded to be one of those.
If all miscarry, yet it will not grieve,
Or grieve the less, to die with company.
 Wife. That name of death already martyrs me.
 Stuk. Tut, never fear. And if I chance to die,
Thou being a lusty widow, there's enow   720
Will gladly sue to be received of thee.
The worst is, I confess, I leave thee poor,
As taking with me all the jewels thou hast,
And all the coin was given me for thy dower:
But I do leave thee with a wealthy father
And one that will not see thee want, I know.
Beside thou hast a jointure of such lands [1]
As I am born unto. And therefore cease
And let me seal thy lips up with this kiss.
 Wife. Stay but a day or two and then depart.   730
 Stuk. Are not my soldiers ready? what a shame
Were it to send them forward, and myself

---

[1] Stucley was born to no lands.

Come lagging after like [to] one that fears
Or went unwillingly unto [the] wars
As thou respects me, talk no more to me.
  Wife. Am I so odious that I may not speak?
Well, I have listened when you talked e'er now,
Or words had been the harvest of your hope;
But since to silence I am so enjoined
I would my life might likewise have an end. 740
  Stuk. March hence away, or still there will be cast
Some let or other to detract our haste.

         [*As they are marching enter* CURTIS *and* OLD STUCLEY.

  Cur. Bones a Dod man, lay down thy tabor-sticks
And hear me speak, or with my Dudgen dagger
I'll play a fit of mirth upon thy pate.
Why hear me Tom, hear me son Stukeley,[1] ha,
What here to-day and gone to-morrow? See
Thy wife laments, canst thou behold her weep?
  Stuk. Sound drums I say: I will not hear a word.
  Old Stuk. Wilt thou not hear thy father graceless boy? 750
  Stuk. Father, unless you mean I shall be thought
A traitor to her Majesty, a coward
A sleepy dormouse, and a carpet squire
Mix not my forward summer[2] with sharp breath
Nor intercept my purpose being good.
  Old Stuk. I come not, wilful boy, as a reprover

---

[1] Dudgen-dagger, wooden dagger.
[2] Cf. 'Titus Andronicus,' V. ii. line 140—

   'Here stands the spring whom you have stain'd with mud;
   This goodly summer with your winter mix'd.'

Of any virtuous action thou intends
But to reprove thy lack of husbandry
And the unthrifty courses thou hast used.
Learn to be sober, and not rashly thus 760
To rush into affairs of such great moment.

 Stuk. Father, I know not what you term rashness
But any time since I was of the skill
Or strength to wield a sword, I vowed in heart
To be a soldier; and the time now serves,
And now my vow shall be accomplished.
For any thing betwixt my wife and me,
We are agreed, however sour cheer
Do at our parting show the contrary;
If you as well as she can be persuaded 770
Why, so:
If not, sound drums; I will not hear no more.

 Cur. Nay Tom, son Tom, thou art deceived in me
I am not grieved that thou shouldst serve thy prince
Nor do I take exceptions at thy mind
So long as honour is thy object, Tom;
But that without our knowledge thou departs
And on the sudden; body of me, 'tis that
That strikes a discontentment in us all.

 Stuk. I cannot help it sir; with all my heart 780
And in all reverend duty of a son
I take my farewell, fathers; of you both
Thus much entreating if I ne'er return
Ye would have both a care unto my wife. [*Exit.*

 Old Stuk. Well brother Curtis, hope the best of him

He may return a comfort to us all
And were a not my son I would commend
His resolution—'tis heroical.

Cur. There is no remedy now but patience ;
But, were the bargain to begin again   790
I would be twice advised ere I'd bestow
My daughter so. I'wis, so large a sum
Is more than I had thought should fly with wings
Of vain expenses into Ireland.
But all is one : come daughter, never mourn
I will not see thee want whilst I do live.

Old Stuk. I hope she hath the like conceit of me ;
Then comfort, girl ! fear no extremity.   [*Exeunt.*

Enter O'NEALE, O'HANLON, *and* NEALE MAKENER.

O'Neale. O'Hanlon.

Hanlon. Ow.

O'Ne. Tread softly on the stones,
The water tells us we are near the town :   800
Neale Makener come on, fix all our eyes
Upon the walls of this bewitched Town
That harbours such a sort of English churls,
To see if any signal be set out
Where we shall enter to surprise Dundalk.

Mackener. O'Neale speak softly, we are near the walls ;
The English sentinels do keep good watch ;
If they descry us all our labour's lost.

Han. Our labour lost, for we can see no sign

Of any white that hangeth over the wall 810
Where we shall enter, by our spies within.

 O'Neale. A plague upon the drowsy drunken slaves
Bryan MacPhelim and that Neale O'Quyme
Who being drunk or sleeping with his drabs
Forget the business that they have in hand.

 Mac. O'Neale be patient, and suspect the worst;
They may unto the English be betrayed;
Or else, perceiving strong watch everywhere,
Dare not approach the walls or gates for fear.

 Han. O'Neale, thy secretary says very true; 820
The English, knowing all thy power so near,
Will be more watchful than their custom is;
So both our spies and friends dare not assay
To hang out signal, nor come near the Port.

 Neale. Why so it is; I know within Dundalk
I have ten friends to one the English have;
I mean of townsmen; but sure policy
Cannot of might attain our entrance in,
That we might cut off all the English heads
Of theirs that watch, and theirs that sleep in beds. 830
Let us withdraw unto our troops again
Tomorrow comes O'Kane with Gallinglasse
And Teague Magennies with his lightfoot kerne
Then will we not come miching thus by night
But charge the town and win it by daylight.
O'Hanlon, Captain Harbart shall be thine,
And Gainsford's ransom shall be Mackener's.

 Han. Thanks great O'Neale.

Mack. Be whist, I hear one stir.   [*One coughs within.*

O'Neale. Some English soldier that hath got the cough.   840
I'll ease his grief by cutting off his head.

Mack. These English churls die if they lack their bed
And bread and beer, porridge, and powdered beef.

Han. O Marafastot [1] shamrocks are no meat
Nor bonny clabbo,[2] nor green water-cresses [3]
Nor our strong butter, nor our swell'd oatmeal
And drinking water brings them to the Flixe.[4]

O'Neale. It is their niceness, silly puling fools.

Mack. There be of them can fare as hard as we
And harder too; but drunkards and such like   850
As spend their time in ale-house surfeiting
And brothel-houses, quickly catch their bane.

O'Neale. One coughs again; let's slip aside unseen
Tomorrow we will ease them of their spleen.

Enter SHANE O'NEALE, O'HANLON, NEALE MACKENER
softly as by night.[5]

O'Neale. O'Hanlon.

Humlon. Owe.

O'Neale. Fate is the token? fate siegne that Brian Mack Phelem
said he would hang oot?

Han. I' feate, I kno not; ask the Shecretary.

---

[1] Marafastot, an oath.   [2] bonny clabbo, curds.
[3] watercresses. *Dekker*, ii. p. 276, calls the Irish 'shamrock eaters.'
[4] Flixe, flux.
[5] This is an alternative scene, instead of the preceding one

O'Neale. Neale Mackener. 860

Mack. Hest, O'Neale, Hest, pease! too art at the vater seed.

O'Neale. Fate is the token bodeaugh breene? that I sall see
Ovare the valles of this toone of Dundalke?

Mack. I' feat O'Neale thoo art Saint Patrick his cushin and a
great Lord, but thou art not weeze.. The siegne is a paire
Of feet trouzes, or a feet shurt, or some feete blankead
To be hang oote over the valles, fan we sall be let in at the lettle
    Booygh dore by the abbay.

O'Neale. Esta clamper, thoo talkest too much, the English
Upon the vall will heare thee, lake, feagh, bodeaugh
Dost thou see any thing feete. 870

Mack. No by this hand, Shan O'Neale, we see no feat thing.

                                  [*One coughs within.*

Han. Cresh blesh us, fo ish tat ishe coughes?

Mack. Saint Patrick blesh us we be not betraid

O'Neale. Mackener, Mac Deawle, marafastot art thou a feete
    liverd kana: Tish some English churle in the toone
That coughes, that is dree, some prood English souldior hees a
    dree cough, can drinke no vater, The English churle dees
If he get not bread and porrage and a hose to lee in: but looke is
    the sicegne oote? zeele cut his troate and Help him of his cough
    fan I get into Dundalk.

Mack. Bee this hand O'Neale der is no siegne, zee am afraid
    Brian Mack Phelemy is wid his streepo, and forgeats To hang a
    siegne or let us in.

O'Neale. No matter; come, no noyse, 'tis almost day 882
Softly, let us creepe abootc by the valles seed, ane awan sone at night
Even at shuttene of the gates fan O'Cane and Magennis

Come from Carlingford, we will enter lustily the town
Mackener, O'Hanlon, zee will give you tree captaines to ransom.
> *Han.* Zee will take tree prishoners, and give thee too, and take
> de turd myself.
> *O'Neale.* Speake softly O'Hanlon, and gow, make ready oore
> kerne and gallinglasse against night, and bid my bagpiper be
> ready to peep Ballootherie soon, for I will sleep in Dundalke
> at night. Come, go back into the Fewes again. 892
> *Han.* Slave haggat Bryan Mac Phelemy.
> *Mack.* Slave, let's Rorie beg. [*Exit.*

Enter HERBART *at one door with soldiers, and* VERNON *at another.*

Harb. Good morrow master Vernon,
Ver. Good morrow captain Harbart.
Harb. Is it your use to be so early up?
Such vigilance doth fit us soldiers best
[1] And search our garrisons for fear of spies.
Ver. And travellers that use to walk the round 900
Of every country to survey the world
Must not be friend [2] with sleep and idleness.
But in plain terms, I do prevent mine hour
By reason of a gentleman's report
That is a soldier, and did walk the round,
Who coming in this morning to his rest
Said, the enemy was about the town to night.[3]
Lieut. So said this soldier that stood sentinel

---

[1] Perhaps 'And' should be 'To.' [2] friend, *i.e.* friendly. Ed. frend.
[3] to night, *i. e.* last night.

Now, this last watch, at dawning of the day,
That he did hear, hard by the water side, 910
Near the North gate that opens toward the Fewes,
Some trampling on the gravel up and down;
He did but cough and thought to call to them,
And they were gone. Soldier, was it so?

Sol. Yes governor, I know 'twas Shane O'Neale
They were so whist whilst they were near the walls
Pray God they have no spies within the town.

Harb. Thou prayest too late, the townsmen [all] are spies,
And help, and store them with provision;
And love them better than us Englishmen. 920

Ver. It behoves you therefore to be circumspect.

Lieu. Fear not you that, I'll search the town myself
And place a double guard at every gate.
How stands the wind?

Ver. From England very fair.

Harb. We look for fresh supplies to come from thence
To strength[1] our garrison, for it is but weak.
And we must bear the brunt of all the North.

Ver. Your men are healthful.

Harb. There's no soldier sick 930
But he that drinks, or spends his thrift at dice.

[*Sound a drum afar off.*

What drum is this?

Ver. A drum without the town.

Harb. Some band of men from England new arrived
Or else some company of the English pale.

---

[1] strength for strengthen

Bid Captain Gainsford guard the Southern Port
Toward Tredagh, and take that company in.
I'll see our troops in readiness this day
For I expect the Irish soon[1] at night.
 Ver. What will you do? I'll to the Southern Port   940
To see what Captain leads this band of men.
 Harb. I make ye lieutenant Governor for the time.   [*Exeunt.*

  Enter STUKLEY, *his Lieutenant, Ancient, Drum,*[2] *Soldiers, and Company.*

 Stuk. I muse what Lord is governor of this town
That comes not forth to welcome Stukley in.
 Lieut. The town's so long, he cannot hear our drum
And if he did he knows not whose it is.
 Stuk. Drum, thump thy tapskins[3] hard about the pate
  [*Drum sounds. Enter* VERNON, GAINSFORD, *and Soldiers.*
And make the ram-heads hear that are within:
Zounds, who is that? Vernon with a partisan?[4]
Is he a soldier? Then the enemy's dead.   950
 Ver. Is Stukley come, whom I desire to shun?
And must he needs to Ireland follow me?
I will not draw that air wherein he breathes;
One kingdom shall not hold us, if I can.
 Gains. Is not this lusty Stukley with his men?
 Ver. Yes Captain Gainsford, this is lusty Tom.

---

[1] Ed. soune.   [2] drum, *i.e.* drummer.
[3] tapskins of the drum—drum-sticks which tap the skins, or the skins which are tapped?
[4] partisan—a pike ending in a sword, sharp on both sides.

Stuk. These gallants are grown ceremonious,[1]
They stand at gaze as if they knew me not,
Or else they strain a further compliment
To see if I will vail my bonnet first.   960
I'll eat my feather ere I move my hat
Before I see their crowns uncovered.

   Lieut. Cherish that humour; it becomes your port.[2]

   Ver. He doth expect we should salute him first

   Gains. 'Tis fit we should, for hee's but new arrived.

   Ver. You're welcome into Ireland Captain Stukeley

   Stuk. Gramercies master Vernon, and well met,
I did not dream that you professed arms.

   Ver. It is not my profession but my pleasure.
The Governor being busy in the town   970
Makes me Lieutenant Governor for the time.

   Gains. Brave Captain Stukley, welcome to Dundalk

   Stuk. Thanks Captain Gainsford even with all my heart.

          [STUKLEY'S *Lieutenant delivers a letter to* VERNON.

   Ver. To me Lieutenant? from whom I pray ye.

   Lieut. From an old friend.

   Ver. I'll see what friend it is.

   Stuk. What enemy lies there near about this town?

   Gains. The rebel Shane O'Neale and all his power

   Stuk. Why do ye not beat them home into their dens?

   Gains. We have enough ado to keep the town.   980

   Stuk. To keep the Town? dare they beleaguer it?

   Gains. Aye, and assault it.

   Stuk.   Hang them, savage slaves

---

[1] Ed. ceremonies.   [2] port, rank, carriage.

Belike they know you dare not issue out.
Who is governor here?

 Gains.   That's Captain Harbart Sir

 Stuk. S'death, I am bewitched, mine enemy Governor!

               [*Aside alone.*

Well 'tis no matter, I'll about with him.
So soon as ere I see him, by this light—
Tis marvel he'll indure their proud approach.
Harbert is valiant; but the slaves are proud [1]
And have no boot to fetch worth following them.   990

 Gains. Yes Captain Stukley they have gallant horse;
The best in Ireland are of Ulsters breed.
They have a prey of Garrans cows and sheep
Well worth a brace of thousand pounds at least.

 Stuk. Hang cows and sheep, but have among their horse
I'll lose this head but I'll have hobbies from them
What news from England that ye read so long? [*To* VERNON.

 Ver. The largest news concerns yourself.

 Stuk.   Wherein?

 Ver. Will Mallerye writes, ye do not love your wife
You are unkind, you make not much of her.   1000

 Stuk. Writes he I have not made much of my wife?
I'll tell ye Captain how much I have made: [*To* GAINSFORD.
I have made away her portion and her plate
Her borders bracelets chains and all her rings,
And all the clothes belonging to her back
Save one poor gown: And he that can make more

---

[1] proud should probably be poor; 'proud' occurs in the previous line, which accounts for the mistake.

Of one poor wife, let him take her for me.

Ver. Well, had I known you would have made so much
You should not have been troubled with my love.

Stuk. Come, strike up drum, let's march into the town.   1010

[*Exeunt all but* VERNON.

Ver. Well, go thy ways. A kingdom is too small
For his expense, that hath no [1] mean at all.
Doubtless if ever man was misbegot [2]
It is this Stukley; of a boundless mind
Undaunted spirit, and uncontrolled spleen,
Lavish as is the liquid Ocean,
That drops his crowns even as the clouds drop rain.
Yet once I loved him better than myself,
When, like myself,[3] too prodigal in love,
I gave my love to such a prodigal.   1020
For which I hate the climate where he lives,
As if his breath infected all the air.
And therefore, Ireland, now farewell to thee
For though thy soil no venom will sustain
There treads a monster on thy fruitful breast.
If any shipping be for Spain or France
Abroad will I, and seek some further chance.

---

[1] Ed. ny.

[2] misbegot. This and a former passage may contain an obscure hint of the tradition mentioned by the Irish historian, O'Sullevan, that Stucley was an illegitimate son of Henry VIII.

[3] 'myself' ought to be 'himself.' The mistake arises from *myself* being in the previous line.

Enter HERBERT *in a shirt of mail and booted, and his page with him.*

Herb. Boy, bid the Sergeant major shut the gates
And see them guarded with a double ward.
That done, bid him command the companies   1030
To man the walls : then bid the messenger
Haste with these letters to the Deputy.
                              [*Exit page. Enter* STUKLEY.
Come Captain Stukley, wheres your company ?
Draw them with speed unto the Water Port.

   Stuk. Is there for every one a Tankard[1] there ?

   Herb. How do you mean ? a Tankard ?

   Stuk.   Sir, in brief
I made a vow, you know it well enough,
For your kind speeches to my wifes old Dad
Sir Thomas Curtis; that wheresoever we met
I would fight with you; therefore, your tools. [*He draws.* 1040

   Her. What were my speeches ?

   Stuk. That the old knight had cast away his daughter
When ye perceived she was bestowed on me.

   Herb. I spake those words, and thou hast proved them true.

   Stuk. And for those words Harbert, I'll fight with you.

   Harb. Rash hare-brained Stukley, knowst thou what thou dost
To quarrel in a town of garrison
And draw thy weapon on the Governor ?

---

[1] Tankard, water-carrier's vessel.

Stuk. Zounds, have ye logic to defend your skin?
Lay by your tricks and take you to your tools. 1050
Think ye your Governor's title 's rapier-proof?
Come, come, untruss, put off those coward shifts.

Harb. Stukley, thou know'st I am a soldier
And hate the name of carpet-coward[1] to death.
I tell thee but the discipline of war.

Stuk. Gods, you may hang us then by the law.
By law of manhood here I challenge thee
Lay by thy terms, and answer like a man.

Harb. Thou seest the public enemy is at hand
And we shall fight about a private brawl? 1060

Stuk. Nor shall that shift, Tom Harbert, serve thy turn.

Harb. Then give me leave but to disarm myself
Thou know'st I scorn t' have odds of any man.

Stuk. Disarm of what? of school-boys haberdines
Such as they cast at points in every street!
No, arm thy legs, put splinters in thy boots[2]
Casque on thy head, and gantles on thy hands
Would thou wert armed in pistol-proof complete
And nothing bare but even thy very lips,
I hold my head I'll hurt thee in the mouth. 1070
Lay by thy scare-crow name of Governor
And arm thee else unto a finger's breadth.

Harb. Braving braggart, since thou dost seek thy death
Look to thyself; I'll speed thee if I can. [*They fight.*

---

[1] carpet-coward, as in *carpet-knight*, or *carpet-monger*.

[2] splinters in boots. See Patient Grissil, Act II. Sc. i., where Emulo is found to have protected his shins with laths in his boots.

Stuk. Sir your teeth bleeds. This picktooth is too keen.

[*Drum soundeth and a bagpipe.*

Har. Hark, the enemys charges! we must to the walls
Another time I'll pick your teeth as well.

Stuk. Even when ye can. I said I would hit your mouth.

Exeunt ambo. Alarum is sounded, divers excursions, STUKLEY *pursues* SHANE O'NEAL *and* NEALE MACKENER, *and after a good pretty fight his Lieutenant and Ancient rescue* STUKLEY *and chase the Irish out. Then an excursion betwixt* HERBERT *and* O'HANLON, *and so a retreat sounded. Enter* HARBART, GAINSFORD *and some soldiers on the walls.*

Harb. Are all the gates and posterns closed again?
Gai. Aye, every one, and strong guards at them all. '   1080
Harb. Who would have thought these naked savages
These Northern Irish durst have been so bold
T' have given assault unto a warlike town?
Gains. Our suff'rance and remissness gives them heart
We make them proud by mewing up ourselves
In walled towns, whilst they triumph abroad
And revel in the country as they please.
Harb. Well Sergeant Major we will stir abroad.
This sudden sally was performed as men
It cut three hundred rebels throats at least   1090
And did discomfort and disperse them all.
Gains. Had we pursued we had tane a lusty prey.
Harb. Ye see 'tis night, and time we should retire
To guard the town; but hark what drum is this?

Are any of our company without?

Gains. Tis lusty Stukley if any be abroad
He is so eager to pursue the foe
And flesh his soldiers that are new arrived
That he forgot or heard not the retreat
At which gate shall he enter, Governor? 1100

Harb. He shall not enter. Give me all the keys.
I'll teach him duty and true discipline.

Enter STUKLEY, *Lieutenant, Ancient, Drum and soldiers.*
A noise within of driving beasts.

Stuk. Are the gates shut already? open! how!
Herb. Who knocks so boldly?
Stuk. Ha, who's that above?
Herb. Herbert the Governor. Who's that below?
Stuk. Stukley the Captain knocks to be let in.
Herb. Stukeley the Captain comes not in tonight.
Stuk. How? not to night? I am sure ye do but jest.
Herb. I do not use to jest in these affairs.
Stuk. Ye do not jest? and I must stay without? 1110
I trust you'll let my company come in.
Harb. Nor company nor captain comes in here
Until the morning that the gates be ope.
Stuk. We humbly [1] thank ye, honorable sir!
What if the Irish should make head again
And set upon us, would ye rescue us?
Harb. No. Why retired ye not at the retreat

[1] Ed. humble.

As did myself, and all the other troops?

Stuk. Because I meant not to come empty home
But bring some booty to enrich my men.   1120
Besides, in prosecution we have slain
Two hundred Irish since you left the chase
And brought a prey—six hundred cows at least
Forty chief horse, a hundred hackney jades—
And yet the Governor will not let us in![1]

Harb. No sir I will not, and will answer it.
If all your throats be cut you are well served,
To teach ye know the discipline of war.
There is a time to fight, a time to cease
A time to watch, a time to take your rest,   1130
A time to open and to shut the Ports:
And at this time, Stukley, the gates are shut
And till a full time [they] shall not be op't

Stuk. Solomon says with words mild
' Spare the rod and spill the child.'
Wholesome instruction! godly discipline!
This is a simple piece of small revenge.
But this I vow. Who shut me out at night
Shall never see me enter here by day.
Will ye sir let the prey be taken in   1140
For fear the Irish rescue it again?

Gains. 'Twere pity sir to lose so good a prey

---

[1] Perhaps this incident is borrowed from Geo. Gascoyne's experience. Lately landed with his company, he was surprised by 3000 Spaniards, but retired in good order under the walls of Leyden: but the Dutch refused to open the gates, and all were made prisoners.

And greater pity but to lose one man.

Harb. You may let in the prey: but keep them out.

Stuk. Stay Sergeant Major! O white livered lout,
Dost thou respect a bullock or a jade
More than a man to Gods own image made?
Herbert thou get'st not one cow to thy share
Nor a cows tail, unless as Cacus did
I by the tail could draw one from the herd   1150
And cast her at thy head, the horns and all.

Herb. Go make your cabin underneath the wall
And so good night.

Stuk. Farewell. Go pick your teeth. [*Exeunt* HARB. *and* GAINS.
How glad I am my trunks are yet aboard!
Lieutenant, Ancient, fellow soldiers all,
I would we might not part, but needs we must.
Tom Stukeley cannot brook the least disgrace.
To night I'll bide such venture as you shall,
Let's man the bridge, the water flows apace   1160
If the enemy come he dare not pass the flood,
So on this side we with our prey are safe.
How many cows shall fall unto my share?

Lieut. All if ye please; your valour compassed all.

Stuk. Shall all the cows be mine? I'll not have one
Thirty chief horse if you will let me have
To ship from hence to seek a better coast,
Share that amongst ye; there's a hundred pound.   [*His purse.*
And two months pay thats due unto myself
I give you frankly. Drink it for my sake.   1170

Lieut. But Captain will you leave this land indeed?

Stuk. Before the sun the morning doth salute
I'll see my hobbies safely sent aboard
Then follow I, that scorn to be controlled
Of any man thats meaner than a king.
Farewell O'Neale; if Stukley here had stayed
Thy head for treason soon thou shouldst have paid.   [*Exeunt.*

Enter O'NEALE *with a halter about his neck, and* NEALE MACKENER *after him.*[1]

Mack. Oh what intends this great O'Neale by this?
O'Neal. Neal Mackener, I do not wear this cord
As doubting or foredooming such a death;　　　　1180
But thou, who art my secretary, knowst
That my unkind rebellions merit more.
Therefore I bear this hateful cord, in sign
Of true repentance of my treasons past,
And at the Deputys feet on humble knees
Will sue for pardon from her Majesty,
Whose clemency I grieve to have abused.
What sayest thou? is 't not my safest course?
Mack. Can I believe that mighty Shane O'Neale
Is so deject in courage as he seems　　　　1190
Or that his dauntless dragon-winged thoughts[2]
Can humble them at any prince's feet?
O'Neale. What can I do? my forces are dispersed
My kindred slain, my horses made a prey,

---

[1] The materials for this scene are in Holingshed.
[2] Ed. thoght.

O'Kane, O'Hanlon and Magennis killed—
If the Queen's power pursue I am but dead—
If I submit she's merciful
Her Deputy will grant me life in her behalf.
Mack. Thou canst not tell. The state offended stands
And thou condemned in every subjects eye   1200
And I am censured for my practises.
Rather retire thee into Clamgaboy
Where Alexander and MacGilliam Buske
May join their Scots unto thy scattered troops
And reenforce[1] the English with fresh power
If not, at least thy life is safe with them
Until thy friends may reunite themselves
O'Neale. I would embrace thy counsel, but I fear
The wrongs that I have done unto the Scots
Sticks in the breast of Alexander Oge   1210
And he will take occasion of revenge

Enter ALEXANDER OGE *and* MASTER GILLIAM BUSKE, *two Scots.*

Mack. Put it to proof, for here comes he and Buske.
Cast off thy cord, let them not see thy shame.
Alex. Gillam, the news are true of great O'Neale
Dundalk hath dasht his pride and quell'd his power.
Busk. Occasion offers us a fair revenge
For our dear cousin young Mac Angus death.
Alex. Who'll take revenge on weakness that's deprest?

---

[1] reenforce, *i. e.* renew the attack upon, engage again.

Busk. Who'll let his kinsmans blood unwreaked [1] rest?
O'Neal. Do they not see us? or disdain to see us?   1220
Mack. Salute them kindly.
O'Neal.   Gentlemen, good day
Alexander Mac Surlo, and Master Gilliam Busk
Fortune hath frown'd upon your friend O'Neal.
My troops are beaten by the English power.
If therefore you will join your Scottish aid
With the remainder of my followers,
Your means may make recovery of my loss
And you shall bind O'Neale to 'quite your love.
  Alex. How can a rebel or a traitor hope
Of good success against his sovereign?   1230
Awhile perhaps he may disturb the state
And damn himself; but at the last he falls.
  Mack. I thought thou hadst despised the English churls.
  Busk. Admit he did, how can he love O'Neale,
But chiefly thee that was the counsellor
To cut off young Mack Angus our dear cousin.
  Mack. Not my advice, but his too saucy braves
To great O'Neale, did cause his cutting off.
  Busk. Speak such another word, I'll cut thy throat,
Thou traiterous rebel Mackener.   1240
  O'Neal. Mack gilliam Buske, upbraid not Neal Mackener;
I did the deed, and hold it was well done,
Because he braved me in my own command.
  Alex. As thou dost us now in our own command.
For justifying of so foul a fact

[1] unwreaked, unavenged.

Here is revenge.   Traitors have at you both.
[*They draw and fight.* O'NEALE *flies*, ALEXANDER *pursues him out.* BUSK *and* MACKENER *fight, and* MACK *is slain.*
Fly'st thou, thou traiterous coward Shane O'Neale?
I am too light a' foot to let thee scape.   [*Exit after* O'NEALE.

Busk. I'll stop your flight, you shall not follow him.

Mack. I meant it not proud overweaning Scot.   1250

Busk. Have at thee then, rebellious Irishman.

[*They fight,* MACK *is slain.   Enter* ALEX. *with* O'NEALE'S *head.*

Alex. I see we are victors both, Mack Gilliam Busk
Here is the head of traiterous Shane O'Neale.

Busk. And here's his bloody Secretary dead.

Alex. No force[1]; this head for present will I send
To that most noble English deputy[2]
That ministers justice as he were a God
And guerdons virtue like a liberal king.
This grateful present may procure our peace,   1260
And so the English fight and our fear may cease.[3]

Busk. And may all Irish that with treason deal
Come to like end or worse than Shane O'Neale.   [*Exeunt.*

[ACT III.]

Enter HERNAND *with* STUKELEY, *brought in with Bills and Halberts: to them the Governor's wife.*

Stuk. Had I known thus much Governor, I would have burnt

---

[1] no force, no doubt; so in *Faire Em,* I force not for I doubt not.
[2] Perhaps this alludes to Essex. Sidney was deputy at the time described.
[3] Something amiss in this line, perhaps 'fight' should be omitted; it may have been written as an alternative for 'fear,' and both words printed by the composer.

my ships in the haven before thy face, and have fed haddocks with my horses.

Gov. Is thou and all thou hast at my dispose,
And dost deny me upon courtesy
What I may take whether thou wilt or no?
Stukley, if thou be called so   1270
I'll make thee know a governor of Cales.[1]

Stuk. Governor, will nothing but five of my horses serve your turn? Sirra thou gets not one of them, an' a hair would save thy life: if I had as many horses as there be stones in the Island, thou should'st not have one of them.

Gov. Know Stukley too
It had been thy duty to have offered them,
And glad that I would grace thee to accept them.
What is he that dares thrust into this harbour
And not make tender of his goods to me?   1280

Stuk. Why then know Governor here is once one
That dares thrust into this harbour
That will not make thee tender of a mite,
Nor cares not of a hair[2] how thou dost take it.
I will not give one of my hobbies for thy government.

Gov. I will be answerable to thee for thy horses

Stuk. Dost thou keep a toll-booth?[3] Zounds, dost thou make a horse-courser[4] of me?

Gov. Nay sirrah then I'll lay you by the heels
And I will have them, every horse of them.

---

[1] Stucley landed at Vivero in Galicia, not at Cadiz.
[2] cares not of a hair—Latin construction.
[3] toll-booth = receipt of custom.   [4] horse-courser = horse-dealer.

Stuk. Thou get'st not so much as a nail of one of them 1290
No, if thou wouldst draw it with thy teeth.
If you do, I'll clench it with your scalp.

Enter the Governor's wife.

Gov. Call me the Provost hither presently.   [*One goes.*
Lady (*to one of the attendants*). Sirrah, is this the English gentleman
Which brought the horses?
Serv. Madam, it is he; this is the man.
Lady. How do you call him?
Serv. His servants say his name is Signor Stukly.
Lady. Now by my troth, and as I am a Lady   [*Aside.*
I never saw a fairer gentleman   1300
I would it lay in my power to do him good.

Enter the Provost.

Gov. Sirrah, as I have seized your ships and horses
So I commit your body unto prison,
Until his highness pleasure shall be known.
Provost, lay irons upon him, and take him to
Your charge.
Lady. Well, well, for all this might I have my will
In faith his entertainment should be better.   [*Aside.*
Stuk. You muddy slave you may by your power do a little, but
I'll call you to a reckoning for this gear; and Sirrah, see a horse
be not lacking; if he be, I'll make thee on thy bare feet lead him
in a halter after me to the farthest [1] part of Spain.   1312

[1] Ed. pare; perhaps park.

Gov. Go to, thou art a base pirate.

Stuk. Sirrah muchacho, you that have eaten a horse and his tail hangs out of your mouth, you lie. All that thou canst do shall not get a horse; if saint Jaques your saint want a horse he should not get one of them: he should go a-foot else all the days of his life. By this flesh and blood, I'll make thee repent it.

Gov. Away with him. [*Exit* STUKLY.

Lady. Yet good my Lord, consider what you do   1320
Surely the confidence of this man's spirit
Shows that his blood is either great or noble
Or that his fortune's at his own command.

Gov. I hold him rather to be some desperate pirate
That thinks to domineer upon the land
As he is used amongst his mates at sea.

[*Lady*]. Besides, it's less disgrace to bear his braves
Here where your power is absolute and free
And where he wholly stands at your dispose
Than in a place indifferent to either   1330
And where you both should stand in equal terms.

Gov. If I did prize his honour with mine own
Then, wife, perhaps I might allow your reason.

Lady. Besides, perhaps they may be for a present,
Which now his heat restrains him to disclose;
Which should they be to any Prince of Spain
How ill it may be taken at your hands!

Gov. This his committing gives some cause to doubt.
I care not, were they sent unto the Devil,
Where the commission of my government   1340
Gives me as much as I demand of him

Tomorrow I'll unto the court myself
Today I have some business in the Isle
And 'twill be Evening ere I do return.   [*Exit Governor.*

Enter Provost.

 Lady. Provost.
 Pro. Madam
 Lady. Where have you yet bestowed this gentleman?
 Pro. Madam he's here within the Palace yet
Ready to go unto the Marshalsea
He had been gone but that upon some business   1350
I come to know his honour's pleasure in,
And he is gone.
 [*Lady*]   But Provost, since your prisoner
Is not departed, I pray thee bring him hither:
I'll see if by persuasion I can win him
To yield and to submit unto my Lord.
 Pro. Madam I will.   [*He fetcheth him in.*
 Lady. I thank you: give us leave a little.
Fair gentleman, but that it is too late
To call back yesterday, I would have wished
That you had dealt more kindly with my Lord.   1360
Sir it should seem you have been unacquainted
With the hot bloods and temper of our clime,
Or with a Spaniard's noble disposition.
Whereas your kind submission might have wrought
What your high spleen and courage cannot do.
 Stuk. Fair courteous lady, had your beauteous self
Ask't anything, a noble English heart

Had made you mistress of your own desires.
But to be threatened and subjected by him,
Zounds, first I'll fray him out on 's government   1370
And vex his very marrow in his bones.
Thinks he because I am fallen into his hands
I fear his power? s'blood, I'll stare his eyes out first.
He looks not on the sun I dare not brave.
I am Stukly; let him know my name.

  Lady. Brave gentleman! yet I could have wish't
I had but been of counsel with your thoughts
But without breach or touch of modesty
Even for the love I bear unto your country,
Mine honour kept unstain'd, which I protest   1380
I prize beyond the thing I hold the dearest,
Command whatever lieth in my power
To comfort you in this extremity

  Stuk. Madam, how much your noble Spanish courtesy hath power in me
A faithful English heart shall manifest
And I will be the champion of your honour
Wherever I become in Christendom.[1]

  Lady. Yes, know a lady of Spain can be as kind
As any Englishwoman of them all.
What is it Signor I can help you with?   1390

  Stuk. My liberty's the thing I most desire.

  Lady. That presently I cannot warrant you;
But I will labour for it to my Lord
With all the means my wits can all devise.

[1] Wherever I become, wherever I come to be.

Stuk. Then this Madam : might I possibly obtain, but to work some means for me by your best endeavours that I may have but one of my horses that I will choose, and but respite for one day to ride a little way upon some earnest business, now in the absence of your husband, and as I am a soldier and a gentleman, and by the honours of my nation, I will come back by the prefixed hour. 1400

Lady. Sir, should I devise some means for the accomplishment of your desire, and that it should come to my husbands ear before your return, I should hearken for your coming back. Besides, if by this means you should seek to escape, greater treasons might be objected than I hope you are guilty of : and what danger both my life and honour might incur I imagine you are not ignorant.

Stuk. Madam, if all your wits can but hide it from your husband, if he should come before I return, for the other I dare pawn my soul to you that I will hold my word. 1409

Lady. Go to, mine honour and life is your bail; let your return be six a'clock in the evening. I will once trust an Englishman on his word. [*Exeunt.*

Enter KING PHILIP, *with him* ALVA *and* SANCTO DAVILA; *with them the Portingall embassador.*

Phil. Speak reverend intercessor for the state
Of young Sebastian, king of Portingall.
What craves our dear intire beloved cousin
Wherein we may befriend his Majesty ?
  Bot.[1] First sacred king, the sovereign of my faith

---

[1] Botalla.

And Portugals undoubted supreme head
Doth kindly greet your highness in all love.
Next on behalf of your respective care   1420
And the league-bond of natural amity
Which he mistrusts not but combines ye both
As being kinsmen, he intreats this boon;
That whereas lately from the king of Fez
Muly Mahamet, to my royal master
Hath honorable ambassage been sent
And great intreaty made to crave his aid
Against Mullucco, brother to that king,
Who now intrudes upon Mahamets bounds,.
And building on his privilege of age   1430
And inequality of matchless strength,
Strives to deprive him of his diadem—
It would seem good unto your princely self
(As in the like we shall be ready still
As Spains intreaty) to assist my Lord
With some such necessary strength of war
As in this action may conclude a peace
To Portugals great profit and renown.

 Phil. Are then Molucco and his brother king
At civil mutiny among themselves?   1440

 Bot. They are my Lord, and many woful days
Th' afflicted Barbary hath suffered spoil
And been a prey unto her natural subjects.

 Phil. The right is in Molucco: wherefore then
Would Prince Sebastian aid the other part?
Beside, Mahamet is an infidel,

From whose associate fellowship in this
And all things else we Christians must refrain.
 Bot. Grace but his reasons with your mild conceit
Whereon he grounds his lawful resolution   1450
And mighty Philip you shall quickly find
This his intent to be most honorable.
Not for regard of any supreme claim
The stern Mahamet lays unto the crown
Nor any justice that in his behalf
May be presumed upon, doth stout Sebastian
List to this motion, but for honour's sake,
For Portugals chief good, and to advance
The Christian true religion through those parts,
Is he inclined to undertake this war.   1460
 Phil. How can that be? acquaint us with your meaning.
 Bot. This worthy king. Tis not unknown to you
That divers towns and cities situate
Within the borders of rich Barbary
Which King Emmanuel conquered by his blood
And left appropriate still to be enjoyed
Of such as should be kings of Portugal,
[1] Are, but by this prevention, like to fall
And be confiscate to the Moor again
But by an army thither brought in time   1470
Not only these great cities shall be kept
But raising this Mahamet to the crown
And quite distinguishing[2] his brothers claim
When we have planted him; and that by us

  [1] Ed. or.   [2] distinguishing, *i.e.* extinguishing.

The country is subdued and kept in awe
We shall not only still retain our own
But for Mahamet to subscribe to us
And either he and his [to] change their faith
And worship that eternal God we do
[1] Or disannulling be deprived of life   1480
And so assume the government ourselves.

 Phil. This tastes of honour and of policy
Might it with like success be brought to pass.

 Bot. With your assistance there's no doubt my Lord
But what we have imagined shall ere long
Be truly and effectually perform'd.

 Phil. Aye, but Mullucco's army, doth consist
Of dreadless Turks and warlike Saracens,
Is much to be suspected in this case.[2]

 Bot. What can they do, though great their number be,   1490
When for their single force we come in strength
Of Spain of Portingall and Barbary?

 Phil. Your reasons have prevail'd. What power is it
Our loving cousin doth request of us?

 Bot. Of horse and foot indifferently commixt
Only ten thousand will supply his want.

 Phil. Botellio, so I take it you are called,
Give place awhile, till with our faithful lord[s]
We have advised us better on the cause
And then you shall have answer presently. [*Exit* Bot.   1500
Now you supporters of our royal state
Alva and Sanct' Danulo, briefly show

   [1] Ed. and.   [2] Ed. casse.

What your opinion is touching the suit
Of neighbouring Portingales fame-thirsty king?
    Alva. That he attempts an enterprise my liege
Will sooner break his neck than make him great.
    Da. That hereby, if occasion be laid hold on,
That Spain and Portingale shall be unite [1]
And you the sovereign ruler of them both.
    Phil. Express thy meaning, Danulo, in that point.   1510
    Da. It shall not need I stand on circumstance.
Your highness knows, Sebastian once removed,
The way is open solely for yourself,
Either by force or by corrupting gold,
To step into the throne: now for a mean
To cut him off: what better way than this?
To sooth his purpose and to draw him on
With expectation of a strong supply;
But when he is set forth upon his way
And left his country, that without reproach   1520
And scandal to his name he cannot retire,
Then to proclaim, on pain of speedy death,
That not a Spaniard seem to join with him.
So, landed once in desert Barbary,
His weakened soldiers and himself at once
Shall fall before Mullucco's conquering sword.
    Alva. Mean space, to colour your intent the better,
Muster your men as if you meant to aid him;
But with these men, as soon as he is gone,
Approach the borders of fair Portingale   1530

    [1] unite for united.

That if it chance Sebastian do survive
The pagans sword, yet in his absence we
May enter his dominions, sack his towns,
And take possession of the realm by force.
 Da. Withal, despatch embassadors to Rome
And forthwith to intreat the Pope's advice,
Who in no wise, before hand we are sure,
Will licence any Christian potentate
To traffick or converse with heathen kings:
And so his prohibition may excuse   1540
And serve to cloke your breach of promise with,
When 'tis perceived you do not aid, Sebastian.
 Phil. You counsel well and fitting our desire
That many years have wish'd, that Portingal
And fruitful Castile, being one Continent,
Had likewise been the subject of one sceptre.
Call forth th' ambassador: As you have said   [*Enter* BOTTELLA.
So will we dally with our cousins suit.
My Lord Botellio we have weigh'd th' effect
Of your imbassage; and in nature bound   1550
Beside the affection of near neighbourhood
To do our kinsman and your noble king
All offices of kindness that we can
Tell him from us we only not[1] commend
His haughty mind in this attempt of his,
But his discreet and politic proceeding;
And will therein, to further his intent,
Aid him with twice five thousand armed soldiers

[1] only not, *i.e.* not only.

And fifty gallies all well-furnished;
Which on the fourth of June, near to the straits   1560
Of Giberalter, in a haven there
Called El Porto de Sancta Maria, shall wait
His coming on toward Apheryca.[1]
So wishing him a happy prosperous brother
In all we may, we live to do him good.
   Bot. Thanks to the high and mighty king of Spain.
   Phil. Lord Sancto Danulo, bring him on his way;
                                         [*Exit* BOTEL. DAN.
And Alva, now, what think ye of this plot?
Is it not too severe, ambitious
And more deceitful than becomes a king?   1570
   Alva. A kingdoms thirst hath to dispense,[2] my Lord,
With any rigour or extremity;
And that which in mean men would seem a fault,
As leaning to ambition or such like,
Is in a king but well beseeming him.
Upon my life your grace hath well resolved
And howsoever vulgar wits repine
Yet regal majesty must have his course.

Enter DANULO.

   Phil. Danulo, what news? you are so soon return'd.
   Da. A gallant Englishman, my gracious Lord,   1580
Haughty in look and hasty in his business,

---

[1] Apheryca, by the necessity of metre, for Africa.
[2] dispense; is this a common use of the word in illo tempore?

But now arriv'd at the court gate,
Earnestly craves admittance to your presence.
   Phil. An English gentleman—let him draw near—

Enter STUKLY.

   Stuk. Right high and mighty, if to kings install'd
And sacredly anointed it belong
To minister true justice, and relieve
The poor oppressed stranger, then from thee
Renowned Philip, that by birth of place [1]
Upholds the sceptre of a royal king,   1590
Stukeley, a soldier and a gentleman—
But neither like a soldier nor a man
Of some of thy unworthy subjects handled—
Doth challenge justice at thy sacred hands
And succour 'gainst oppression offered him.
   Phil. Oppression offered, and by some of ours?
   Stuk. Yes royal Philip, and in some respect
The vile abuse doth touch your Majesty.
   Phil. Stand up and tell the manner of thy grief
And on our royal name we promise thee   1600
Thoffender shall be sharply punished.
   Alva. A lusty man, believe me, of his limbs.
   Da. Aye, and as knightly in his talk beside.
   Stuk. Thus kingly Philip : having served of late
Under my princes army in the field
Against the rude rebellious Irish, where

---

[1] birth of place for place of birth.

Upon desire to travel, and especially
Upon affection that I had to see
Your princely court so honourably famed
As also to make tender of my love 1610
And duteous service to your Majesty
Shipping myself, with other private goods
Which I had purchased by my dint of sword,
I came to Cales, where, landed with my prey
In number thirty hobbies, for the shore,
One Don Herando, there your governor,
Attacheth both my ship and all therein;
And though I tell them that the hobbies were
A present for your grace, and for that cause
I thither brought them, yet the uncivil Lord 1620
Because he might not have one horse of them
To his own use, clapt irons on my heels,
And in a dungeon like a gripple[1] churl
I think his purpose was to famish me
But that by strange adventure and good hap
I scaped his tyrant fingers: hoping here,
If I might once get opportunity
To let your highness understand thereof,
I should find remedy against his wrong.

   Phil. Have we such base ignoble substitutes 1630
That dare so heinously oppress a stranger?
And such a one as came to offer us
The bounty of his heart in friendly gifts?
Let there be sent a messenger forthwith

[1] a gripple churl, *i.e.* griping.

To bring the wretch to answer his abuse,
And Stukley, welcome to King Philips court,
Repose thyself: thou shalt have right with me
And favour too againe thine enemy.

Stuk. I thank your Majesty, but must intreat
You would vouchsafe to pardon me in this: 1640
I needs must back again to Cales my Lord.

Phil. Be not afraid thy goods shall be purloined
There 's not a mite but he shall bring it forth,
Or of his own purse make it good to thee.

Stuk. It is not that, an' please your Majesty
But I have past my word I will return
And Stukley holds his promise as religion.

Phil. Well then, my Lord of Alva, give in charge
Some of our pensioners attend on him
To bring Herando hither, safely guarded. 1650

Alva. It shall be done my Lord. [*Exeunt.*

Enter Provost and Governor's wife.

Pro. [Madam] What shall we do, the time draws on
The English Captain promis'd to return,
But yet he comes not. If my Lord should miss him
My life were lost, your credit thereby crack'd.

Lady. Content thee Provost: such apparent signs
Of manly disposition shine in him,
Of valour gentry and what not beside
As I presume, if he remain alive,
He will return at his prefixed hour: 1660

As yet the respite that was granted him
Is not expired: I do not doubt ere then
But he will rid us of the fear we are in.

Pro. Had we but, Madam, known which way he went
Or had himself [but] told us of the place
To which he purposed to make his journey
There had been yet some comfort and some hope;
But ignorant of both, how can we choose
But be suspicious and almost despair?

Lady. Thou talk'st absurdly. Had we known the place 1670
The cause which made him, and which way he went,
What thank were that to us to let him go
Where we were sure to find him out again?
Or how should trial of his faith appear
In matters of no weight or jeopardy?
Now being so that of our own accord
Without the least respect but to his promise
He was dismissed, and that he clearly sees
Tis at his charge to stay on his return,
And yet will unconstrained keep his vow, 1680
Approves him truly loyal, us truly loving.

Pro. If I be called in question for his absence,
Madam, I must rely upon your wit.

Enter HERANDO.

Lady. Be that thy refuge. Here Herando comes.
Her. Provost I have bethought me at the last
How to dispose of Stukley and his goods.
Part of his horses I will give the king

And part I will bestow upon my friends.
To these conditions if he condescend
I am content he shall have liberty,   1690
And he, his ship, and men be so discharg'd.
But otherwise I'll cause his ship be sunk
And he and his as pirates suffer death.
Therefore go fetch him to me presently,
I may be certain if he'll yield or no.

   Pro. Ah Madam I am strucken dumb and dead,
What shall I answer to my Lord's demand?

   Lady. Be not so fearful lest thy guilty looks
Argue suspicion of some treachery.

   Her. Dost hear me Provost? fetch me Stukley forth   1700

   Lady. Make it as though thou understands him not.

   Her. Madam, what whispers he into your ear
That he neglects to do as I command?

   Lady. He tells me, my Lord, the English Captain
Is grown submiss and very tractable
And of himself is ready to resign
As much as you require to have of him;
And that even now, after his counsel heard
How best he might crave pardon for his pride
His stiff resistance and audacious words,   1710
Whereto he answered that his readiest way
Was by petition to solicit him
And so he tells me that he left him studying
How to intend some quaint conceited method
Might draw remorse from your displeased mind.

   Her. Is he Provost become flexible?

Pro. Exceeding mild and penitent my Lord.

Her. I thought his stomach would come down at last
Go bid him save a labour with his pen
And tell him we are here. Let it suffice   1720
If with his tongue he do recant his fault.

Lady. Nay let him write, for writing will remain
When words but spoken may be soon forgot.
It makes the better on your side my Lord
That underneath his hand it shall appear
By his consent and not by your constraint
He made surrender of his prize to you
So shall the world, what after chance to fall,
Clear your extorsion and abuse.

Her. It cannot be but he hath done ere this   1730
I prithee see : much matter in few lines
Is quickly cought[1] by one of meaner wit.

Lady. It were not good to trouble him so soon.

Her. I will not subject my desire herein
And wait upon his leisure; look, I say.

Lady. Without some cunning shift we are undone   [*Aside.*

Her. Why stay'st thou Provost when I bid thee go?

Lady. Withdraw thyself to satisfy his mind.

Pro. Help my excuse sweet Madam if I fail.

Lady. Let me alone : my lord, how glad am I   1740
There shall be now atonement of this strife;
And that this English gentleman is pleas'd
To yield obedience, and yourself as willing

---

[1] much matter is quickly *coughed*. See a similar use of the word 'spit,' 'Hen. VIII.,' I. ii. 6, 'Tongues spit their duties out.'

To be appeased at his humility.

Her. I tell thee wife, he stopped in happy time
Or all submission else had come too late

Enter Provost.

Where is he Provost? will he come to us?
   Lady. Is he not yet returned? ⎫
   Pro.   Madam, not yet. ⎬ [*Aside.*
   Lady. Then do I fear our plot will be discovered ⎭

Her. Why speak'st not man? where is thy prisoner?   1750
Pro. He hath not yet my Lord set down his mind
He doth intreat your honour stay awhile
And he will then have made an end of all.
Her. I'll wait no longer on his mastership
Give me the key, I'll fetch him forth myself.
Lady. What will you do?—you fetch him forth yourself?
I would not that for all the wealth in Spain!
Will you so much annoy your vital powers
As to oppress them with the prison stink?[1]
You shall not, if you love me, come so near.   1760
The place is mortally infected lately,
And, as the Provost tells me, divers die
Of strange diseases, and no longer since
Than the last morning two were buried thence,
Ask him my Lord if this be true or no.
   Pro. It is most certain there are many sick

---

[1] the prison stink. See Bacon, Nat. Hist. Cent. X. no. 914. Besides the well-known black assizes at Oxford in 1577, there was a similar outbreak at Exeter in 1586. See Holinshed, IV. 868, and Leicester Correspondence, 224.

And therefore good my Lord refrain the place.

Her. Unless thou bring him straightway to my sight
Nor danger nor intreaty shall prevail
But I will enter at the door myself. 1770

Lady. See once again, it may be he is come
Mean space I'll hold him with some other talk.

Pro. Do gentle Madam.

Lady. If he be not come [*Aside.*
Protract the time as much as in thee lies

Pro. I'll tarry long enough, ne'er doubt of that.

Her. Sirrah, before thou go—bring him forth
Or look to lie in irons as he doth.

Lady. I have not seen you often times, my Lord,
So out of patience and so far from quiet.
You were not wont in things as great as this 1780
But that you'd be persuaded by my words.

Her. I cannot tell how I may think of you,
Your busying of yourself so much herein,
And speaking for this Englishman so oft,
Makes me suspect more than I thought to do.

Lady. Suspect? as how? that I do favour him?
Or is't your meaning that I go about
To set him free? your best accuse me flatly
That I have taught him here to break the prison!
Is this the recompense for my good will? 1790
Have I this thank for being provident,
And careful for your health? go where you will
Suspect thyself and me, cut short thy days
Do anything that may disparage you

Hereafter I will learn to hold my tongue.

Her. How now my love, what? angry for a word?

Lady. Have I not reason when you grow suspicious
Of me, that am yourself, your bosom friend?

Her. I prithee be content, I meant no harm:
I know thou would'st not prejudice my state   1800
To be the empress of all Asia here.

Enter STUKELEY *in gyves.*

Now he comes—

Lady. Then do I cast off fear,
And whilst I live hereafter will I trust
An Englishman the better for his sake.

Her. Where's the submission that ye told me of?
Call ye this repentance for his pride?

Stuk. What craves the unjust governor of Cales?

Her. Obstinate captain, that thou lend thy knee,
And make surrender of what I require,
Or thou and thine like pirates all shall die.   1810

Stuk. I cannot hear, I would you would speak louder.

Her. Dost thou deride me?

Stuk.   Not deride you Sir—
But for my hobbies I'll not spare a hair,
So much of their tails to pick your teeth.

Lady. Sweet Captain, speak him fair at my entreaty.

Stuk. Madam I owe my life to do you service
But for his threats I do not care a rush.

Her. How have I been deluded by your words!
He scorns me still. Knock off his iron gyves

And let an executioner be sent for1820
I will not stir until I see him dead.
 Stuk. Herando, I do dare the worst thou can'st
 Lady. Oh do not provoke him so.
 Stuk. Content you Madam ; Stukeley bears a mind
That will not melt at any tyrants words.

   Enter MARSHALL.

 Her. Call'st thou me tyrant too ? it is enough
In sooth I'll try your patience for that word.
 Mars. Herando, in his majesty's high name
I charge you, presently prepare yourself
To make appearance at the court this night ;1830
And bring this gentleman your prisoner here,
Together with such horses as you have
Of his in your possession : fail you not
As you will answer it unto your peril.
 Her. How knows the king he was my prisoner?
 Mess. What answer make ye? will ye go with me?
 Her. With all my heart. This Stukley is some devil
And with his sorcery hath incensed the king.
 Stuk. Hernando, if your Lordship want a horse
One of my hobbies is at your command.1840
 Her. He flatters me, but I must dissemble with him—
Brave Signor Stukley whatsoe'er hath past
Betwixt yourself and me, conceive the best ;
It was but trial of your fortitude
And now I see you are no less indeed
Than what you seem, a valiant gentleman.

I do embrace you with a brother's love.
Come let us go.   I'll do you any grace
Unto the king my honour extends unto.
   Stuk. When I do need it I will thank ye Sir   1850
But Madam wherein may I quittance [1] you
Whose kindness is the cause of all my good?
   Lady. I crave not more for anything I do
But that you virtuously report of me,
And in remembrance of me wear this scarf.
   Stuk. This on mine arm, yourself within my heart
Doth Stukely vow perpetually to bear.   [*Exeunt.*

Enter VERNON *and a Master of a Ship with the Lantado and two or three officers.*

   Ver. Signor Lantado by your patience
It is no wrack, nor you by law can seize
Upon the ship or goods here cast away.   1860
   Lant. Sir, Sir, your negative is of no force.
You are part owner, haply, of the ship,
Or else cape-merchant [2] ventred in the freight.
Your speech is partial to save ship and goods.
   Ver. Examine then the master of his oath.
   Lan. So we intend
   Ship M. Sir you have known me long
And never knew me falsify my word,
Much less mine oath, which I will freely pawn
My life and all, to testify the truth.   1870
   Lant. Whence was the ship?

---

[1] quittance as verb.   [2] Cape-merchant.

Ship M.   Of London
Lan. What her name?
Ship M.   The pelicane
Lan. What burden was she of?
Ship M.   Two hundred ton.
Lan. And what her lading?
M. Ship.   Packs of English cloth
This gentleman ought neither ship nor goods
But come from Britain[1] as a passenger:
For at St. Mallows we had cause to touch
To take aboard a merchants factor there,
And there we found this honest gentleman
Very desirous to be shipped for Spain.   1880
In luckless hour he brought his trunks aboard
And in more hapless time the same are lost,
  Ver. Small loss were that if all the rest were safe.
The men are lost, only we two survive
Whom you by shows of pity have enforced
To come ashore, and leave the crazed ship
And will ye now forget what ye have sworn,
And seek to make a wrack of that is none?
Let us aboard again and let us bide
The hazard of the tempest and the tide.   1890
  Lant. Ye are ashore, and thank me for your lives.
Which said, why should you value ship or goods?
You swear you are but passenger; let pass
Let th'owners and the merchant bear the loss.
  Ship. What if he should? The master then am I

[1] Brittain, *i.e.* Brittany. St. Mallows, *i.e.* St. Malo.

And were I dead, if any did survive
And live aboard you cannot make a wrack.

   Ver. No, I will kneel before the King of Spain
Before my country men such loss sustain.

   Lan. Proud Englishman, since thou art peremptory   1900
Thou shalt not kneel nor see his Majesty.
Away with them.

Trumpets sound. Enter K. PHILIP, *leaning on* STUKLEY'S *shoulder,*
   ALVA, DAVITA, VALDES *that was the messenger,* HERNANDO
   before bare, and the governor HERNANDO *after, with other.*

   Phil. Heroic Stukley, on our royal word
We never did esteem a present more
Than those fair Irish horse of your frank gift,

   Stuk. Redoubted Philip, royal Catholic King
It pleaseth so the bounty of your spirit
To reckon them that are of little worth.
But if your highness know my inward zeal
To do you service past the worlds compare,
You would esteem these thirty Irish jades   1910
As thirty mites to all the Indian mines.

   Phil. How we esteem your present and yourself
Our instant favours shall advertise you.
Alva and Sancto Danula shall declare
To gallant Stukeley what regard we bear.

   Ver. Cross of all crosses,[1] why should sea and wind
Spare me to live where double death's assigned?
Is 't possible that Stukly, so deject [2]

---

[1] *i.e.* the greatest of calamities, *crux de cruce.*   [2] dejected.

In England, lives in Spain in such respect?
   Phil. Stay, what are these?
   Ver.   Poor suitors to your grace.   1920
An English ship is split here in the race
And this Lantado the Viceadmiral
Coming aboard, and seeing us alive
The sole remainder of a hundred souls
Enticed us by Christian promises
To come ashore, as pitying our case.
Our feet no sooner touched this Spanish earth
Than he would make a wrack of ship and goods.
   Lant. Dread sovereign, true, the ship is split and sunk,
And every billow over-rakes the hull: 1930
This living couple, crept up to the poop
In dread of danger and of present death,
In charity I took to save their lives.
   Ship M. With promise and proviso gracious king
That no advantage should be ta'ne thereof;
Else had I stayed, though he had gone ashore.
   Phil. Why, what are you?
   Ship M.   The Master of the ship.
   Phil. And he the owner or the venturer
And would deceive us of our royalty.
   Ver. Upon my life great king I meant it not.   1940
I am no owner nor yet venturer;
I came but in her as a passenger;
But afore[1] I saw the tide was at the highest,
And ebbing water would have laid us dry,

       [1] afore seems to mean 'because,' and for.

The ship belonging to my place of birth,
I was resolved to bide the utmost brunt
And save the ship and goods for th' English owners.
   Phil. Whereof you may be one.
   Stuk.   Hear me great king.
If you believe this breast have any spark
Of honour or of vulgar honesty   1950
Then, credit me, this gentleman that speaks
Was never owner of a ship in 's life
Nor merchant venturer, though both trades be good—
But well deriv'd, of rich and gentle birth,
Holds it his bliss to be a traveller.
   Phil. Your protestations have persuaded us,
Lantado, leave them, and discharge the ship;
And gentlemen and shipper, stay without;
This honourable countryman of yours
Shall bring our further pleasure for your good.   1960
   Ver. If in the Basilisks fore-prizzing [1] eye
Be safety for the object it beholds
Then Stukley may to Vernon comfort bring
Else men are safe at sea when Syrens sing.
                [*Exit* VERNON, *Ship Master, and* LANDATO.
   Phil. Now gallant Stukley, boast of Philips grace
By such employments as we have assigned.
The king our cousin, Don Sebastian,
Solicits us for aid to Africa
In hope to conquer the barbarians.
The farther princes of that parched soil   1970

          [1] fore-prizzing, like sur-prising.

Are in contention who shall wear the crown
And the young King of Portingall believes,
And so do we, their strife shall breed him peace.
And for he stands engaged by royal oath
To help the King of Fez against his foe
And craves assistance from us of his blood,[1]
We have consented with condition
To give it him if Rome doth hold it fit.
And you brave Stukley are the man select
To carry to the Pope our embassy   1980
And we will furnish you for these affairs.
Do not admire the strangeness of our choice
In pointing you before our native nobles,
But think our love, our hope, or your desert
Or all conjoined advance you to this place.

   Stuk. Most sacred and [most] mighty King of Spain,
Though many reasons might withstand belief
That you would choose me your ambassador
Yet since your highness twice hath spoke the word
I humbly credit, and accept the charge.   1990

   Phil. And to defray your charge in our affairs
Our bounty shall exceed her usual bounds
First, for it is the time of Gubilie [2]
Next, for you go from Philip King of Spain,
And last, for high regard we hold you in.

   Stuk. Which [3] favour I will study to deserve.

   Phil. It is deserved: Valdes, deliver you

---

[1] us of his blood—his kinsmen.
[2] This jubilee was that of 1575. Stucley was then at Rome on a mission from Philip, but not in behalf of Sebastian.   [3] Ed. *with.*

Five thousand ducats in Don Stukley's hands.
Here are our letters and commission
With such instructions as concern the cause.   2000
So much for that: now for your countrymen
Whose ship miscarried here upon our coast;
We do allow them all convenient help,
For your sake, to recover ship and goods;
And that their loss may seem so much the less
We do acquit them of all custom fees,
So gallant Stukeley carry them these news
And make you ready for these great affairs.

    Stuk. Ready to serve and follow your command   [*Exit* STUK.

    Phil. Are not these English like their country fish   2010
Called gudgeons that will bite at every bait?
How easily the credulous fools believe
The thing they fancy or would wish of[1] chance,
Using no precepts of art prospective
To see what end each project sorteth to.
Hernandes tell me what is thy conceit
Of our election, and of Stukley's worth?

    Her. Most gracious and dread sovereign, pardon me
To speak of Stukley in particular,
Because your frowns lies heavy on me yet   2020
For that I did and offered him at Cales.
But generally I censure th' English thus—
Hardy but rash, witty but overweaning,
Else would this English hot-brain weigh th' intent
Your Highness hath in thus employing him.

[1] Probably we should read 'to chance.'

Phil. Thou judgest rightly, it is not for love
We bear this nation that we grace him thus
But use him as the agent of our guile.
For if the matter were of great import
Or that we would keep-touch [1] with Portingall   2030
And aid his voyage into Barbarie,
Stukley should have no hand in these affairs.
But now we deal as Lords of Vineyards use—
Stop with one bush two gaps into their ground:
One must we send to Rome to Jubile
And Stukley for his gift must have reward.
One bounty gilded with employment's grace
Serves both the turns, and sends proud Stukeley hence.
Valdes, five thousand ducats; pay him that.
So are we rid of a fond Euglishman.   [*Exit Omnes.*   2040

Enter STUKELEY *with* VERNON *and the Shipmaster.*

Stuk. But is it certain that my wife is dead.
Ship M. Sure as I live I saw her buried
First died the mother, then the daughter next,
Then old Sir Thomas Curtis lived not long
And died not rich; [2] but what was left he gave
Part to his brother, part to the hospital.
Stuk. Then where's the part he left his son-in-law?
Ver. Your part and grand part [3] were consumed too soon
To have a portion left you at the last.

---

[1] keep touch; to perform an agreement exactly.
[2] Anne Stucly administered Sir Thomas Curtis' goods as his heir, and Stucley inherited, and wasted his wealth.   [3] Ed. graund-part.

Stuk. Friend Vernon leave such discontenting speech; 2050
Your melancholy overflows your spleen,
Even as the billows over rack your ship,
Whose loss the King for my sake will restore.
Then tax me not good Vernon with graund parts
What 's twenty thousand pound to a free heart?
Twenty weeks charges for a gentleman
A thousand pound a week 's but fair expense.
   Ver. Your wife died not worth such a weeks expense.
   Stuk. What remedy? yet Stukley will not want.
She 's gone, and all her friends their heads are laid. 2060
Good resurrection have they at the last
Then shall we meet again. In the mean space
Tom Stukley lives, lusty Tom Stukley
Graced by the greatest King of Christendom.

Enter one of the K. men.

Nuncio. The governor of Cales Hernandez stays
To cry you mercy and to take his leave.   [*Exit* NUNCIO.
   Stuk. There let him stay; I leave him to himself
I love him not, nor malice [1] one so mean.

Enter VALDES.

Val. The King Don Stukeley prays to speak with you
But even a word, he will not stay you long. 2070
   Stuk. I shall attend his highness by and by— [*Exeunt* VALDES.
For old acquaintance and for country sake

[1] malice, as verb.

Vernon and Master, let me banquet you.
It shall be no disgrace to feast with me
Whom the King useth with so great respect.

Ship M. Pardon, sir, I must go see my ship
Whose owner shall be thankful for your favour.

Stuk. What says Master Vernon?

Ver. I some other time
May trouble you although it be not now. 2080

Stuk. As your occasions shall induce you sir. [*Exit* STUKELEY.

Ver. Good master see if any thing of mine
May from the ship be safely brought a-shore
And I will see your pains considered.

Ship M. I do not doubt but all your stuff is safe
The hatches are as close as any chest
Nothing takes hurt but what is in the hold
Because the keel is split upon the sands.
I'll send your trunks ashore and then provide
To seek our drown'd men and to bury them. [*Exit.* 2090

Ver. Not all the drown'd, but those are drown'd, and dead—
For I am drownd in my conceit alive!
Some sin of mine hath so offended heaven
That heaven still sends offence unto mine eye.
What should I think of Stukley or myself?
Either was he created for my scourge
Or I was born the foil to his fair happes,
Or in our birth our stars were retrograde.
In Ireland, then he braved his governor,
In Spain, he is companion to the King. 2100
His fortunes mounts, and mine stoops to the ground;

16

He as the Vine, I as the Colewort grow;
I live in every air but where he breathes;
His eye is as the Gorgons head to me,
And doth transform my senses into stone.
Some hold Spains climate to be very hot
I feel my blood congeal'd to ice in Spain.
The Leopard lives not near the Elephant
Nor I near Stukeley.   Spain, farewell to thee
Either I'll range this universe about   2110
Or I will be where Stukeley hath no being.   [*Exit.*

Enter STUKELEY, VALDES, STUKELEYS' *page, and one bearing bags sealed.*

Stuk. How many ducats did the King assign?
Val. Five thousand.
Stuk.   Are they all within these bags?
Val. Well near.
Stuk.   How near?
Val.   Perhaps some twenty want.
                    [*The bags are set on the table.*
Stuk. Why should there want a Marmady,[1] a mite?
Doth the King know that any ducats lacks?
Val. He doth, and saw the bags would hold more
And sealed them with his signet as you see.
Stuk. Valdes return them; I will have none of them
And tell thy master the great king of Spain   2120
I honour him, but scorn his niggardice. [*Cast the bags on the ground.*

[1] Marmady, *i.e.* Maravedi.

And spurn abridged bounty with my foot.
Abate base twenty from five thousand ducats!
I'll give five thousand ducats to my boy!
If I had promised Philip all the world
Or any kingdom, England sole except,
I would have perished or perform'd my word,
And not reserved one cottage to myself
Nor so much ground as would have made my grave.
Foutre for ducats if he take the tythe.   2130
Tell him I'll do his business at Rome
Upon my proper cost; but for his crowns
Since they come curtail'd, carry them again.
Come boy, to horse, away.   Spaniard, farewell.
   Val. Stay sir I pray ye till I move the King
   Stuk. Thou mov'st a mountain sooner than my mind.
                    [*Exit* STUKELEY *and his page.*
   Val. What a high spirit hath this Englishman
He tunes his speeches to a kingly key
Conquers the world, and casts it at his heels—

        Enter PHILIP *and his Lords.*

Here comes the King.
   Phil.   How now, is Stukeley gone?   2140
   Val. Gone, and will do your business in Rome
Though he refused the ducats you assigned
   Phil. How so?
   Val.   Because that twenty ducats want.
   Phil. Amongst five thousand may not twenty lack?

Val. [1] No; he supposeth you repent your gift
If you abridge your bounty but a mite.

Phil. Not for the world shall Stukeley go without
Go add a thousand ducats more to these
And post, and pray him not to be displeased.
Tell him I did it but to try his mind   2150
Which I commend above my treasury.
If England have but fifty thousand such
The power of Spain their coast shall [never] touch
Come Lords to horse ; to [2] Cyvilt lies our way
Valdes, I charge you to eschew delay.   [*Exeunt omnes.*

Enter SEBASTIAN, ANTONIA, HERANDO, *the* CARDNALL *and*
BOTELLIO.

Seb. The great and honour'd promise thou return'st us
From our brave kinsman Philip King of Spain
My dear Botellio adds a second life
Unto the action that we have in hand
The joyful breath that issues from thy lips   2160
Comes like a lusty gale to stuff our sails
Curling the smooth brows of the Afric deep.
O let me hear thy tongue sound once again
The cheerful promise of our new supplies

Bot. Why thus imperial Spain bid me return
Unto the great puissant Portingall—
Ten thousand foot of gallant Spanish blood
Men borne in honour and exploits in war,
And not one Indian or base bastard Moor—

[1] Ed. no, no.   [2] Seville.

Fifty his gallies, of the proudest vessels   2170
That to this day yet ever bare an oar
To meet you at the Port de Sant Maria
The fourth of June.

   Seb. The fourth of June at Port de Sant Maria
Ten thousand foot and fifty of his gallies
By land and sea, and at a certain time,
Oh what a gallant harmony is here!
Methinks that I could stand and still repeat them
A month together, they so please my soul—   2179
Ha Antonio! oh what an army's here.   *[Turning to the King of*
I tell thee cousin, never Christian king   *Portingall.*[1]
Came with so proud a power to Africa.

   Ant. And yet the greatness of your royal spirit
Makes all this nothing, so your glory shines
Above the power of Spain and Portingall.

   Seb. Cousin Antonio, to pay Botello back
The interest of his Spanish embassy
As you have taken muster of our powers
Report the number, what our army is.

   Ant. Unto the number of ten thousand Spaniards   2190
In the Kings army; add to this Botellio
Three thousand mercenary Spanish moors
Of voluntary valiant Portingalls
Three thousand threescore special men of arms
The garrison of Taieer,[2] and light horsemen
Five thousand and four hundred
Five thousand Germans and Italians

---

[1] Antonio is here called King of Portingall.   [2] Tangier.

My power three thousand, and the Duke Averos
Doubles my number, if [not] fully more
Besides the power that we do expect from Rome   2200
Thirty seven thousand we are now complete.

   Seb. Our army joined with that Mahamet brings
His barbarians and his mountain Moors
Brought from the deserts of burnt Africa
His valiant Turks trained up in spoil of war
His soldiers of Morocco and of Sirus
To fifty thousand as his promise is—
Ha brave Antonio there will be a power
To affright the very walls of Fez
And make stout Afric tremble at the sight   2210
Where we shall brave her on the sun-burn'd plains
And with our cannons crush her wanton head.
O my Antonio how I long to see
How Spanish blood and Turkish will agree.

   Ant. How shall it please your sacred Majesty
To appoint the several charges of this war.

   Seb. Cousin Antonio in this heat of war
For the safety of our royal kingdom
Let us yet speak of things concern our peace
Although but brief. First our dearest cousin   2220
For your princely self
Your right unto the crown of Portingall
As first and nearest of our royal blood
That, should we fail, the next in our succession
'Tis you and yours to sit upon our throne
Which is our pleasure to be published.

Ant. Long may my liege and sovereign Lord Sebastian
Sit on the royal throne of Portingall
    Seb. We thank you princely cousin.
Our dear and reverend uncle Cardinal—   2230
Unto ourself commit our wars in Africa—
For the great trust we reposse in you
We do bequeath our kingdoms government
As one whose wisdom and nobility
Deserves the great protection of our realm.
    Card. The most unworthy of that royal place
Whose many years and imbecility
Are but too weak to underprop the burthen.
But may the remnant of my age be spent
To Portingal's relief and your content.   2240
    Seb. Now Antonie unto our several charges.
Yourself will share the fortunes in these wars.
We do commit a garrison of Tanieers
Unto the leading of Alvares Peres
Our voluntary Portingalls to Lodovico Cæsar
The mercenary Spaniards to Alonzo
Mereneces Lieutenant general of our forces
Tanara for the German colonel—
And now set forward, let our ensigns fly
Either victorious, or if conquer'd die.   2250

                Enter Chorus.

    Cho. Thus far through patience of your gentle ears
Hath Stukley's life in comic history

Bin new reviv'd, that long ago lay rakte
In dust of Afric with his body there.
Thus far upon the steps of high promotion
His happy stars advanced him. Now at highest
As clearest summer days have darkest nights
And everything must finish; so in him
His state declining draws unto an end.
For by the Pope created, as you've heard 2260
Marquess of Ireland, with that new honour
Embark'd and victual'd think him on the sea
And that the time Sebastian had set down
To meet with Philip's promised aid is past
Toward Afric he, toward Ireland the other
Are both addrest upon the boisterous waves
But meeting what strange accident befel
How he was altered from his first intent
And be deluded by the hope he had
To be ascribed by the Castile King 2270
Regard this show, and plainly see the thing.

Enter at one door PHILIP *K. of Spain,* ALVA *and Soldiers; they take their stand: then enter another way* SEBASTIAN, DON ANTONIO, AVERO *with drums and ensigns: they likewise take their stand. After some pause* ANTONIO *is sent forth to* PHILIP *who with obeysance done approaching, away again very disdainfully; and as the Spanish soldiers are about to follow* ANTONIO, PHILIP *with his drawn sword stops them and so departs. Whereat* SEBASTIAN *makes show of great displeasure, but whispering with his Lords, each encouraging other as they are about to depart. Enter* STUKELEY *and his Italian band, who keeping aloof,* SEBASTIAN *sends* ANTONIO *to him, with whom* STUKELEY *draws near toward the King, and having a while conferred, at last retires to his soldiers to whom he makes show of persuading them to join with the portugeese: at first they seem to mislike, but last they yield, and so both armies meeting embrace, when with a sudden thunderclap the sky is on fire and the blazing star appears, which they prognosticating to be fortunate departed very joyful.*

So far was Philip as you have beheld
From lending aid unto the Portigeese
Is not content to undergo the blot
Of breach of promise, but with naked sword
Of unavoided justice threatens such
As should but offer to depart the Land:
Whereby the prince, though very much disturbed
Yet not dismay'd, so haughty was his mind,
Resolveth still to prosecute his journey   2280
And whilst they are debating on the cause
Stukley by weather is driven in to them
Who being known what countryman he was
What ships he had and what Italian bands
And whereto he was bound : th' offence thereof
The great dishonour and impiety
Laid open by Sebastian, straight recants
And moves his soldiers, which with much ado
At last are won to make for Barbary
No sooner was this fellowship contrived   2290
And they had join'd their armies both in one
But heaven, displeas'd with their rash enterprise,

Sent such a fatal comet in the air
Which they misconstruing shone successfully
Do haste the faster, furrowing through the deep.
And now suppose—but woe the wretched hour,
And woe that damned Mahamet [by] whose guile
This tender and unskilled but valiant king
Was thus allured unto a timeless death—
That in Tyrill a town in Barbary   2300
They all are landed; and not far from thence
Do meet that straggling fugitive the Moor
With some small forces; what doth then ensue
We may discourse, but Christendom shall rue.   [*Exit.*

Enter MULY MAHAMET *with* CALIPOLIS *drawn in their chariot,
with them a messenger from* SEBASTIAN.

Maham. Go, let ten thousand of our guard be sent
To entertain the great Sebastian
And welcome Christian to the King of Fez
And tell the Portingall thy royal master
That Afric makes obeisance to his feet
And stoops her proud head lower than his knee   2310
Tell him mine eyes are thirsty for his presence.
   Mess. I will return to tell your highness pleasure.
   Maha. Do so, begone,
And let our chariot be drawn softly forward
Where I and my Calipolis will sit
To grace the entrance of great Portingale.
Now fair Calipolis, rouse thy proud beauty

And strike their eyes with verder of thyself
 He leaps from his chariot. Enter SEBASTIAN *at the sound of trumpets.*
Dismount thee Muly from thy chariot wheels
To entertain the mighty Christian King.   2320
Welcome Sebastian King of Portingale.

 Seb. Thanks to the mighty and imperial Fez [1]
Why thus alights the mighty emperor?

 Muly. That I will do great Portingall the grace
To set thee by Callipolis my Queen

 Seb. Let mighty Muly's self supply that place
And give me leave to attend upon your love.

 Muly. Mount thee Sebastian, Muly doth command
It is my pleasure, I will have it so,
Mount thee brave lord and sit thee on her side   2330
And say Sebastian that the son of Phœbus
Upon his fathers fiery burnish'd car
Ne'er sat so glorious as the Portingale
Jove would exchange his sceptre for thy seat
And would abandon Junos godlike bed
Might he enjoy my fair Calipolis.
Welcome Sebastian, love, to Africa.

 Calip. All welcome that Calipolis can give
To the renowned mighty Portinguyse
Here sit sweet prince and rest thee after toil   2340
I'll wipe thy brows with leaves more sweet and soft
Than is the down of Cithereas fans
I'll fan thy face with the delicious plumes

[1] Ed. Fesse.

Of that sweet wonder of Arabia
With precious waters I'll refresh thy curls
Whose very savour shall make panthers wild,
And lively smell of those delicious sweets
And with such glorious liquors please thy taste
As Helens goblet never did contain
Nor never graced the banquet of the Gods.   2350

  Muly. Then speak, the comfort of great Mulys life
Her teeth more white than Caucase frosty clots
Where she unlocks the portals of her lips
Beauty a Phœnix burneth in her eye
Which there still liveth, as it still doth die

  Stuk. Why here's a gallant, here's a king indeed
He speaks all Mars
Tut, let me follow such a lad as this
This is pure fire; every look he casts
Flasheth like lightning; there's mettle in this boy   2360
He brings a breath that sets our sails on fire
Why now I see we shall have cuffs indeed.

  Ant. Now afore God he is a gallant prince

  Muly. What princes be these in your company?

  Seb. That is our cousin Prince Antonio
The other Stukley the brave Irish Marquess

  Muly. Noble Antonio and renowned Marquess
Ten thousand welcomes into Africa

  An. Thanks to great Muly.

  Stuk.   To your mightiness

  Muly. Next now the neighing of our warlike horse   2370
Shall shake the palace of commanding Jove

Our roaring cannons tear the highest clouds
And fright the sun out of his wonted course
Afric, I'll dye thy tawny sands in blood
And set a purple on thy sun-burnt face
This is the day thy terror first began
Before great Muly and Sebastian
Drive on and I will lacky by thy side
These Christian Lords I trust will take no scorn
When Muly-hamet bears them company.   2380
Away.   [*Exeunt.*

Two trumpets sound at either end: Enter MULY HAMET *and* ANTONIO.

  Ant. Second thy sonne[1] whatere thou be 'st that call'st
And with thy proud importance greet our ears.
  Muly ham. What African or warlike Portingale
Comes forth to answer?
  Ant.   Muly hamet, I.
  Mul. Antonio?
  Ant. The same proud Moor: that proud Portugal
  Mul. Where is Sebastian? he comes not forth
Himself to answer me.

Enter SEBASTIAN, MAHAMET *and the train.*

  Seb. Here Muly hamet, here stout African   2390
What wouldst thou Hamet with the Portugise
Where's Abdelmelek thy proud haughty brother?

---

[1] sonne, sound.

Enter ABDELMELEK *and his train.*

Abd. Here brave Sebastian King of Portingal.

Seb. O art thou there? Thyself in presence then
What wouldst thou beg? proud Abdelmelek speak.

Abd. Beg, 'tis a word I never heard before
Yet understand I what thou mean'st thereby
There's not a child of manly Zariks line
But scorns to beg of Mahomet himself.
We shall lead Fortune with us bound about   2400
And sell her bounty as we do our slaves
We mount her back and manage her for war
As we do use to serve Barbarian horse
And check her with the snaffle and the reins [1]
We bend her swelling crest and stop and turn
As it best likes us, haughty Portingales.

Seb. We'll spur your Jennet lusty African
And with our pistols we'll prick her pampered sides
Until with yarking she do break her girths
And fling her gallant rider in the field   2410
And say proud Moor that so said Portingall.

Abdel. Thy words do sound of honour, Christian King
Which makes me therefore pity thee the more
And sorrow that thy valour should be sunk
In such a vasty unknown sea of arms
Where thy old courage [2] cannot bear that sail
That thy proud haughty spirit would gladly have
Therefore Sebastian cast aside these arms

[1] Ed. razins.   [2] qu. cordage.

That thou unjustly bears against thy friend
And leave that traitor that but trains thee on 2420
Unto the jaws of thy destruction.

 Muly. Brave young Sebastian king of Portingall
And Don Antonio, hear me gallant Lords—
Muly Mahamet, but you are in presence,
Would think himself damn'd everlastingly
But to hold wrack¹ with so base a slave
Whose coward melting soul for very fear,
Comes frighted up and down within his bosom
And fain would find a message from his breast
So daunted with the terror of our arms 2430
That he is mad his soldiers will not fly
That with some colour he might turn his back
See'st thou the power of Africs in my hand
Like furious lightning in the hand of Jove
To dash thy pride, and like a raging storm
To tear those Turkish flags that spread their silks
Upon the strands of peaceful Africa
And quak'st not slave with terror of the same?

 Hamet. Dare but my brother's bastard and a slave
That should have knelt at Abdelmeleks feet 2440
Send these proud threats from his audacious lips?

 Maha. Down dog, and crouch before the feet
Of great Morocco [and] of mighty Fez
But why vouchsafe language to this slave?
Hear me Sebastian, thou brave Portuguise
I Muly hamet King of mighty Sus

   ¹ wrack, should be converse, or the like.

Whose countrys bounds and limits do extend
From mighty Atlas over all those lands
That stretch themselves to the Atlantic sea
And look upon Canaræs wealthy Isles   2450
And on the West to Gibaltaras straights
Those fruitful forelands and the famous towns
Assure Sebastian King of Portingall
Most glorious and triumphant victory.

 Abdel. Hear me Sebastian, hear me youthful King
And Abdelmelek will receive thee yet
And clip thee in the arms of gentle peace
Forsake this tyrant and join hands with me
And at thy pleasure quietly possess
The towns thou holdest in Afric at this day   2460
Aginer, Zahanra, Seuta, Penon, Melilla
Which Muly Mahamet will dispossess thee of
If by thy means he should obtain the day.

 Seb. Say Abdelmelek, tell me, wilt thou yet
Dismiss thy power, break these rebellious arms
Which now thou bearest 'gainst the King of Fez
And great Sebastian King of Portingale
Yet of Mahamet will obtain thy life.

 Hamet. Look on the power that Abdelmelek brings
Of brave resolved Turks and valiant Moors   2470
Approved Alarkes, puissant Argolets
As numberless as be these Afric sands
And turn thee then and leave thy petty power
The succour failing you expect from Spain
And bow thy knees for mercy Portingall.

Ant. Our very slaves, our negroes, muleteers
Able to give you battle in the field
Then think of those that you must cope withal
The Portingall and his approved power.
Muly Mahamet and his valiant Moors   2480
The Irish Marquess Stukley and his troops
Of warlike Germans and Italians
Alvares, Cæsar, Menesis and Avero
Proud Abdelmelek kneel and beg for grace.
 Abd. Then proud Sebastian I deny all means.
 Maha. Therefore Mahamet and Sebastian farewell.

EXCURSIONS.

Enter SEBASTIAN ANTONIO AVARO *and* STUKELEY *in counsel together.*

 Seb. Advise us Lords if we this present night
Shall pass the river of Mezaga here
Upon whose sandy banks our tents are pitch'd
Or stay the morning fresh approaching sun.   2490
 Ave. In my opinion let us not remove
The night is dark, the river passing deep
And we ourselves and all my troops my Lord
Exceeding weary with the last days march.
 Ant. My Lord Avero counsels well methinks
 Seb. What's your opinion Marquess of Ireland?
 Stuk. My Lord might I persuade, neither to night
Nor in the morning should ye cross the river

Our men are weak, the enemy is strong
Our men are feeble, they in perfect health;   2500
Beside his better discipline I judge
To let them seek us here than we them there
Considering what advantage may be had
Gainst them that first attempt to pass the river.
Again, on this side whatsoever fall
We have Larassa and Morocco both
Strong towns of succour to retire unto.

   Seb. Retire unto! talks Stukeley of retreat?
Are you invested with a Marquess name
Graced with the title of a fiery spirit   2510
Renown'd, and talkest so of fortitude?
And lurks there in your breast so mean a thought
Can there issue from your lips a term
So base and beggarly as that of flight
I rather thought that Stukeley would have said
We baite here, and are not swift enough
In seeking fit time to begin the fight

   Stuk. Conceit me not Sebastian at the worst.
You crav'd my counsel, and in that respect
I speak my conscience; if you like it not   2520
Condemn me not therefore of cowardice
For what I said was as a faithful friend
Careful we should embrace the safest course.
But as I am Tom Stukeley and a Captain
Never known yet to stand in fear of death
Rise when you will; his foot that is the foremost
His sword that[s] soonest drawn, my foot and sword

Shall be as forward and as quickly drawn
Nay do but follow and I'll lead the way
I'll be the first shall wade up to the chin   2530
Or pass Mezagas channel, and the first
Shall give assault unto the enemy.
So little do I fear thextremest brunt
Or hardest fortune that attends on war.

Enter MULY.

Muly. To arms brave king, to arms courageous lords
Bright crested victory doth waft us on
And all advantage[s] that may be had
Offer to fill our hands with wished spoil
And cheer our hearts with endless happiness.
False Abdelmelek mortally is sick   2540
For fear I think that we shall vanquish him
His soldiers mutinise, and his best friends
Begin to waver and mistrust the cause
Of which three thousand of his stout Alarks
Men very expert with the shield and lance
This night are fled to us, who likewise tell
Of many thousands more that will revolt
Were we but ordered once within the field
I dare assure ye had not crossed the river
As now the day-break calles us to labour   2550
So that there might be expeditious means
For such as do affect us to depart
Half Abdelmelcks army would forsake him.

Sebast. No longer great Mahamet will we linger
We gave direction by our pioneers
So soon as any beams of light appear'd
Within the East, to settle to their work
And make our passage smoother through the ford.
And lest they loiter we ourself in person
Will overlook them that by ten o'clock   2560
Within yonder plain adjacent to Alcazar
The lot of happy fortune may be cast.
Come Lords, and each unto his several charges.
  Muly. Bravely resolved, my self will follow you.
And so it happen that Mahamet speed
I wreck not who, or Turk or Christian, bleed.   [*Exeunt.*

The trumpets sounding to the battle. Enter ABDELMELEK *and*
  SEBASTIAN *fighting: after them again* MULY MAHAMET *and*
  MULY HAMET : *then* ANTONIO *with some other passing away;
  then they retired back and* ABDELMELEK *alone in the battle.*

  Abd. Fetch me one drop of water, any man
And I will give him Taneers wealthy town.
The sands of Afric are so parching hot
That when our blood doth light upon the earth   2570
The drops do seethe like caldrons as they stand,
Till made like ink it cleave unto the hoove
Of our fierce Jenets, which sunk underneath us
Overcome with heat ; some water, water howe !
  Sold. [*running in haste.*] My Lord you have been very lately sick.
And scarcely yet recovered your disease

Withdraw yourself out of the murdering press
Hazard not so the safety of us all.

Abdel. Go slave and preach unto the droughty earth
Persuade it if thou canst to shun the rain　　　　　　2580
My soul to death is thirsty for revenge
Rush through the ranks, let the proud Christians know
That Abdelmelek was their overthrow—　　　　*[Exit running.*

Enter SEBASTIAN.

Seb. The sun so heats our armour with his beams
That it doth burn and scar our very flesh
That when we would stretch out our arms to strike
Our parched sinews crack like parchments scrolls
And fly in sunder, that our arms stands out
Stiff as our lances, and our swords fall down　　*[Panting for breath.*
And stick their envious points into the earth.　　　　2590

Muly Mah. There never yet was such a heat before
Since Phaeton set this universe on fire
That the earth fearing he had liv'd again
And got into the chariot of the sun
Opens her wide mouth like a gaping wall.

Seb. [*hastily.*] Muly Mahamet, say, how stands the day.

Muly Mah. Fly fly Sebastian, for the foe prevails
Dugall, who led five thousand men of war
Is now revolted to the enemy
Farewell Sebastian, this our latest night　　　　　　2600
I will assay to save myself by flight.

Enter a Company, set upon SEBASTIAN *and kill him ; they go out.*
Enter a soldier bringing in ABDELMELEK *on his back*, MULY
MAHAMET *following.*

Muli Mahan. I ever fear'd that my courageous brother
Would wade so far into this storm of war
That he would be too lavish of his person.
   Sol. My Lord, he died not by the dint of sword
But being overcome with toil and heat
Not well recovered of his dangerous sickness
Sank down for faintness, and gave up his soul.
   Muly. In the secret'st manner that thou canst devise
Convey his royal corse into our tent   2610
For if his death should once be blown abroad
It were a means to overthrow the day.
        [*Enter a soldier running. Exit soldier carrying his body.*
Speak slave who has the advantage of the day
   Sol. Our valiant Turks and Moors have got the field
Sebastian slain; Muly Mahamet fled
And Abdelmelek crown'd with victory
   Muly. Shine glorious sun and bear unto the West
News of our conquest; and fright those that dwell
Under our feet with terror of our name
Rein in thy fiery palfreys yet awhile   2620
And trot them softly on those airy planks
To look upon the glory of the day.   [*Exit.*

Enter DON ANTONIO *disguised like a Priest, fearfully looking about him.*

 Ant. Oh poor Antonio, which way canst thou take ;
But dreadful horror dogs thee at the heels?
Sebastian slain, Muly Mahamet fled,
All Portingales brave Infantries slain
And not a man of mark or note alive.
Thou glad to hide thee in a priests disguise
Thy Chaplain, that came with thee to the war
And in this battle likewise lost his life.   2630
Heaven (be thou pleas'd) this may yet stand in sted.
If not, thy will then be accomplished.

    Enter three ar four Turkish soldiers.

 1 *Sol.* See here, a priest yet left alive
Sirra come hither, how hast thou scap'd?
What shall we kill him?
 2 *Sol.* No kill him not, first let us ransack him
What hast thou Sirrah that may save thy life?
 Ant. All that I have my friends I'll give ye freely
So it may please ye but to save my life
Which to destroy will do ye little good.   2640
 2 *Sol.* Come then, be brief, let's see, what hast thou?
 Ant. This purse containeth all the coin I have
These bracelets my dead Lord bestow'd on me
That if 1 scaped I might remember him
In my devotions and my daily prayers.
 2 *Sol.* Whose priest wast thou?

Ant. Ferdinands, Duke of Averos.

2 *Sol.* Well listen fellows, 'twill do us little good
To kill him, when we may make benefit
By selling of him to be some mans slave   2650
And now I call to mind the wealthy Moor
Amalek that dwells here in the Fesse, He'll give as much
As any man; how say ye, shall it be so.

[1] 2 *Sol.* No better counsel can be.

Ant. Thy will O God be done, whatere become of me

Chorus.

Thus of Alcazars battle in one day
Three kings at once did lose their hapless lives
Your gentle favour must we needs entreat
For rude presenting such a royal fight
Which more imagination must supply   2660
Than all our utmost strength can reach unto
Suppose the soldiers who you saw surprised
The poor dismayed prince Antonio
Have sold him to the wealthy Moore they talk'd of
And that such time as needs must be allowed
Already he hath passed in servitude
Sit now and see unto our story's end
All those mishaps that this poor prince attend.

After Antonio's *going out Enter* Muly Hamet *with victory.*

The certain number that can yet be found
And of the Christian Lords   2670
The Duke of Averro, and the bish of Cambra, and Portua [1]

---

[1] *i.e.* The Bishops of Coimbra and Oporto, and Christopher de Tavora.

The Irish Marquess Stukley, Count Tanara
Two hundred of the chief nobility of Portingale
And Muly Hamet, passing of the ford
Of swift Larissa to escape by flight
His horse and he both drowned in the river.

Muly. See that the body of Sebastian
Have Christian and Kingly burial
After his country manner; for in life
A braver spirit never lived upon the same   2680
And let the Christian bodies be interr'd.
For Muly Mahamet, let his skin be flea'd
From off the flesh from foot unto the head
And stufft within, and so be borne about
Through all the parts of our dominions
To terrify the like that shall pursue
To lift their swords against their sovereign
And in memorial of this victory
For ever after let this fourth of August
Kept holy to the service of our God   2690
Through all our kingdoms and dominions.

Enter STUKLEY *faint and weary, being wounded, with him* VERNON.

Stuk. Come noble Vernon that I meet you here
Were the day far more bloody than it is
Our hope more desperate and our lives beset
With greater peril than we can devise
Yet should I laugh at death, and think this field
But as an easy bed to sleep upon.

Ver. Oh Master Stukeley, since there now remains

No way but one, and life must here have end
Pardon my speech, if in a word or two 2700
Whilst here we breathe us, I discharge my soul.
I must confess, your presence I have shunned,
Not that I hate you, but because thereby
That grief which I did study to forget
Was still renewed, and therefore when we met
In Ireland, Spain, and at the last in Rome
And that I saw I could no way direct
My course but always you were in my way
I thought if Europe I forsook, that then
We should be far enough disjoin'd. But lo 2710
Even here in Aphrick we are met again.
And now there is no parting but by death.

   Stuk. And then I hope that we shall meet in heaven.
Why Master Vernon, in our birth we two
Were so ordain'd to be of one self heart
To love one woman, breathe one country air
And now at last, as we have sympathized
In our affections, led one kind of life,
So now we both shall die one kind of death
In which let this our special comfort be 2720
That though this parched earth of Barbary
Drink no more English blood but of us twain
Yet with this blood of ours the blood of kings
Shall be commixt, and with their fame our fame
Shall be eterniz'd in the mouths of men.

   Ver. Forgive me then my former fond conceits
And ere we die let us embrace like friends.

Stuk. Forgive me rather that must die before
I can requite the friendship you have shown.   *[Embrace.*
So this is all the will and testament
That we can make.   Our bodies we bequeath
To earth from whence they came; our souls to heaven;
But for a passing bell to toll our knell
Ourselves will play the sextons, and our swords
Shall ring our farewell on the burganets
Of these blood thirsty and uncivil Turks.

Enter four or five Italian soldiers.   They lay hands on him.

See where he is; lay hands upon him sirs.
  Stuk. Soldiers what mean ye? will ye mutinize?
  Ver. He is your leader—Do ye seek his life?
  2. To lead us to destruction—but if he
Had kept his oath he swore unto the Pope
We had been safe in Ireland, where now
We perish here in Aphrick.   But before
We taste of death, we vow to see him dead.
Then brave Italians, stab him to the heart
That hath so wickedly bereaved[1] your lives
  Ver. First villains you shall triumph in my death
And either kill me too, or set him free.
  Stuk. Hear me you bloody villains.
  2. Stab him soldiers.
    [VERNON *fights with some of them to save* STUKLEY, *and is
slain of them; in the mean while the rest stab* STUKLEY.

---

[1] Ed. behavide.

Stuk. O have you slain my friend?

2. Yet doth he prate?

Stuk. England farewell! what fortune never yet
Did cross Tom Stukeley in, to show her frown
By treason suffers him to be overthrown.   [*Dies.*

FINIS.

NOTE.—Since the foregoing was in type, Dr Brinsley Nicholson has given me the title of a book in his possession, which he supposes to have furnished Peele with some of his materials for *The Battle of Alcazar*.

Historia | De bello Africano | *In quo* | Sebastia-|nus Serenissi-|mus Portugalliæ | Rex, periit ad diem 4 Aug. | Anno 1778 | *Vnd cum* | ortu et Fami-|lia Regum, qui nostro | *tempore in illis Africæ regioni-*|*bus imperium tenne-*|*runt* | Ex Lusitano sermone primo in | Gallicum: inde in Latinum | translata | per Ioannem Thomam | Freigivm D. | Noribergæ | CIƆ IƆ XXC.| PP. 71, but no pagination. Col. Imprimebatur Noribergæ in Officina Catharinæ Gerlachin, & Hæredum Iohannis Montani.

Dr Nicholson informs me that Stucley is barely mentioned in the book. It seems however that some of the details of Battle in the foregoing play (*e.g.* l. 2543, sqq. and 2671) are taken from it. A translation of it (?) by Munday and Chettle was published in 1601.

NOBODY AND SOMEBODY.

Nobody and Somebody is an anonymous play. In construction and intention it corresponds to the better known, but not better, drama *A merry knack to know a knave*. In both a plot is taken from what purported to be records of British History, and this over-plot was made the vehicle of a half-comic, half-satirical underplot reflecting on the most prominent social questions and classes of the Elizabethan world. The 'historical' part of *Nobody and Somebody* is from Geoffrey of Monmouth's mythical chronicles of British Kings. The argument may be given in the words of Spenser (Fairie Queen, Bk ii., c. x. st. 44, 45) :—

> Five sonnes he [Morindus] left, begotten of one wife
> All which successively by turnes did rayne
> First Gorboman, a man of vertuous life;
> Next Archigald, who for his proud disdayne
> Deposed was from Princedome soverayne,
> And pitteous Elidure put in his sted;
> Who shortly it to him restored agayne,
> Till by his death he it recovered;
> But Peridure and Vigent him disthronized :

> In wretched prison long he did remaine,
> Till they out-raigned had their utmost date,
> And then therein reseized was againe,
> And ruled long with honorable state,
> Till he surrendred realme and life to fate.

The comic personages of the play in their names retain the abstract character of the old moralities. And the abuses which are satirized are the same as those lashed in such archaic productions as the *Three lords and three ladies of London*, and the *Three ladies of London*. The decay of hospitality, the racking of rents, the extorsions of usurers, the offences against the protectionist code which forbad all export of raw material, wool, corn, or metal. 'Nobody' does all the good, 'Somebody' all the ill, which he puts off upon 'Nobody.' 'Nobody' therefore first in the country, then 'in the city, then in Court has to bear the blame of 'Somebody's' misdeeds, till at the end the true knave is smelt out and punished, and 'Nobody' is rewarded.

The joke of all this was of venerable age at the time when the play was probably written. The Stationers' Registers tell us of a license to Rowland Hall in 1561 for *a letter of Nicholas Nemo*, who was also a character in the play of *The three ladies of London*. In 1568 Singleton was licensed to print *the return of old well-spoken Nobody*. The same kind of witticism is seen in Sir Edward Dyer's *Praise of Nothing*, 1585, and in William Lisle's *Nothing for a new-year's Gift*, 1603, with its motto, 'Nihil est ex omni parte beatum.' The matter of the invective points to no more definite date than the form of the plot does. The same stuff is found in the plays I have mentioned, and in the *Pedlar's Prophecy* long before 1590, and it continues to be the theme of social reformers and satirists long afterwards. The only hopeful note of date in the play is when Nobody, after promising to 'build up Paul's steeple without a collection,' observes, 'I see not what becomes of these collections.' The steeple was burned in 1561; in 1563 a collection was made throughout the kingdom for its restoration, and the repairs thus paid for were all finished in 1566. But there seems to have been some idea prevalent that the funds had been misapplied. In 1576 the Queen wrote to complain that no progress was made in repairing the steeple; but the Council persuaded her that she could not order subsidies for it in the city, because of the heavy contributions the citizens already paid to the government. In 1583 Aylmer, the Bishop of London, suggested to the Council that payments for commutations of penances should be suppressed, what had been paid refunded, and applied to the repairing of Paul's, 'which would well help to make good a good piece of it.' Aylmer's were not safe hands to hold money. When Bancroft became Bishop in 1597, it was proved that the ruins and dilapidations of the Church and Bishop's houses came to £6,513 14s. 0d. And he obtained judgment against Aylmer's son for £4,210 1s. 8d.; Fletcher, the intermediate Bishop (father of the Dramatist), was, I presume, answerable for the rest. Any how, there were scandalous rumours on the matter, and in 1592, two years before Aylmer's death, Verstegan, Parson's intelligencer at Antwerp, in his *Declaration of the true causes of the great troubles, &c.* thus alludes to them. 'But it is a wonder to consider what great and grievous exactions have from time to time been generally imposed upon the people, as all the loans, the lotteries, *gathering for the steeple of Pauls*, new imports,' &c. Bacon, in his official reply, *observations on a libel*, 1592, says upon this—'Now to the point of levies and contributions of money, which he calleth exactions. First very coldly he is not abashed to bring in the gathering of Pauls steeple and the lottery; trifles, and past long since; whereof the former, being but a voluntary collection of that men were freely disposed to give, never grew to so great a sum as was sufficient to finish the work for which it was appointed, and so, I imagine, was converted to some better use; like to that gathering which was for the fortifications of Paris [one MS. reads Barwick] save that that came to a much greater, though, as I have heard, no competent sum.' Bacon's reply proves that there were rumours of the misappropriation of the fund, and he retorts by referring to a similar accusation against the French government. This, so far as it goes, seems to point to 1592 as the date of the play. As that was the date of the revival of the *Knack to know a knave*, by Lord Strange's company, and as it is certain that the popularity of that play induced Henslowe to get some one to write the *Knack to know an honest man* for the Lord Admiral's company, it seems probable enough that a third company should follow suit with *Nobody and Somebody;* where the relationship, not apparent in the title, is much more evident in the body of the play.

But it was evidently revised, perhaps re-written, when it was revived in the time of King James. The edition bears no date, but claims to be 'the true copy, as it hath been acted by the Queen's Majesty's servants.' These were Queen Anne's players, who had been the Earl of Worcester's, and were perhaps transferred to the Queen in 1603. Their patent, however, bears date April 15, 1609. Thomas Heywood was one of them. This edition is alluded to in Shakspere's *Tempest*, where Ariel's music is said to be 'played by the picture of Nobody.' There are two wood-cuts, one at the beginning of the book, the other at the end, representing the stage dress of the two chief characters. 'The picture of Nobody' at the beginning represents him in a huge pair of slops, all legs, head and arms, but no body.[1] Somebody

---

[1] See an allusion to this in the play, p. 303.

has an equally exaggerated doublet, with no legs to speak of. Perhaps this plate may throw some light on a joke frequent in plays about the year 1600 and later, that 'a man borne upon little legs' was 'a gentleman;'—for he was Somebody. Other notes of a date after 1603 are—1. England is called Britain. But this is not decisive; for the play relates to a time when the Island as yet contained no Englishmen; and even in Elizabeth's days, perhaps out of compliment to the Tudor dynasty, the Island was so called. Thus Puttenham—

> Elizabeth, regent of the Great Britain Isle,
> The English Diana, the great Briton maid.

But, 2. The following allusion is more to the point—

> ——When the King
> Knighted the lusty gallants of the land
> No-body then made dainty to be knighted.

This looks like a reference to James' fiscal distribution of the honour. He made altogether 2323 knights, of whom 900 in his first year. John Philpot, who made a catalogue of them, published in 1660, says—'If you observe the history of those days you will find many knighted who in the time of the late Queen had showed small affection to that King of peace. But he was wise, and best knew how to make up a breach.' The Somerset Herald, 'a devout servant of the royal line,' omits to say that each knight had to pay his fee.

Nobody and Somebody is one of the plays, acted in Germany, of which a German translation was published in 1620. Some extraordinary liberties are taken with the text; Ex. g. in the scene, p. 292, instead of the lady boxing Lord Sycophant's ears, he beats her with a stick. In one place of the translation Elidure's title is said to be King of England, Scotland, and Ireland, showing that the translation was made after the Union of the Crowns. Herr Cohn, however, supposes that all the plays in the volume of 1620 were acted in Germany in or about the year 1600.

On the character of the Lord Sycophant it may be noted that possibly it was aimed at Lord Cobham. The Earl of Essex, Wotton tells us, 'was not prone and eager to detract openly from any man; only against one man he had forsworn all patience, namely Henry Lord Cobham, and would call him (per excellentiam) the Sycophant (as if he had been an emblem of his name), even to the Queen herself, though of no small insinuation with her.' Remembering how generally the dramatists were in the interest of Essex, this allusion must be considered probable. The scene, p. 293, seems distinctly to allude to Cobham's appointment in 1596 to the Wardenship of the Cinque Ports, in spite of the warm endeavours of Essex in favour of Sir Robert Sydney.

No-body and Some-body.

With the true Chronicle Historie of Elydure, who was fortunately three several times crowned King of England.

The true copy thereof, as it hath been acted by the Queens Maiesties Servants.

Printed for John Trundle, and are to be sold at his shop in Barbican, at the signe of No-body.

THE PROLOGUE.

A subject, of no subject, we present,
   for No-body, is Nothing :
   Who of nothing can something make?
It is a worke beyond the power of wit,
   And yet invention is rife :
A morrall meaning you must then expect
   grounded on lesser than a shadowes shadow :
Promising nothing where there wants a toong;
   And deeds as few, be done by No-bodie :
Yet something out of nothing we will show
To gaine your loves, to whome our selves we owe.

No-body and Some-body.

Enter CORNWELL *and* MARTIANUS.

Corn. My Lord *Martianus.*
Mar. My Lord of *Cornwell.*
Corn. Morrow.
Mar. Morrow.
Corn. You are sad my Lord.
Mar.   You melancholy.
Corne.   So
The state itselfe mournes in a robe of Wo
For the decease of *Archigalloes* vertues.
  Mar. I understand you, noble-minded *Cornwell.*
What generous spirit drawes this Brittish ayre
But droops at *Archigalloes* government?
  Corn. And reason, *Martianus.* When the Sunne
Struggles to be delivered from the wombe
Of an obscure Eclipse, doth not the earth   10
Mourne to behold his shine envelloped?
O *Corbonon*, when I did close thine eyes
I gave release to *Britaines* miseries.

Enter ELYDURE.

  Mar. Good morrow to Prince *Elydure.*

Elid. The same to you and you: you are sad my Lordes;
Your harts I thinke are frosty, for your blood
Seemes crusted in your faces, like the dew
In a September morne. How fares the King?
Have you yet bid good morrow to his highnes?
    Corn. The King's not stirring yet.   20

                Enter VIGENIUS *and* PERIDURE.

    Perid. Yonder's old Cornwell; come Vigenius
Weele have some sport with him.
    Vig. Brother, content.
    Perid. Good morrow to you brother *Elydure*
    Cornwel. God morrow to *Cornwell*
    Vig. Morrow old gray-beard
    Corn. My beards not so gray as your wits greene
    Vig. And why so?
    Perid. We shall ha you come out now with some reason that
was borne in my great grandsires time.   28
    Corn. Would you would prove as honest princes as your great
grandsire was, or halfe so wise as your elder brother was! Theres
a couple of you! Sfoote I am ashamed you should be of the blood
royall.
    Perid. And why, father Winter?
    Corn. You do not know your state. There's *Elydure*
Your elder brother next unto the King;
He plies his booke; when shall you see him trace
Luscivious *Archigallo* through the streets,
And fight with common hacksters hand to hand
To wrest from them their goods and dignities?

Perid. You are to[o] saucy, Cornwell. 40
Vig. Bridle your spirit.
Elyd. Your words are dangerous, good honest subject,
Old reverent states-man, faithful servitor:
Do not traduce the King, hees vertuous.
Or say he tread somewhat besides the line
Of vertuous government, his regality
Brookes not taxation: Kings greatest royalties
Are, that their subjects must aplaud their deedes
As well as beare them. Their prerogatives
Are murall interponents twixt the world
And their proceedings. 50
Corn. Well, well, I have served foure Kings,
And none of all those foure but would have ventured
Their safeties on old *Cornwels* constancy.
But thats all one; now I am cald a dotard.
Go to, though now my limbes be starke and stiffe
When Cornwels dead, Brittayne I know will want
So strong a prop. Alasse, I needs must weepe
And shed teares in abundance, when I thinke
How *Archigallo* wrongs his government.
Vig. Nay, now youle fall into your techy humor. 60

Enter LORD SICOPHANT.

Sicoph. My Lords,—Princes I should have said, and after, Lords
—I am the Usher and Harbinger unto the Kings most excellent
person; and his Majesty—
Vig. —Is fourth-comming——
Sicoph. Or comming fourth, hard by or at hand. Will you

put your gestures of attendance on, to give his Maiestie the *Bon-ioure?*

Enter ARCHIGALLO *and two Lords,* MORGAN, MALGO.

All. Good morrow to our soveraigne *Archigallo.*
Arch. Morrow.
Corn. Why do you frowne upon your servants, King? 70
We love you, and you ought to favor us.
Will you to Counsel? Heeres petitions,
Complaints, and controversies twixt your subjects,
Appealing all to you.
Arch. Lets see those papers. A controversie betwixt the Lord *Morgan* and the Lord *Malgo,* concerning their Tytles to the Southerne Island.
We know this cause and what their titles be.
You claim it by inheritance?
Morg. My liege, I do.
Arch. You by the marriage of Lord *Morgans* mother, 80
To whom it was left joynture?
Malgo. True gratious Soveraigne.
Arch. Whose evidence is strongest? To which part
Inclines the censures of our learned Judges?
Morgan. We come not heer to plead before your grace
But humblie to intreat your Maiestie
Peruse our evidence and censure it
According to your wisdome.
Arch. What I determine, then, youle yeeld unto?
Both. We will, my Soveraigne.
Arch. Then that Southerne Ile

We take to our protection, and make you 90
Lord governor thereof.

Sicoph. I humblie thanke your highnesse.

Mal. I hope your Maiesty——

Arch. Replie not, I but take it to myselfe
Because I would not have dissention
Betwixt two peeres. I love to see you friends;
And now the Islands mine your quarrell ends.
What's next? A poore No[r]thern mans humble petition. Which
is the plaintive?

Enter clowne, Wench, and RAFE.

Rafe. I; If it please your Maiestie I was betrothed to this maid.

Arch. Is this true my Wench? 100

Wench. Tis verie true, and like your maiestie, but this tempting fellow after that most felloniously stole my hart awaie fro me, caried it into the church, and I, running after him to get my hart againe, was there married to this other man.

Clown. Tis verie true, and like your maiesty; though Raphe were once tooke for a propper man, yet when I came in place it appeared otherwise: if your highnesse note his leg and mine, there is ods; and for a foot, I dare compare. I have a wast to[o]; and though I say it that should not saye it, there are faces in place of Gods making. 110

Arch. Thou art a proper fellow, and this wench is thine by lawfull marriage.

Clown. Rafe, you have your answer, you may be gon; your onely way to save charges is to buy a halfpenniwoorth of Hobnailes for your shoes. Alasse, you might have looked into this, before: go silly Rafe, go, away, vanish.

Arch. Is not this lasse a pretty neat browne wench?

Sicoph. She is my liege, and mettell, I dare warrant.

Arch. Fellow, how long hast thou been married? 119

Clown. I was, as they say, coupled the same day that my countryman Raphe begunne the law: for to tell your Majestie the truth, we are yet both virgins, it did never freese betwixt us two in a bed I assure your grace.

Arch. Didst never lie with thy wife?

Clown. Never yet, but nowe your Majestie hath ended the matter, Ile be so bold as take possession.

Arch. Harke my wench, wilt leave these rusticke fellowes and stay with me?

Wench. What will your highnes doe with me?

Arch. Why, Ile make thee a Lady. 130

Wench. And shall I goe in fine clothes like a Lady?

Arch. Thou shalt.

Wench. Ile be a Lady then, that's flat. Sweet heart, farewell, I must be a Lady, so I must.

Clow. How now, how now? but hear you Sis.

Wench. Away you Clowne, away.

Clown. But will your highnes rob me of my spouse?

Arch. What we will we will. Away with those slaves..

Clown. Zounds, if ever I take you in Yorkshire for this!

Sicoph. Away, you slaves. 140

Corn. My Lord, these generall wrongs will draw your highnesse Into the common hatred of your subjects.

Arch. Whats that to thee? Old doting Lord, forbeare. Whats heere? Complaints against one *Nobody* For over much releeving of the poore,

Helping distressed prisoners, entertayning
Extravagants and vagabonds. What fellowes this?

Corn. My liedge I know him; he's an honest subject
That hates extortion, usury, and such sinnes
As are too common in this Land of Brittaine. 150

Arch. Ile have none such as he within my kingdome;
He shall be banisht.

Sicoph. Heare my advise my liedge : I know a fellow
Thats opposite to *Nobody* in all thinges :
As he affects the poore, this other hates them;
Loves usurie and extortion. Send him straight
Into the Country, and upon my life
Ere many monthes he will devise some meanes
To make that *Nobody* bankrout, make him flie
His Country, and be never heard of more. 160

Arch. What doost thou call his name?

Sicoph. His name is *Somebody* my liedge.

Arch. Seeke out that *Somebody*, wele send him straight.
What other matters stay to be decided
Determine you and you. The rest may follow
To give attendance.

[*Exeunt all but the Lords.* MANENT CORNWELL *and* MARTIANUS.

Mart. Alls nought already, yet these unripe ills
Have not their full growth; and their next degree
Must needes be worse than nought : and by what name
Doe you call that? 170

Cornw. I know none bad enough :
Base, vild, notorious, ugly, monstruous, slavish,
Intollerable, abhorred, damnable !

Tis worse than bad! Ile be no longer vassaile
To such a tirannous rule, nor accessarie
To the base sufferance of such outrages.

Mart. Youle not indure it?—How can you remedie
A mayme so dangerous and incurable?

Corn. There is a way: but walls have eares and eyes.
Your eare, my Lord, and counsell.

Mart.   I have eares
Open to such discourse, and counsell apt,   180
And to the full recovery of these wounds
Made in the sick state, most effectual.
A word in private.

Enter PERIDURE *and* VIGENIUS.

Perid. Come brother, I am tyrde with revelling,
My last Caranta made me almost breathlesse.
Doth not the Kings last wench foote it with art?

Vige. Oh rarely, rarely, and beyond opinion.
I like this state where all are Libertines
But by ambitions pleasure and large will.—
See, see, two of our strict-lived Counsellors   190
In secret conference: they cannot indure
This freedome.

Perid.   Nor the rule of Archigallo
Because tis subject to his libertie.
Are they not plotting now for some installement
And change of state? Old gallants, if you be
Twill cost your heads.

Vige. Bodies and all for me.

List them ; such strict reproovers should not live
Their austere censures on their kings to give.
    Corn. He must then be deposd.
    Perid. Ey, are you there? that word sounds treason.   200
    Vig. Nay, but farther heare.
    Mart. The King deposd, how must it be effected?
What strengths and powers can sodenly be levied?
Who will assist this busines, to reduce
The state to better forme and government?
    Vig. Ey mary, more of that.
    Corn. All Cornwells at my becke ; Devonshire our neighbour
Is one with us ; you in the North command.
The oppressed, wrongd, dejected and supprest
Will flock on all sides to this innovation :
The Clergie late despisd, the Nobles scornd,   210
The Commons trode on, and the Law contemnd,
Will lend a mutuall and combyned power
Unto this happie change.
    Perid. Oh monstrous treason !
    Mart. My Lord, we are betraide and over-heard
By the two princes.
    Corn. How? betraide?
    Mart. Our plots discovered.
    Corn. Ile helpe it all ; doe you but sooth me up
Wele catch them in the trap they lay for us.
    Mart. Ile doot.
    Corn. Now sir, the King deposd
Who shall succeed?
    Mart.   Some would say *Elidure*.

Corn. Tush, he's too milde to rule.   220
But there are two young princes, hopefull youths
And of rare expectation in the Land.
Oh, would they daigne to beare this weightie charge
Betwixt them, and support the regal sceptre
With joynt assistance, all our hopes were full!

Vig. A sceptre!

Perid.   And a crown!

Mart. What if we make the motion? We have wills
To effect it, we have power to compasse it.

Vig. And if I make refusall, heaven refuse me.

Perid. These Counsellors are wise, and see in us   230
More vertue then we in ourselves discerne.
Would it were come to such election!

Corn. My honord Lord, wele breake it to those princes,
Those hopefull youths, at our convenient leasure.

Mart. With all my hart.

Corn.   You that our footsteps watcht
Shall in the depth of your owne wiles be catcht.   [*Exeunt.*

Vig. A King!

Perid. And were a crowne, a crowne imperiall!

Vig. And sit in state.

Perid.   Command.

Vig.   And be obeyed.

Perid. Our Nobles kneeling.   240

Vig.   Servants homaging
And crying *Ave.*

Perid. Oh brother, shall we through nice folly
Despise the profferd bountie of these Lords?

Vig. Not for the world. I long to sit in state
To purse the bountie of our gracious fate.
Perid. To entertaine forreine Embassadors.
Vig. And have our names ranckt in the course of kings.
Perid. Shadow us, State, with thy majesticke wings!

Enter KING, CORNWELL, MARTIANUS, *and* ELIDURE.

Vige. Now sir, my brother *Archigall* deposde
Corn. Deposd! did you heare that my Lord? 250
Vig. For his licensious rule, and such abuses
As wele pretend gainst him in parliament—
Arch. Oh monstrous brothers!
Elidu.   Oh ambitious youthes!
Vig. Thus wele divide the Land: all beyond Trent
And Humber, shall suffise one moitie:
The southpart of the Land shall make the tother,
Where we will keepe two Courts, and raigne devided,
Yet as deere loving brothers.
Arch. As vild traitors.
Perid. Then Archigall, thou that hast sat in pompe
And seene me vassaile, shalt behold me crownd, 260
Whilst thou with humble knees vailst to my state.
Arch. And when must this be doone? when shall my crowne
Be parted and devided into halfes?
You raigne on this side Humber, you beyond
The river Trent! When do you take your states?
Sit crownd and scepterd to receive our homage
Our dutie, and our humble vassalage?

Perid. I know not when.

Arch.   Nor you?

Vige.   Nor I.

Arch. But I know when you shall repent your pride,
Nor will we use delayes in our revenge.   270
Ambitious boyes, we doome you prisonment;
Your Pallace royall shall a Jaile be made,
Your thrones a dungeon, and your sceptres Irons,
In which wele bound your proude aspiring thoughts.
Away with them, we will not mount our chayre
Till their best hopes be changd to black despaire.

Perid. Heare us excuse ourselves.

Vige.   Or lets discover
Who drew us to this hope of soveraigntie.

Arch. That shall our further leysures arbitrate.
Our eares are deafe to all excusive pleas.   280
Come unambitious brother *Elidurus*,
Helpe us to lavish our abundant treasures
In masks, sports, revells, riots, and strange pleasures.   [*Exeunt*

           Enter SOMEBODY, *with two or three servants.*

Somb. But is it true the fame of Nobody
For vertue, alms-deeds, and for charity
Is so renowned and famous in the country?

Serv. O Lord, sir, ay, he's talkd of far and near
Fills all the boundless country with applause;
There lives not in all Britain one so spoke of
For pity, good mind, and true charity.   290

Som. Which Somebody shall alter e'er 't be long.

Serv. You may, my Lord, being in grace at Court
And the high favours of King Archigallo,
Exile this petty fellow from the land
That so obscures the beauty of your deeds.
  Som. What doth this Nobody?
  Serv.   You shall hear, my Lord.
Come twentie poore men to his gate at once,
Nobody gives them mony meate and drinke;
If they be naked, clothes. Then come poore souldiers
Sick, maymd and shot, from any forraine warres,   300
Nobody takes them in, provides them harbor,
Maintaines their ruind fortunes at his charge.
He gives to orphants, and for widdowes buildes
Almes-houses, Spittles, and large Hospitals:
And when it comes in question, who is apt
For such good deeds, tis answerd, *Nobody*.
Now *Nobodie* hath entertaind againe
Long banisht Hospitalitie, and at his boord
A hundred lustie yeomen daily waites,
Whose long backs bend with weightie chynes of biefe   310
And choise of cheere, whose fragments at his gate
Suffice the generall poore of the whole shire.
Nobodies table's free for travellers,
His buttry and his seller ope to all
That starve with drought, or thirst upon the way.
  Somb. His fame is great; how should we helpe it?
  Serv. My Lord, tis past my reach, tis you must doe it,
Or 't must be left undone.
  Somb.   What deedes of note

Is he els famous for?

Serv.   My Lord, Ile tell you.
His Barnes are full, and when the Cormorants   320
And welthy Farmers hoord up all the graine
He empties all his Garners to the poore
Under the stretcht prise that the market yeelds.
Nobody racks no rents, doth not oppresse
His tenants with extortions. When the King
Knighted the lustie gallants of the Land
Nobody then made daintie to be knighted,
And indeed kept him in his known estate.

  Somb. The slave's ambitious, and his life I hate.

  Serv. How shall we bring his name in publick scandall?   330

  Sombo. Thus it shall be, use my direction.
In Court and country I am *Sombody*,
And therefore apt and fit to be employed:
Goe thou in secrete, beeing a subtile knave,
And sowe seditious slaunders through the Land.
Oppresse the poore, suppresse the fatherlesse,
Deny the widdowes foode, the starv'd releefe;
And when the wretches shall complaine their wrongs,
Beeing cald in question, sweare twas *Nobody*.
Racke rents, raise prises,   340
Buy up the best and choise commodities
At the best hand, then keepe them till their prises
Be lifted to their height, and double rate;
And when the raisers of this dearth are sought,
Though *Sombody* doe this, protest and sweare
Twas *Nobody*, fore Judge and Magistrate:

Bring scandalls on the rich, raise mutinous lyes
Upon the state, and rumors in the Court,
Backbite and sow dissention amongst friends,
Quarrels mongst neighbors, and debate mongst strangers,   350
Set man and wife at ods, kindred at strife;
And when it comes in question, to cleere us
Let every one protest and sweare for one,
And so the blame will fall on *Nobody*.
About it then; if these things well succeede
You shall prevaile, and we applaude your speede.

Enter NOBODY *and the Clowne.*

See where he comes: I will withdraw and see
The event and fortunes of our last pollicie.

Nobod. Come on, myne owne servaunt, some newes, some newes, what report have I in the country? how am I talkt on in the Citty, and what fame beare I in the Court?   361

Clowne. Oh Maister, you are halfe hangd.

Nobod. Hangd, why man?

Clowne. Because you have an ill name: a man had as good almost serve no Maister as serve you. I was carried afore the constable but yesterday, and they tooke mee up for a stravagant: they askt me whom I served; I told them *Nobody:* they presently drew me to the post, and there gave me the law of armes.

Nobody. The law of armes?

Clow. Ey, as much lawe as their armes were able to lay on; they tickled my Collifodium; I rid post for a quarter of an houre, with switch though not with spurre.   372

Nobod. Sure *Sombody* was the cause of all.

Clow. Ile be sworne of that. *Sombody* tickled me a heate, and that I felt. But Maister, why doe you goe thus out of fashion? you are even a very hoddy doddy, all breech.

Nobod. And no body. But if my breeches had as much cloth in them as ever was drawne betwixt Kendall and Canning street, they were scarce great enough to hold all the wrongs that I must pocket. Fie fie, how I am slaunderd through the world. 380
Nobody keepes tall fellowes at his heeles,
Yet if you meete a crew of rogues and beggars,
Aske who they serve, theile aunswere, *Nobody.*
Your Cavaliers and swaggerers bout the towne
That dominere in Taverns, sweare and stare,
Urge them upon some termes: theile turne their malice
To me, and say theile fight with *Nobody;*
Or if they fight, and *Nobody* by chaunce
Come in to part them, I am sure to pay for it,
And *Nobody* be hurt when they scape scotfree: 390
And not the dastardst coward in the world
But dares a bout[1] with me. What shall I doe?

Somb. Doe what thou wilt, before we end this strife
Ile make thee tenne times weary of thy life.

Clown. But do you heare Maister, when I have serv'd you a yere or two, who shall pay me my wages?

Nobo. Why, *Nobody.*

Clowne. Indeede if I serve *Nobody*, *Nobody* must pay me my wages, therefore Ile even seeke out *Sombody* or other to get me a new service; but the best is, Maister, if you runne away, you are easie to be found againe. 401

[1] *orig.* about

Nobod. Why so sir?

Clowne. Mary, aske a deafe man whom hee heares, heele straignt say *Nobody*, aske the blindest beetle that is, whom hee sees, and heele aunswere *Nobodie*. He that never saw in his life can see you, though you were as little as a moate; and hee that never heard can heare you, though you treade as softlie as a Mouse, therefore I shall be sure never to loose you. Besides you have one commoditie, Maister, which none hath besides you; if you should love the most fickle and inconstants wench that is in the world, sheele be true to *Nobody*, therefore constant to you.   411

Nobod. And thou sayest true in that my honest servant.
Besides, I am in great especiall grace
With the King *Archigallo* that now raignes
In tiranny and strange misgoverment.
Nobody loves him, and he loves *Nobody*.
But that which most torments my troubled soule,
My name is made mere opposite to vertue;
For he is onely held peacefull and quiet
That quarrels, brawles and fights with *Nobody*.   420
He 's honest held that lies with *Nobodies* wife,
And he that hurts and injures *Nobody*,
All the world saies, ey, thats a vertuous man.
And though a man have doone a thousand mischiefes,
And come to prove the forfeit made to law,
If he can prove he hath wrong'd *Nobody*,
No man can touch his life. This makes me mad,
This makes me leave the place where I was bred,
And thousand times a day to wish me dead.

Somb. And Ile pursue thee where so ere thou fliest,   430

Nor shalt thou rest in England till thou diest.

Clowne. Maister, I would wish you to leave the Country, and see what good entertainement you will have in the Cittie. I do not think but there you will be most kindly respected. I have been there in my youth; there's Hospitalitie, and you talke of Hospitalitie, and they talke of you, bomination to see. For there, Maister, come to them as often as you will, foure times a day, and theyle make *Nobody* drinke; they love to have *Nobody* trouble them, and without good securitie they will lend *Nobody* mony. Come into Birchin Lane, theyle give *Nobody* a sute, chuse where hee list; goe into Cheapeside, and *Nobody* may take up as much plate as he can carrie. 442

Nobod. Then Ile to London, for the Country tires me
With exclamations and with open wrongs.
Sith in the Cittie they affect me so.

Clowne. O Maister, there I am sure *Nobody* may have anie thing without mony; *Nobody* may come out of the Tavern without paying his reckoning at his pleasure.

Enter a man meeting his wife.

Nobody. Thats better then the Country. Who comes heere?
Man. Minion, where have you been all this night? 450
Wife. Why do you aske, husband?
Man. Because I would know, wife.
Wife; I have beene with *Nobody.*
Nobod. Tis a lie good man, beleeve her not, shee was not with mee.
Man. And who hath layne with you to-night?
Wife. Lye with me, why *Nobody.*

Nobod. Oh monstrous, they would make me a whore-maister.
Man. Well, I doe not thinke but *Sombody* hath been with you.
Sombo. *Sombody* was indeed. 460
Wife. Gods life, husband, you doe me wrong, I lay with *Nobody*.
Man. Well minion, though *Nobody* beare the blame,
Use it no more, least *Sombody* bide the shame.
Nobod. I will endure no longer in this Clymate,
It is so full of slaunders. Ile to the Cittie,
And there performe the deedes of charitie.

Enter the 2 man and a prentice.

2. *Man.* Now, you rascall, who have you beene withal at the ale-house?
Prent. Sooth, I was with *Nobody*.
Nobod. Not with me. 470
2 *Man.* And who was drunke there with you?
Prent. Sooth, *Nobody* was drunke with me.
Nobod. O intollerable! they would make me a drunkard to[o].
I cannot indure any longer, I must hence;
No patience with such scandals can dispence.
2 *Man.* Well sirra, if I take you so againe, Ile so belabour you;
O neighbour, good morrow.
1. *Man.* Good morrow.
2 *Man.* You are sad, me thinkes. 479
1 *Man.* Faith sir, I have cause; I have lent a friend of mine a hundred pounde, and have *Nobodyes* worde for the payment; bill nor bond, nor any thing to shew.
2. *Man.* Have you *Nobodies* worde? Ile assure you that Nobodie is a good man; a good man, I assure you, neighbor; *Nobodie*

will keepe his worde; *Nobodies* worde is as good as his bond.

 1. *Man.* Ey, say you so? nay then, lets drinke down sorrow;
If none would lend, then *Nobody* should borrow.

 Nobody. Yet there's one keepes a good tongue in his head,
That can give *Nobody* a good report;
I am beholding to him for his praise.   490
But since my man so much commends the Cittie,
Ile thether, and, to purchase me a name,
Take a large house of infinite receipt,
There keepe a table for all good spirits,
And all the chimneyes shall cast smoake at once:
There Ile give schollers pensions, Poets gold,
Arts their deserts, Philosophy due praise,
Learning his merrit, and all worth his meede.
There Ile release poore prisoners from their dungeons,
Pay Creditors the debts of other men,   500
And get myself a name mongst Cittizens,
That after-times, pertakers of all blisse,
May thus record, *Nobody* did all this.
Country, farewell, whose slaunderous tongues I flie!
The Cittie now shall lift my name on hie.

 Sombody. Whether Ile follow thee with Swallowes wings
And nimble expedition, there to raise
New brawles and rumors to eclipse thy praise.
Those subtile slie insinuating fellowes
Whom *Sombody* hath sent into the country   510
To rack, transport, extort, and to oppresse,
Will I call home, and all their wits employ
Against this publique Benefactor, knowne

Honest, for all the rumors by us sowne.
But howsoever, I am sworne his foe,
And opposite to all his meriting deedes.
This way must doe; though my devining thoughts
This augurie, amidsts their changes have,
That Sombody will at length be proov'd a knave.   [*Exeunt*

Enter QUEEN, SICOPHANT *and* LADY ELIDURE *severallie.*

Sicoph. Good day to you both, faire Ladies!   520
But fairest of them both, my gratious Queene!
Good day to your high Majestie! and madam,
The royall Lady of great *Elidure*,
My Soveraignes brother, unto you I wish
This morning proove as gracious and as good.

Queene. Those greetings from the Lady *Elidure*
Would pleasingly sound in our princely eares.

Lady. Such greetings from great *Archigalloes* queene
Would be most gratious to our princely eare.

Queene. What, no good morrow, and our grace so neere?   530
Reach me my glove.[1]

Lady.   Whom speakes this woman to?

Queene. Why, to my subject, to my waiting maid;
Am I not mightie *Archigalloes* queene?
Is not my Lord the royall English King?
Thy husband and thy selfe my servitors?

Lady. Is my Coach ready? where are all my men

---

[1] Compare II. Hen. VI., I. iii. l. 141, where the Queen tells the Duchess of Gloucester to pick up her fan, and gives her a box on the ear—pretending to take her for some one else.

That should attend upon our awfull frowne?
What, not one neere?

   Queene.   Minion, my glove.
   Sicoph. Madam, her highnes glove.
   Lady. My scarfe is falne, one of you reach it up.   540
   Queene. You heare me?
   Lady. Painted Majesty, begone!
I am not to be countercheekt by any.

   Queen. Shall I beare this?
   Sicoph.   Be patient, I will schoole her.
Your excellence greatly forgets your selfe
To be so dutilesse unto the Queene;
I have seene the world; I know what 'tis to obey
And to commaund. What if it please the Queene
That you her subject should attend on her
And take her glove up, is it meete that I   550
Should stoope for yours? You're proud, fie, fie, you're proud!
This must not be twixt two such royall sisters
As you by marriage are; go to, submit,
Her Majestie is easie to forgive.

   Lady. Sawcie Lord, forbeare; there's for your exhortation!
                             [*Strikes him, see p.* 297.]
   Queene. I cannot beare this, tis insufferable:
Ile to the King; and if he save thy life,
He shall have mine: madnes and wrath attend,
My thoughts are leveld at a bloody end.   [*Exit.*
   Lady. Shee's shadow;   560
We the true substance are: follow her those
That to our greatnesse dare themselves oppose.

Enter CORNWELL, MARTIANUS, MORGAN *and* MALGO.

Cornw. Helth to your Ladiship, I would say Queene
If I might have my minde, bir lady, Ladie.
Mart. I had a sute unto the King with this Lord
For the great office of high Seneshall,
Because of our good service to the state.
But he in scorne, as he doth every thing,
Hath tane it from us both, and gin 't a foole.
Morg. To a Sicophant, a courtly parasite.   570
Sicoph. Beare witnes, Madam, Ile goe tell the King
That they speake treason.
Malgo.   Passe upon our swords,
You old exchecker of all flatterie.
I tell thee, *Archigallo* shall be deposd,
And thou disroab'd of all thy dignitie.
Sicoph. I hope not so.
Cornw.   See heere the Counsels hands,
Subscrib'd to Archigallos overthrow.
The names of sixteene royall English Peeres
Joynd in a league that is inviolate;
And nothing wants, but *Elidurus* grant   580
To accept the kingdome when the deede is done.
Sicoph. Nay then, Ile take your parts, and joyne with you.
Mart. We will not have a Clawbacks hand comixt
With such heroick peeres.
Sicoph.   I hope, my Lady
Is not of their minds. My most gratious Queene,
What I did speake in reprehensive sort

Was more because her Majestic was present,
Then any offence of yours, and so esteeme it.
God knowes I love your highnes and these Lords.
 Lady. Which of you will persuade my *Elidure*   590
To take upon him Englands royaltie?
 Mart. Madam, we all have so importund him,
Laying unto his judgement every thing
That might attract his sences to the crowne;
But he, frost-braind, will not be obtaind
To take upon him this Realmes government.
 Malg. Hee is the verie soule of lenitie.
If ever moderation liv'd in any,
Your Lord with that rich vertue is possest.
 Lady. This mildnes in him makes me so despisd   600
By the proude Queene, and by her favourits.

Enter ELIDURE

 Cornw. See, Maddam, where he comes, reading a booke.
 Lady. My Lord and husband, with your leave, this booke
Is fitter for an Universitie,
Than to be lookt on, and the Crowne so neere.
You know these Lords, for tyrannie, have sworne
To banish *Archigallo* from the throne,
And to invest you in the royaltie:
Will you not thanke them, and with bounteous hands
Sprinckle their greatnes with the names of Earles,   610
Dukes, Marquesses, and other higher terms?
 Elid. My deerest love, the essence of my soule,
And you my honord Lords; the sute you make,

Though it be just for many wrongs imposd,
Yet unto me it seemes an injurie.
What is my greatnes by my brothers fall,
But like a starved body[1] nourished
With the destruction of the other lymbes?
Innumerable are the griefes that waite
On horded treasures, then much more on Crownes.   620
The middle path, the golden meane for me!
Leave me obedience, take you Majestie.

   Lady. Why, this is worser to my lofty minde
Then the late checks given by the angry Queene.

   Corn. If you refuse it, knowe we are determined
To lay it elsewhere.

   Lady.   On your younger brother,
And then no doubt we shall be awde indeed,
When the ambition of the elders wife
Can scarsly give our patience any bounds.
England is sicke of pride and tirrany,   630
And in thy goodnes only to be curde.
Thou art cald foorth amongst a thousand men
To minister this soveraigne Antidote;
To amend thy brothers cruelty with love;
And if thou wilt not from oppression free
Thy native Country, thou art vilde as he.

   Elid. I had rather stay his leasure to amend.

   Lady. Men, heaven, gods, devills, what power should I invoke
To fashion him anew? Thunder, come downe!
Crowne me with ruine, since not with a Crowne.   640

   [1] *Qu.* belly?

Corne. Long life unto the Kingly *Elidure!*
Trumpets, proclaim it, whether he will or no.
  Lady. For that conceit, Lords, you have wonne my hart.
In his despight let him be straight waies Crownd,
That I may triumph while the trumpets sound.
  Elid. Carry me to my grave, not to a Throne!
  Lady. Helpe, Lords, to seate him! nay, helpe every one!
So should the Majestie of England sit,
Whilst we in like state do associate him.
  Elid. Never did any less desire to raigne   650
Then I; heaven knowes this greatnes is my paine.
  Lady. Paine me in this sort, great Lords, every day;
Tis sweete to rule.
  Elid.   Tis sweeter to obay.
  Cornw. Live King of England long and happily!
As long and happily your Highnes live!
  Lady. We thanke you, Lords; now call in the deposd!
Him and his proud Queen, bring unto our sight,
That in her wrongs we may have our delight.

Enter ARCHIGALLO *and his* QUEENE *bound.*

  Archi. Betrayd, tane prisoner, and by those that owe
To me their duty and allegiance!   660
My brother, the usurper of the Crowne!
Oh, this is monstrous, most insufferable!
  Elid. Good brother, grieve not! tis against my will
That I am made a King. Pray take my place;
I had rather be your subject then your Lord.
  Lady. So had not I; sit still my gracious Lord,

Whilst I looke through this Tyrant with a frowne.
Minion, reach up my glove.

    Queene. Thinkst thou because
Thy husband can dissemble piety,   670
And therein hath deposd my royall Lord,
That I am lesser in estate than Queene?
No, thine owne answere lately given to me
I thus revet.[1] Stoope thou, proud Queene, for me!

    Sicoph. Nay then, as I did lately to her Highnes,
I must admonish you. Dejected lady,
You do forget yourself, and where you are.
Duty is debt; and it is fit, since now
You are a subject, to beare humble thoughts.
Follow my counsell, Lady, and submit;   680
Her Majestie no doubt will pardon it.

    Queene. There's for your paines!   [*Strikes him*
    Sicoph.   Which way soere I goe,
I have it heere, whether it ebbe or flowe.

    Lady. That pride of thine shall be thy overthrowe.
And thus I sentence them.

    Elid.   Leave that to me.

    Lady. No, you are too mild; judgment belongs to me.
Thou, *Archigallo*, for thy tirannie,
For ever be excluded from all rule
And from thy life!

    Elid.   Not from his life, I pray.

    Lady. He unto whom the greatest wrongs are done,   690
Dispatch him quickly.

---

[1] revert.

Morg. That will I.

Malg. Or I.

Elid. And therein, Lords, effect my tragedie.

Lady. Why strike you not? Oh, tis a dangerous thing
To have a living subject of a King:
Much treason may be wrought, when in his death
Our safety is secur'd.

Elid. Banish him rather. Oh sweete, spare his life!
He is my brother.

Archi. Crownd, and pray thy wife?

Elid. Oh brother, if you roughly speake, I knowe
There is no hope but your sure overthrowe.   700
Pray be not angry with me for my love.
To banishment! since it must needes be so.
His life I give him, whosoere saies no.

Lady. What? and his Ladies to?

Elid. I, hers and all.

Lady. But Ile not have you banisht with the King.
No, minion, no, since you must live, be assur'd
Ile make thee meanest of my waiting Maides.

Queene. I scorne thy pride.

Archi. Farewell, deceiving state!
Pride-making Crowne! my deerest wife, farewell!   710
I have been a Tyrant, and Ile be so still.   [*Exit.*

Elid. Alas, my brother!

Lady. Dry up childish teares,
And to these Lords that have invested you,
Give gracious lookes and honorable deedes.

Elid. Give them my Crowne, oh, give them all I have!

The¹ throne I reckon but a glorious grave.
   Lady. Then from my selfe these dignities receive.
The Iland wrested from you, I restore;
See it be given them backe, Lord Sicophant.
The office of hie Seneschall bereft you,   720
My Lord of *Cornwell*, to your grace we give.
You, *Martianus*, be our Treasurer;
And if we find you faithfull, be assured
You shall not want preferment at our hands.
Meanetime this office we impose on you;
Be Tutor to this Lady; and her pride,
With your learnd principles whereof you are full,
Turne to humility, or vex her soule.
   Queene. Torment on torment! tutord by a foole!
   Sicoph. Madam, it is her Highnes will; be pleased.   730
   Lady. Young *Peridurus* and *Vigenius*, Lords,
Release from prison; and because your King
Is mightely affected unto Yorke,
Thether dismisse the Court incontinent.
   Sicoph. Shall it be so, my Liedge?
   Lady.   Are not we King?
His silence saies it; and what we ordaine,
Who dares make question of? This day for ever
Thorough our raigne be held a festivall,
And tryumphe, Lords, that England is set free
From a vild tyrant and his crueltie.   740
   Elid. On to our funerall; tis no matter where:
I sin I knowe, in suffering pride so neere.   [*Exeunt*

¹ Ed. Thy.

Enter NOBODY *and the Clowne.*

Nobody. Ahem boy, Nobody is sound yet, for all his troubles.

Clow. And so is Nobodies man, for all his whipping. But Maister, we are now in the Citty, wald about from slaunder; there cannot a lie come in but it must runne thorough bricke, or get the good will of the warders, whose browne bills looke blew upon all passengers.

Nobody. O this Citty, if Nobody live to be as old againe, be it spoken in secret, 750
Ile have fenst about with a wall of brasse.—

Clowne. Of Nobodies making—that will be rare.

Nobody. Ile bring the Tems through the middle of it, empty Moore-ditch at my own charge, and build up Paules-steple without a collection. I see not what becomes of these collections.

Clowne. Why, Nobody receaves them.

Nobody. I, knave?

Clowne. You, knave: or as the world goes, Somebody receives all, and Nobody is blamd for it.

Nobody. But is it rumord so thorough out the Citty? 760

Clowne. Doe not you knowe that? Theres not an orphants portion lost out of the Chamber, but Nobody has got it; no Corne transported without warrant, but Nobody has donne it; no goods stolne but by Nobody, no extortion without Nobody: and but that truth will come to light, fewe wenches got with child, but with Nobody.

Nobody. Nay, thats by Somebody.

Clowne. I thinke Somebody had a hand in 't, but Nobody some times paies for the nursing of it. 769

Nobody. Indeede I have taken into my charge many a poore infant left to the almes of the wide world; I have helpt many a vertuous maide to a good husband, and nere desird her maiden-head: redeemed many Gentlemens lands, that have thankt Nobody for it; built Pest-houses and other places of retirement in the sicknes time[1] for the good of the Cittie, and yet *Nobody* cannot get a good word for his labor.

   Clowne. Tis a mad world, Maister.[2]

   Nobody. Yet this mad world shall not make me mad. I am All spirit, *Nobody*. Let them grieve
That scrape for wealth; I will the poore relieve.   780
Where are the Maisters of the severall prisons
Within and neere adjoyning to the Citty?
That I may spred my charity abroad.

   Clowne. Heere they be Sir.

Enter three or four.

   Nobody.   Welcome, gentlemen!
You are they that make poore men housholders
Against their wills, and yet doe them no wrong:
You have the actions and the cases of your sides,
Whilst your Tenants in comon want money to fill them.
How many Gentlemen of lesse revenewes than *Nobody*
Lie in your Knights ward for want of maintenance?   790

   1. I am, Sir, a Keeper of the Counter, and there are in our wards above a hundred poore prisoners, that are like nere to come foorth without satisfaction.

   Nobody. But *Nobody* will be their benefactor. What in yours?

   3. Double the number, and in the Gayle.

---

[1] Years of plague were 1593 and 1603.
[2] Middleton's 'A mad world, my Maisters,' was published in 1608.

Nobody. Talke not of the Gayle; tis full of limetwigs, lifts, and pickpockets.

1. Is it your pleasure, Sir, to free them all?

Nobody. All that lie in for debt.

2. Ten thousand pound, and ten to that, will not doe it.   800

Nobody. Nobody, Sir, will give a hundred thousand,
Ten hundred thousand! *Nobody* will not have a prisoner,
Because they all shall pray for *Nobody*.

Clowne. Tis great pitty my Maister has no body, and so kind a hart.

[*A noise within. Follow, follow, follow.*

Nobody. What outcries that?

Enter SOMEBODY, *with two or three.*

Somebody. This is the gallant, apprehend him straight.
Tis he that sowes sedition in the Land
Under the couler of being charitable.
When search is made for such in every Inne,   810
Though I have seene them housd, the Chamberlaine,
For gold, will answere there is *Nobody*.
He for all bankrouts is a common baile;
And when the execution should be servd
Upon the sureties, they find *Nobody*:
In private houses, who so apt to lie
As those that have beene taught by *Nobody*?
Servants forgetfull of their Maisters friends,
Being askt how many were to speake with him
Whilst he was absent, they say, *Nobody*.   820
Nobody breakes more glasses in a house

Then all his wealth hath power to satisfie.
If you will free this Citty then from shame,
Sease *Nobody*, and let him beare the blame.
    Const. Lay hold upon him.
    Nobody. What, on *Nobody?* Give me my sword, my morglay!
My friends, you that doe know how innocent I am,
Draw in my quarrell, succor Nobody!
What? Nobody but Nobody remaining?
    Clowne. Yes Maister, I, Nobodies man.   830
    Nobody. Stand to me nobly then, and feare them not!
Thy Maister Nobody can take no wounds.
Nobody is no coward; Nobody
Dares fight with all the world.
    Somebody.   Upon them, then.
    [*a fight betwixt Somebody and Nobody; Nobody escapes*]
What, has he scapt us?
    Const.   He is gone, my Lord.
    Somb. It shall be thus, now you have seene his shape:
Let him be straight imprinted to the life;
His picture shall be set on every stall,
And proclamation made, that he that takes him
Shall have a hundred pounds of *Sombody*.   840
Country and Citty I shall thus set free,
And have more roome to worke my villanie.   [*Exeunt.*
    Nobody. What? are they gone? Then, Citty, now adew;
Since I have taken such great injury
For my good life within thy government,
No more will *Nobody* be charitable,
No more will *Nobody* relieve the poore.

Honor your Lord and Maister *Somebody*,
For *Somebody* is he that wrongs you all.
Ile to the Court; the changing of the ayre   850
May peradventure change my injuries.
And if I speede no better, being there,
Yet say that Nobody liv'd every-where.   [*Exit.*

Enter ARCHIGALLO.

Archi. I was a King, but now I am [a] slave.
How happie were I in this base estate
If I had never tasted royaltie !
But the remembrance that I was a king,
Unseasons the content of povertie.
I heare the hunters musicke; heere Ile lie
To keepe me out of sight till they passe by.   860

Enter MORGAN and MALGO

Morgan. The stag is hearded; come, my Lord,
Shall we to horse, and single him againe ?
Malgo. Content, the King will chase; the day is spent
And we have kild no game.   To horse, away !   [*Exeunt*

Enter ELIDURE

Elid. Hearded,? goe single him, or couple straight,
He will not fall to day.   What fellowes this ?
Archi. I am a man.
Elid.   A banisht man, I thinke.
My brother *Archigallo*, ist not so ?
Archi. Tis so, I am thy brother, *Elidure ;*

All that thou hast is mine; the Crowne is mine, 870
Thy royaltie is mine; these hunting pleasures
Thou doost usurpe. Ambitious *Elidure*,
I was a King.

   Elidu. And I may be a wretch! Poore Archigallo!
The sight of thee, that wert my Soveraigne,
In this estate, drawes rivers from mine eyes.
Will you be King againe? If they agree,
Ile redeliver all my royaltie,
Save what a second brother and a subject,
Keepes in an humble bosome; for I sweare 880
The Crowne is yours that *Elidure* doth weare.

   Arch. Then give it me; use not the common sleights
To pittie one, and keepe away his right.
Seest thou these ragges? Do they become my person?
O *Elidure*, take pittie on my state,
Let me not still live thus infortunate.

   Elidu. Alas, if pittie could procure your good,
Insteed of water, Ide weepe teares of blood,
To expresse both love and pittie. Say, deere brother,
I should uncrowne my selfe, the angry Peeres 890
Will never let me reach the imperiall wreathe
To *Archigalloes* head. There's ancient *Cornwell*,
Stout *Martianus*, *Morgan*, and bold *Malgo*,
From whom you tooke the pleasant Southerne Ile,
Will never kneele to you: what should I say?
Your tirannie was cause of your decay.

   Arch. What! shall I die then? Welcome be that fate,
Rather then still live in this wretched state!

Enter CORNWELL, MARTIANUS, MORGAN *and* MALGO.

Corn. Yonders the King. My soveraigne, you have lost
The fall of a brave stagg; he's dead, my liedge. 900
What fellow 's this?
  Elidu.   Knowest him not, Cornwell?
  Corn. No, my liedge, not I.
  Arch.   I am thy King.
  Elid. Tis *Archigallo*, man.
  Corn. Thou art no King of mine; thou art a traytor;
Thy life is forfeit by thy stay in Brittaine.
Wert thou not banisht?
  Elidu.   Noble *Cornwell*, speake
More gently, or my piteous hart will breake.
Lord *Martianus, Morgan,* and the rest,
I am awearie of my government,
And willinglie resigne it to my brother. 910
  Mart. Your brother was a tyrant, and my knee
Shall never bow to wrong and tirannie.
  Elidu. Yet looke upon his misery. His teares
Argue repentance. Thinke not, honourd Lords,
The feare of dangers waiting on my Crowne
Makes me so willing to resigne the same;
For I am lov'd, I know : But justice bids.
I make a resignation; 'tis his right;
My call 's but usurpation.
  Corn.   *Elidure,*
If you are wearie of your government, 920
Wele set the Crowne upon a strangers head

Rather then *Archigallo*. Harke ye, Lords,
Shall we make him our King, we did depose?
So might our heads be chopt of. Ile loose mine,
Ere my poore Country shall endure such wrongs
As that injurious tyrant plagues her with.

Mor. Keepe still your Crowne, my Liedge; happy is Brittaine
Under the government of *Elidure*.

Arch. Let it be so.
Death is the happy period of all woe. 930
The wretch thats torne upon the torturing wrack
Feeles not more devilish torment than my hart,
When I but call to minde my tirannie.
I record heaven,[1] my Lords, my brothers sight,
The pittie that he takes of my distresse,
Your love and true allegiance unto him,
Hath wrought in me a reconciled spirit.
I doe confesse my sinne, and freely say
I did deserve to be deposd.

Elidu. Alas good Prince! my honorable Lords, 940
Be not flint-harted! pitty Archigallo!
I know his penitentiall words proceede
From a remorcefull spirit. Ile ingage
My life upon his righteous government.
Good *Cornwell*, gentle *Martianus*, speake!
Shall *Archigallo* be your King againe?

Arch. By heaven, I not desire it.

Elidu.   See, my Lords,

[1] I call heaven to witness, my Lords, that the sight presented by my brother, &c.—G.

Hee's not ambitious. As thou lov'st me, *Cornwell*,
As thou didst love our Father, let his sonne
Be righted; give him backe the government   950
You tooke from him.

   Corn. What should I say? faith, I shall fall a weeping;
Therefore speake you.

   Elid.   Lord *Martianus*, speake.

   Mart. What say these Lords that have been wrongd by him.

   Elidu. Morgan and *Malgo*, all I have in Brittaine
Shall be ingag'd to you, that *Archigallo*
Will never more oppresse you, nor impose
Wrong on the meanest subject in the Land.

   Morg. Then weele embrace his government.

   Elidu.   Saies *Malgo* so?

   Malg. I doe my Lord.

   Elidu.   What saies *Martianus?*   960

   Mar. Faith, as my Lord of *Cornwell*.

   Corn. I say that I am sorry, he was bad,
And now am glad hee's chang'd. His wickednes
We punisht, and his goodnes, there's great reason
Should be rewarded. Therefore, Lords, set on.
To Yorke then, to his Coronation.

   Elidu. Then happie *Elidurus*, happie day!
That takes from me a kingdomes cares away.

   Arch. And happie *Archigallo*, that have rangd
From sin to sin, and now at last am changd!   970
My Lords and friends, the wrongs that you have seene
In me, my future vertues shall redeeme.
Come, gentle brother! Pittie, that should rest

In women most, is harbor'd in thy brest.   [*Exeunt.*

Enter QUEENE, LADY ELIDURE, *and Flatterer.*

Lady. Come, have you done your taske? Now doe you see
What 'tis to be so proude of Majestie?
We must take up your glove, and not be thought
Worthy the name of Sister! Thus, you minx,
Ile teach you ply your worke, and thanke me to:
This paines will be your owne, another day.   980

Queene. Insulting, over-proude, ambitious woman—
Queene I disdaine to call thee,—thou dost wrong
Thy brothers wife, indeed thy Kings espousd;
And mauger all thy tyrannie, I sweare,
Rather then still live thus, Ile perrish heere.

Sicoph. You are not wise, dejected as you are,
To bandie braves against her Majestie.
You must consider you are now her subject.
Your tongue is bounded by the awe of dutie.
Fie, fie; I needes must chide you, since I see   990
You are so sawcie with her soveraigntie.

Queene. Time was, base spaniell, thou didst fawne as much
On me, as now thou strivest to flatter her.
O God, that one born noble should be so base,[1]
His generous blood to scandall all his race!

Lady. My Lord, if she continue these proude terms,
I give you libertie to punish her.
Ile not maintaine my prisoner and my slave
To raile 'gainst any one that honours me.

---

[1] 'Be' is superfluous for sense and metre. 'Base' is 'abase.'

Enter MORGAN *and* MALGO.

Morg. Health to the Queene, and happines to her   1000
That must change states with you, and once more raigne
Queene of this Land.

Queene. Speake that againe, ô I will blesse my fate
If once more I supply my former state.

Malgo. Long may your highnes live. Your banisht Lord
Is by his brother *Elidurus* seated
Once more in Britaines throne.

Lady. O, I could teare my haire! Base *Elidure*,
To wrong himselfe, and make a slave of me.

Queene. Now minion, Ile cry quittance with your pride, 1010
And make you stoope at our imperiall side.
But tell me, *Morgan*, by what accident
You met with my beloved *Archigallo*.

Morg. Even in the woods where we did hunt the stagge,
There did the tender-harted *Elidure*
Meete his distressed Brother, and so wrought
By his importunate speech, with all his Peeres,
That, after much deniall, yet at last,
They yeelded their allegiance to your Lord,
Whom now we must acknowledge our dread King,   1020
And you our princelie Queene.

Lady. Thou Screchowle, Raven, uglie throated slave,
There's for thy newes!   [*She strikes him.*]

Queene.   Restraine her good my Lord.

Sicoph. Fie, madam! fie, fore God, you are to blame,
In presence of my soveraigne ladie Queene

To be thus rude. It would become you better
To shew more dutie to her Majestie.

Lady. O monstrous! was not I thy Queene, but now?

Sicoph. Yes, when your husband was my King, you were.
But now the streame is turnd, and the States currant   1030
Runnes all to *Archigallo*. Blame not me;
Wisedome nere lov'd declined Majestie.

Enter ARCHIGALLO *crownd*, ELIDURE, PERIDURE, VIGENIUS,
    CORNWELL, MARTIANUS *and others.*

Queene. Welcome from banishment, my loving Lord,
Your Kinglie presence wraps my soule to heaven.

Arch. To heaven, and my kind brother *Elidure*,
Faire Queene, we owe chiefe thanks, for this our greatnes.
Next them, these honourable Lords.

Corn.   Great Queene,
Once more the tribute of our bended knees
We pay to you, and humbly kisse your hand.

Mart. So doth *Martianus.*

Perid.   And I.

Vigen.   And I.   1040

Queene. Our brothers, by how much that name exceedes
The name of Lord, so much the more this dutie
Deserves requitall; thanks both, and thanks to all.

Arch. Set on there.   [*Exeunt all but Lady and Sicophant*

Sicoph. Madam, you are not wise to grieve at that
Heaven hath decreed, and the state yeelded to.
No doubt her Majestie will use you well.

Lady. Well, saiest thou? No, I looke that she should treble

All the disgraces I have layd on her.
I shall turne Laundresse now, and learne to starch   1050
And set, and poke, and pocket up such basenes
As never princesse did.   Did you observe
What lookes I cast at *Elidure* my husband?

Sicoph. Your lookes declard the passion of your hart:
They were all fire.

Lady.   Would they had burnt his eyes out,
That hath eclipsd our state and Majestie.

Enter QUEENE, MORGAN, *and* MALGO.

Queene. Bring hether the proude wife of *Elidure*.

Sicop. It shall be done.

Queene. Our shoe string is untied, stoope minion, stoope.

Lady. Ile rather stoope to death, thou moone-like Queene, 1060
New-changd, and yet so proude!   There's those are made
For flexure, let them stoope; thus much[1] Ile doe,
You are my Queene, tis but a debt I owe.

Queene. Bring me the worke there; I will taske you to
That by the howre; spin it, I charge you, doe.

Lady. A distaffe and a spindle, so indeed!
I told you this!   *Diana* be my speede.

Morg. Yet for his Princelie worth that made you Queene,
Respect her, as the wife of *Elidure*.

Enter CORNWELL

Corn. Wheres the Queene?   1070

Queene. What newes with *Cornwell*, why so sad my Lord?

[1] Probable stage action of stiffish obeisance here (as contrasted with stooping to tie the Queen's shoe) not indicated in original.—G.

Corn. Your husband on the suddaine is falne sicke.

Queene. How? sicke?

Lady. Now if it be thy will, sweet blessed heaven,
Take him to mercie!

Quee. Doe not heare her prayers, heaven, I beseech thee!

Enter MARTIANUS

Mart. Madam, his highnes—

Queen. Is he alive or dead?

Mart. Dead, Madam.

Queene. O my hart!

Corn. Looke to the Queene, let us not loose her to.[1]
She breathes, stand of! Where be those wemen there?　　1080
Good Queene that shall be, lends a helping hand,
Helpe to unlace her.

Lady. Ile see her burst first!

Queene. Now, as you love me, let no helping hand
Preserve life in me; I had rather die,
Then loose the title of my soveraigntie.

Lady. Take back your Distaffe—Yet, wele stay our rage,
We will forbeare our spleene, for charitie,
And love unto the dead, till you have hearsd
Your husbands bones. Conduct her, Lords, away;　　1090
Our pride, though eager, yet for foode shall stay.

Sicoph. Wilt please your high imperiall Majestie
Commaund my service; I am humbly yours.

Lady. We doe commaund what we well know youle doe.
Follow the stronger part, and cleave thereto.　　　　[*Exeunt.*

---

[1] i. e. lose her too.

Enter ELIDURE *crownd, all the Lords and Ladies attendants.*

Elidu. Once more our royall temples are ingirt
With Brittaines golden wreath. All-seeing heaven,
Witnes I not desire this soveraigntie.
But since this kingdoms good, and your Decrees
Have laid this heavy[1] loade of common care   1100
On *Elidure*, we shall discharge the same
To your content, I hope, and this Lands fame.
Our brother once interd, we will not stay
But then to Troynovant weele speede away.   *[Exeunt*

Enter two Porters.

1. *Porter.* Come fellow Porter, now the Court is heere
Our gaines will flie upon us like a tide.
Let us make use of time, and whilst theres plentie,
Stirring in Court, still labour to increase
The wealth which by our office we have got.

2 *Porter.* Out of our large alowance we must save   1110
Of thosands that passe by us, and our office;
We will give entertainment to No body.

Enter NOBODY

No-body. My name is *No-body*.

1. *Port.* You are welcome sir. Ere you peruse the Court,
Tast the Kings beere heere at the Porters lodge.
A dish of beere for maister *No-body!*

Nobody. I thanke you sir.

2. *Port.* Heere, maister *No-body*, with all my hart;

[1] *orig.* heaven

A full Carouse, and welcome to our Office.

Nobo. I thanke you, sir: and were your beere tems[1] water,
Yet Nobody would pledge you.   To you sir!   '   1121

1. *Port.* You are a stranger heere, [2]how in the Citty.
Have you bin long in towne?

Nobo. I sir, too long, unlesse my entertaine
Had bin more pleasing; for my life is sought.
I am a harmelesse well dispos'd plaine man,
That injure none, yet what so ere is done
Amisse in London is impos'd on me.
Be it lying, secret theft, or anything
They call abuse, tis done by Nobody.   1130
I am pursued by all, and now am come
To see what safety is within the Court
For a plaine fellow.

2. *Por.* You are welcome hether, sir.
Methinkes you do looke wilde : as if you wanted
Sufficient sleepe.

Nobo.   O do not blame me, sir.
Being pursued, I fled.   Comming through Poules,
There No-body kneeld downe to say his prayers,
And was devout, I wis: comming through Fleetstreet,
There at a tavern doore, two swaggerers   1140
Were fighting; being attacht, twas askt, who gave
The first occasion? twas answered, *nobody*.
The guilt was laid on me, which made me fly
To the Thems side; desired a Waterman

[1] Thames: spelt 'Thems' in l. 1144 below.—G.
[2] for 'how' read 'now.'

To row me thence away to Charing-crosse;
He askt me for his fare; I answered him
I had no money; whats your name? quoth he;
I told him Nobody; then he bad me Welcome:
Said he would carry Nobody for nothing.
From thence I went   1150
To see the law Courts, held at Westminster;
There, meeting with a friend, I straight was askt
If I had any sute?   I answered, yes,
Marry, I wanted money.   Sir, qouth he,
For you, because your name is *Nobody*,
I will sollicit law; and *nobody*,
Assure yourselfe, shall thrive by sutes in Law.
I thankt him, and so came to see the Court,
Where I am very much beholding to your kindnesse.

 1. *Port.* And Maister *nobody*, you are very welcome.   1160
Good fellow, lead him to the Hall.
Will you walke neare the court?

 Nobo. I thanke you sir.   [*Exeunt* NOBODY *and Porters.*

Enter SOMEBODY *and a Bragart.*

 Som. Fie, what a toil it is to find out *nobody*.
I haye dogd him very close, yet is he got into the Court before me.
Sir, you have sworne to fight with *nobody;*
Do you stay heere, and watch at the court gate,
And when you meet him, challenge him the field,
Whilst I set Lime-twigs for him in all Offices.
If either you or I but prosper right,   1170
He needs must fall by policy or slight.   [*Exit*

Brag. I would this round man *nobody* would come.
I, that professe much valor, yet have none,
Cannot but be too hard for *nobody*.
For what can be in *nobody*, unlesse
He be so cald because he is al spirit?
Or say he be all spirit; wanting limbes,
How can this spirit hurt me? Sure he dies;
And by his death my fame shall mount the skies.

Enter NOBODY.

Nobody. By thy leave, my sweet friend,   1180
Theres for thy farewell.

Brag. Stay.

Nobo Thats but one word; let two go to the bargain, if it please you. Why should I stay?

Brag. I challenge thee.

No. I may chuse whither ilc answer your chalenge, by your leave.

Bra. Ile have thee picturd as thy picture, unles thou answer me.

No. For what sir? pray, why wold you have me printed?

Brag. For cowardice.   1190

Nobo. Methinkes, your picture would doe better for the picture of cowardice, then mine sir. But pray, whats your will with me?

Brag. Thou hast abusd one *Somebody.*

Nobo. So have my betters abusd Sombody in their time.

Brag. Ile fight with thee for that.

No. Alas, sir, I am *nobody* at fighting, yet thus much let mee tell you, *nobody* cannot run away: I cannot budge.

Brag. Prepare thee, then, for I will spit thy body upon this weapon.

Nobo. Nay, by faith, that you cannot, for I have no bodye. 1200
Brag. Thy bowels then.
No. They are the fairer mark, a great deal; com on, sir, come on!
Brag. Have at thy bellie.
Nobo. You must either hit that, or nothing.
Brag. Ill kill and quarter thee.
Nobo. Youle hardly find my joynts, I think, to quarter me;
I am so well fed. Come on, sir.

Fight; nobody is downe.

Brag. Now thou art at my mercie.
No. What are you the better to have *nobody* at your mercy?
Brag. Ile kill thee now. 1210
Nobo. I thinke youle sooner kill me then any body. But let me rise againe.
Brag. No, I will let *No-body* rise.
Nobo. Why then let me, sir, I am *no-body*.

Enter Clowne.

Clown. How now, O fates, O heavens, is not that my M?
What shall I do? Be valiant, and reskue my sweet maister.
Avant thou Pagan, Pug, what ere thou be!
Behold I come to set thy prisoner free.
Brag. Fortune, that giddy Goddesse, hath turnd her wheel:
I shall be matcht, thus will I gore you both. 1220
Hold, captains!
Not Hercules himself would fight with two.
I yield.
Clown. Twas your best course. Down, vassall, down!

And kisse my pumpe.

Brag. Tis base, O base!

Clow. Zounds, Ile naile thy lips to limbo, unlesse thou kis.

Brag. Tis done.

Nobo. Thanks, honest servant.

Clow. Zounds, if I say ile doet, ile doet indeed.

Nobo. For this, Ile carry thee into the Court.   1230
Where thou shalt see thy Maister, Nobody,
Hath friends, will bid him welcome.   So farewell.

Clown. Farewell maister Braggart, farewell, farewell.   [*Exeunt.*

Brag. Ile follow, I shall meet with Some-body
That will revenge.   Ile plot, and ert be long,
Ile be reveng'd on Nobody for this wrong.   [*Exit.*

Enter VIGENIUS, PERIDURE *and the* QUEENE.

Queene. Your hopes are great, fair brothers, and your names
Shall, if in this you be advisd by us,
Be rankt in scroule of all the Brittish kings.
Oh take upon you this so weighty charge,   1240
To great to be dischargd by Elidure.

Vig. Deere sister Q. how are we bound to you!
In neerer bonds then a fraternal league,
For this your royall practise to raise us
Unto the height of honor and estate.
Let me no longer breath a prince on earth,
Or thinke me woorthy of your regall blood,
If we imbrace not this high motion.

Perid. Imbrace it brother.   We are all on speed;
My princely thought inflamed with Ardency   1250

Of this imperiall state, and Scepterd rule.
My Kinglie browes itch for a stately Crowne;
This hand, to beare a round Monarchall Globe;
This, the bright sword of Justice and stern aw.
Deere sister, you have made me all on fire;
My kingly thoughts, beyond their bounds aspire.

   Vig. How shall we quit your love, when we ascend
The state of Elidure?

   Queen.   All that I crave
Is but to make the imperious Queene my slave,
That she, that above Justice now commands,   1260
May tast new thraldome, at our royall hands.

   Perid. The Queene is yours. The King shalbe depos'd,
And she disgraded from all Soveraignty.

   Queen. That I might live to see that happy houre,
To have that sterne commandresse in my power!

   Vig. Shees doomd alreadie and at your dispose;
And we, prepard for speedy execution
Of any plot, that may availe our pompe,
Or throne us in the state of Brittany.

               Enter Morgan *and* Malgo.

   Perid. Heere comes the Lords of this pretended league.   1270
How goes our hope? Speake, valiant English[1] Peeres,
Are we in way of Soveraignty? or still stand we
Subjects unto the aw of *Elidure?*

   Mor. Long live the valiant brothers of the King,
With mutual love to weare the Brittish Crowne.

---

[1] 'English' is an oversight for 'British.'

Two thousand Souldiors have I brought from Wales,
To wait upon the princely Peridure.

Malg. As many of my bold confederates
Have I drawn from the South, to sweare allegiance
To young Vigenius.

Vig.   Do but cal me King,   1280
The charming Spheres so sweetly cannot sing.

Malg. To King *Vigenius.*

Vig. Oh, but wheres our Crowne,
That make knees humble when their soveraignes frowne?

Mal. King *Elidurus* shall his state resigne.

Perid. Say *Morgan* so, and *Britains* rule is mine.

Mor. King *Peridure* shall raigne.

Perid. And sit in state?

Morg. And thousand subjects on his glory waite.

Perid. Then they that lifts us to the imperiall seate,   1290
Our powers and will shall study to make great.

Vig. And thou that raisest us, as our best friend,
Shall, as we mount, the like degrees ascend.

Queen. When will you give the attempt?

Perid. Now, royall sister:
Before the King have notice of our plot.
Before the Lords that love his government
Prepare their opposition.

Vig.   Well determined;
And like a king in *Esse*, now, this night,
Lets make a hostile uprore in the Court;   1300
Surprize the King; make ceazure of the Crowne;
Lay hands upon the Counsell, least they scape

To levy forces——Those Lords
That serve the King, and with austere reproofes
Punish the hatefull vices of the Land,
Must not awe us. They shall not raigne. We will
Those that applaud us, raise; despise us, kill.

  Perid. I see a kind of state appeare already
In thy majestick brow. Cal in the souldiors,
Man the Court gates, barricade al the streets,   1310
Defend the waies, the lands[1] and passages;
And girt the pallace with a treble wall
Of armed souldiors; and in dead of night,
When all the peeres ly drownd in golden[2] sleepe,
Sound out a sodaine and a shrill Alarum,
To maze them in the midst of horrid dreames.

  Vig. The King and Crowne is ours!

  Q. The Queen, I claim.

  Perid. It shal go hard, but I the shrew will tame.
Trumpets and drums, your dreadfull clamors sound!   1320

  Vig. Proclaime me captive, or a King new crownd!

Alarum, they watch the doores, Enter at one doore CORNEWELL.

  Corn. Treason, treason!

  Perid. Thou art mine, what ere thou be.

  Corn. Prince Peridure!

  Perid. I, Cornwell, and thy king.

  Corn. He discords taught, that taught thee so to sing.

---

[1] lanes.

[2] 'there golden sleep doth reign.'—*Romeo and Juliet*, II. iii.—G.

Alarum, enter at another doore MARTIANUS.

Mar. Who stops this passage?

Vig. Martianus, we.

Mar. Vigenius?

Vig.   Unto whom thou owest thy knee.

Mar. My knee to none but *Elidure* shall bend.   1330

Vig. Our raign beginning hath when his lines end.

Alarum, Enter at another doore [LADY] ELYDURE, *stopt by the* QUEENE.

Lady. What traitrous hand dares interdict our way?

Queene. Why that dare ours, tis we command thee staie.

Lady. Are we not Queene?

Queene.   Ist you? Then happily met:
I have owed you long, and now Ile pay that dept.

Lady. Vild traitresse, darest thou lay a violent hand
On us thy Queene?

Queene.   We dare commaund thee stand.
Thou wast a Queene, but now thou art a slave.

Lady Before such bondage, graunt me, heaven, a grave!

Alarum, Enter ELIDURE.

Elidure. What seeke ye Lords? What meane these loud
   Alarums,   1340
In the still silence of this hunnied night?

Perid. King, we seeke thee.

Vig.   And more, we seeke thy Crowne.

Elidure. Why, Princely brothers, is it not our owne?

That tis ours, we plead the law of kings,
The guift of heaven, and the antiquety on earth,
Election from them both.

Vig. We plead our powers and strength, we two must raign.

Perid. We were borne to rule, and homage we disdaine.

Corn. Do not resigne, good King.

Perid.   How, saucy Lord?

Corn. Ile keepe still thy Crowne.

Perid.   I say that word   1350
Shall cost old Cornwels life.

Corn.   Tush, this for care[1]:
Tirants good subjects kills, and traitors spare.

Vig. Wilt thou submit thy Crowne?

Mar.   Dread soveraigne, no.

Vig. He hates his own life that adviseth so.

Mar. I hate all traitors, and had rather die
Then see such wrong done to his soveraignty.

Queen. Give up thy state to these two princely youthes,
And thy resigment shal preserve thy life.

Lady. Wilt thou so much wrong both thyselfe and wife?
Hast lived a king, and canst thou die a slave?   1360
A royal seat doth aske a royall grave.
Though thousand swords thy present safety ring,
Thou that hast bin a Monarch, dye a king!

Queen. Whether he live or dye, thou sure shalt be
No longer Queene, but Vassayle unto me.
Ile make ye now my drudge.

Lady.   How, mynion, thine?

---

[1] 'this for care:'—care for this, or note this axiom.—G.

Queene. Thart no more Queen: Thy husband must resigne.
Corn. Resigne? to whom?
Perid.   I am one.
Vig.   And I another.
Lady. Canst be so base to see a younger brother,
Nay, two young Boyes plast in thy throne of state?   1370
And thou, their sodaine [1], in their traines to waite?
Ile dye before I endure it.
Perid.   So shall all,
That do not prostrate to our homage fall.
Shall they not brother King?
Vig.   They shall, by heaven!
Mar. Come, kill me first.
Corn.   Nay make the number even,
And kill me to, for I am pleasd to dye,
Rather then this indure.
Lady.   The third am I.
Queene. Nay strike her first.
Perid.   Rage, give my fury way.
Vig. Strike, valiant brother king.
Elid.   Yet heare me, stay!
Perid. Be brief, for Gods sake, then.   1380
Elid. O heaven, that men so much should covet care!
Septers are golden baites, the outsides faire:
But he that swallowes this sweete sugred pill,
Twill make him sicke with troubles that grow, stil.
Alasse, you seeke to ease me, being wearied,
And lay my burthen on your able loines!

            [1] ? Soudan, sultan, *or* sovraine.

My unambitious thoughts have bin long tird
With this great charge, and now they rest desird.
And see the kinde youths coveting my peace.
Bring me of all these turmoiles free relcase. 1390
Here, take my Crown.

 Lady.   Wilt thou be made a stale [1]?
Shall this proud woman, and these boyes, prevaile?
Shal I, for them, be made a publike scorne?
Oh, hadst thou buried bin as soone as borne,
How happy had I bin!

 Elid.   Patience, sweete wife:
Thinkst thou I praise [2] my Crowne above thy life?
No, take it Lords, it hath my trouble bin,
And for this Crowne, oh give me back my Queene.

 Queene. Nay, shes bestowed on me.

 Elydure.   Then, what you pleese:
Here take my trouble, and resigne your ease. 1400

 Sicoph. My Lords, receive the crowne of Elydure.
Faire hopefull blossoms of our future peace,
Happy am I, that I but live to see
The Land ruld by your dubble soveraignty

 Vig. Now let the king discend, to be disposd of
At our high pleasure. Come, give me the Crowne.

 Perid. Why you the Crown, good brother, more then we?

 Vig. Weele prove it, how it fits our kingly temples,
And how our brow becomes a wreath so faire.

---

[1] 'a stale'—here, as in *Tempest*, IV. i., and *Taming of the Shrew*, I. i. l. 58, means 'a trap,' or 'a decoy.'—G.

[2] appraise, probably.—G.

Perid. Shall I see you crownd, and my selfe stand bare? 1410
Rather this wreath majestick let me try,
And sit inthrond in pompious[1] Majesty.
   Vig. And I attend whilst you ascend the throne?
Where, had we right, we should sit crownd alone.
   Perid. Alone? Darst thou usurpe upon my right?
   Vig. I durst do much, had I but power and might.
But wanting that, come, let us raigne togither,
Both Kings, and yet the rich crowne worne by neither.
   Perid. Content. · The king doth on our sentence waite;
To doome him, come, lets take our dubble state. 1420
What, shall he live or dye?
   Elid. I know not how I should deserve to dye.
   Lady. Yes, to let two such usurpers live.
   Sicoph. Nay, *Madam*, now I needes must tell your grace,
You wrong these kings, forget both time and place.
It is not as it was; now you must bowe
Unto this dubble state; Ile shew you how.
   Ladi. Base flattring groome! slavish parasite!
   Vig. Shall I pronounce his sentence?
   Perid.   Brother, doe.
   Vig. Thy life we graunt thee and that Womans to; 1430
But live devided, you, within the Tower,
You, prisoner to that princesse.
   Lady.   In her power?
Oh dubble slavery!
   Perid.   Convay both hence.
   Elid. My doomes severer then my small offence.

[1] pompous.—G.

Queene. Come, Minion, will you goe?

Lady To death, to hel,
Rather then in thy base subjection dwell.

Vig. Cornwell and *Martianus*, you both see
We are possest of this imperiall seate;
And you that were sworne liedgemen to the Crowne
Should now submit to us that owe the same. 1440
We know, without your grave directions,
We cannot with experience guide the land,
Therefore weele study to deserve your loves.

Perid. Twas not ambition, or the love of state,
That drew us to this businesse, but the feare
Of *Elidurus* weakenesse, whom, in zeal
To the whole land, we have deposd this day.
Speake, shall we have your loves?

Corn. My lords and kings,
Tis bootlesse to contend gainst heaven and you.
Since without our consent the kings deposd, 1450
And we unable to support his fall,
Rather then the whole land should shrinke
You shall have my assystance in the state.

Mar. Cornwell and I will beare the self same state.

Perid. We now are Kings indeede, and Brittaine sway
When *Cornwell* and his brother *Vive* say.

Vig. Receive our grace, keepe still your offyces,
Imbrace these peeres that raisd us to the throne.
Brittaine rejoice, and Crowne this happy yeare,
Two sonnes at once shine in thy royall sphere! 1460

Corn. And thats prodigious! I but waite the time,

To see their sodaine fall, that swiftly clime.[1]

Mar. My Lord, much honor might you win your land,
To give release unto your sister Queene,
Being a Lady in the land belovd.

Vig. You have advisd us well, it shall be so.

Corn. Shold you set free the Princesse, might not she
Make uprors in the land, and raise the Commons,
In the releasment of the Captive King?

Perid. Well counseld, *Cornwell*, she shall live in bondage. 1470

Mar. Renowne yourselfe by being kind to her.

Corn. Secure your state by her imprisonment.

Vig. Weele have the Queene set free

Perid. Weele have her guarded
With stricter keeping and severer charge.

Mar. Will you be braved by one thats but your equall,
Having no more then party government?

Corn. Or you be scornd by one to you inferior,
In generall estimation of the land?

Vig. Set free the 'Princesse; say the king commands.

Perid. Keepe her in thraldome still, and captive bands. 1480

Vig. Weele not be countermaunded.

Perid. Sir, nor we.

Vig. Before Ile be halfe a king, and contrould
In any[2] regality, ile hazard all.
Ile be compleat, or none.

Perid. Before ile stand
Thus for a Cipher, with my halfe command,
Ile venture all my fortunes. How now, Pride,

---

[1] 'aside,' but not so noted in original.—G. [2] my.

Percht on my upperhand?
   Corn.   By heaven, well spyed[1]!
   Vig. Tis ours by right, and right we will injoy.
   Perid. Claimst thou preheminence? Come down proud boy!
   Vig. Then lets try maistries, and one conquer all.   1490
We climd at once, and we at once will fall.

They wrastle, and are parted.

   Perid. They that love Peridure devide themselves
Uppon their part.
   Corn.   That am I.
   Mor.   And I.
   Vig. They that love us, on this side.
   Mar.   I.
   Mal.   And I.
   Vig. Then to the field, to set our sister free!
   Perid. By all my hopes, with her Ile captive thee!
   Vig. Trumpets and Drums, triumphant musick sing!
   Perid. This day a captive, or a compleat king!   [*Exeunt.*

Alarum. Enter SOMEBODY *and* SICOPHANT.

   Somb. Sir you have sworne to manage these affaires,
Even with your best of judgement.   1500

Enter CLOWNE.

   Sicoph. I have, provided you will let me share
Of the grand benefit you get by dice,
Deceitfull Cards, and other cozening games

---

[1] Ironically (and of course aside). Equivalent to—aptly discovered!—G.

You bring into the Court.

C. O rare! Now shall I find out crab[1], som notable knavery.

Somb. You shall have equall share with *Somebody*,
Provided you will help to apprehend that *Nobody*,
On whom the guilt shall lye,
Of all those cheting tricks I have devisd. 1509

C. O, the fates! treason against my m. person! But I beleeve
Somb. will pay fort. Ile tickle your long wast[2] for this, ifaith.

Sico. Give me some bales of dice. What are these?

Som. Those are called high Fulloms.[3]

Clo. Ile Fullom you for this.

Som. Those low Fulloms.

C. They may chance bring you as hie as the Gallowes.

Som. Those Demi-bars.

Clow. Great reason you should come to the barre before the gallowes.

Som. Those bar Sizeaces. 1520

Clo. A couple of Asses, indeed.

Som. Those Brisle dice.

Clo. Tis like they brisle, for I am sure theile breed anger.

Sicop. Now, sir, as you have compast all the Dice,
So I for cards. These for the game at maw:
All, saving one, are Cut next under that.
Lay me the Ace of Harts, then cut the Cards,

---

[1] Crab: Perhaps this is a nickname for Sycophant, who crawls, and crawls backward, too.—G.

[2] *Somebody* was personated on the stage as having a very long body and hardly any legs. See p. 272.—G.

[3] Fulloms, low and high—loaded dice.—See *Merry Wives of Windsor*, I. iii. 95; and Green's *Art of Juggling*, &c., 1612.—G.

O your fellow must needs have it in his first tricke.

Clow. Ile teach you a trick for this, yfaith.

Sicop. These for Premero; cut upon the sides,   1530
As the other on the ends.

Clow. Marke the end of all this.

Sicop. These are for post and paire. These for saunt.
These for new cut.

Clown. Theile make you cut a fether, one day.

Sico. Well, these disperst, and Nobody attacht,
For all these crimes, shall be hangd.

Clow. I, or els you, shall hange for him.

Sico. Come, shals about our busines?   1539

Som. Content, lets straight about it.   [*Exeunt*

Clow. O, my hart! that it was my fortune to heare all thys; but beware a lucky man whilst you live. Alasse, if I had not rescued my maister, the swaggering fellowe woulde have made Nobody of him. Againe, if I had not overheard this treason to his person, these Cunnicatching knaves would have made lesse than Nobody of him; for indeed, they wold have hangd him. But heeres my maister. O, sweete maister, how cheere you?

Enter NOBODY.

Nobo. O excellent, admirable, and beyond comparison!
I thinke my shape inchants them.   1549

Clo. I think not so, for if I wer a Lady I should never abide you: But Maister, I can tell you rare newes; you must be apprehended for a Cheater, a Cozener, a Libiller, and I know not what.

Nobo. Not I, I am an innocent, no Cheater, no Cozener, but a simple honest man, hunted from place to place by *Somebody*.

Clo. 'Tis true sir, it is one *som.* that would attach you, therefore looke to your selfe. But Mai., if you be tooke, never feare, I heard all their knavery, and I can cleare you, I warrant.

Enter SOMEBODY, *and officers.*

Som. O have I found you? This is he, my frends,
We have long sought: You know when twas inquird
Who brought the false Dice and the cheating cards   1560
Into the court, twas answered *Nobody.*

Clo. No. (qd. tha?) I am affraid youle prove the knave *som.*

Som. Lay hold upon him; beare him to the prison.

No. To prison—say you well? If I be guilty,
This fellow is my partner; take him to.

Som. Are you confederate in this treason sirra?

Clo. If I be not, sir, *somebody* is, but if I be guilty I must beare it off with head and shoulders.

Som. To prison with them! Now the bird is caught
For whom so long through *Britaine* have I sought.   1570

Clow. I beleeve I have a bird in a box shall catcht you for all this.

Someb. Away with them I say!   [*Exeunt*

Enter, severally, PERIDURE, VIGENIUS, CORNEWELL, MARTIANUS, MORGAN, MALGO, *with drum and Coulors.*

Vig. In Armes well met, ambitious *Peridure.*

Perid. Vigenius, thou salutes me with a title
Most proper to thy selfe.

Vig.   Art thou not proud?

Perid. Onely to meet thee on this bed of death,
Wherein the Title to the English[1] Crowne
Shall perish with thy selfe.

    Vig.   Faire is the end
Of such as die in honourable warre;   1580
Oh far more faire then on a bed of downe.

    Mar. Warre is the souldiors harvest: it cuts downe —

    Perid. The lives of such as hinder our renowne.

    Vig. Such as are apt for tumult —

    Perid. Such as you,
That to our lawfull Soveraigne are untrue.

    Vig. Blushes not *Peridure,* to brave us so?

    Perid. Blushes, Vigenius,—at thy overthrow.
Who wast that told me he would submit?

    Sicoph. Twas I, my Lord.   1590

    Vig. Peace foole! thou dost forget
Tis not an hower since, to our princely eare,
Thou saidst thou didst desire us to forbeare.

    Sicoph. True, my good Lord.

    Perid.   True, that I sought to stay?

    Vig. That I would basely my ritcht hopes betray?

    Sico. I did it of mine own head, to make you friends.

    Perid. Still playing of the Sicophant.

    Vig.   What still?

    Perid. A glose, I see, to insinuate our goodwill.

    Vig. That whosoever conquerd, he might gaine

    Perid. The favour of us both, that was his trayne   1600

    Vig. But henceforth we cashiere thee from the filde.

---

[1] 'English'—again an oversight for 'British.'—G.

Perid. Never heerafter beare a souldiers shield,
A souldiers sword, nor any other grace,
But what is like thine owne, a doubble face.

Sicoph. Now I beseech *Jove* heare my praier, let them bee both slaine in the battell!   [*Exit.*

Perid. If there be any other of his hart,
We give them free licence to depart.

Corn. Cornwell hates flattery.

Mar. So does *Martianus.*   1610

Malg. Malgo is resolute for all affaires,

Morg. And so is *Morgan*, for he scornes delayes.

Vig. Then, where the fielde consists of such a spirit,
He that subdues conquers the Crowne by merit.

Perid. Thats I.

Vig.   Tis I.

Perid.   Ryvers in blood declare it!

Vig. Grasse turne to crimson if *Vigenius* spare it!

Perid. Aire be made purple with our reaking gore.

Vige. Follow, my friends.

Perid. Conquer, or neare give ore.

Alarum, Excursions, PERIDURUS *and* VIGENIUS *fight, and both slaine. Enter* CORNWELL, MARTIANUS, MORGAN *and* MALGO.

Mar. This way I saw Vigenius, on the spur.   1620

Corn. I *Peridurus*, this way

Morg. A strang sight! My Lord is breathlesse.

Malg. My deare Lord is dead!

Mar. True brothers in ambition, and in death.

Corn. Yet we are enemies, why fight we not

With one another for our generals losse?

Mar. To much blood already hath beene spent,
Now, therefore, since the difference in themselves
Is reconsiled in eithers overthrow,
Let us be as we were before this Jar;   1630
And joyning hands like honorable frends,
Inter their bodyes, as becomes their state,
And (which is rare) once more to *Elidure*,
Who now in prison leades a wearied life,
With true submission, offer Englands Crowne.
Of all the charges[1] of tumultuous fate
This is most strange, three times to flow in state. [*Exeunt*

Enter QUEENE *and* SICOPHANT.

Sico. Madam.

Queene. You are welcome; what new flatteries
Are a coyning in the mint of that smoth face?   1640

Sicoph. Where is the Lady *Elidor*, I pray?

Q. Amongst my other waiting maides at worke.

Sicoph. Tis well. Yet, Madam, with your gratious leave,
I wish it better.

Queene.   What, in love with her?
Canst thou affect such a dejected wretch?
Then I perceive thy flattery is folly,
Or thout prove honest, loving one so poore.

Sico. I know not, *Madam*, what your highnesse gathers
Out of my troubled words; I love you well;
And though the time should alter, as I am sure   1650

---

[1] 'Changes' reads best; but 'charges' is in original.—G.

It is impossible, yet I would follow
All your misfortunes with a patient hart.
   Queene. I have seene too much of thee, to credit thee.
   Sico. Now in your height of glory use your servant,
Now *Madam*, whilst the noble *Peridure*,
That loves you dearer then the Brittish Crowne,
Whilst hees conqueror, use me to destroy
Your greatest enemy, and I will doe it.
   Queene. Thou wilt not.
   Sicoph.   Be it *Elidure* the king,
The prisoner I should say, Ide murder him,   1660
To shew how much I love your majesty.
   Q. Thou wouldst not poyson for me his base Queene,
Whom I so often have triumphed ore,
That torment now is her beatitude
And tedious unto me?
   Sico.   No more; shes dead.

         Enter LADY ELIDURE.

   Queene. See where she comes, dispatch her presently,
For, though the Princely *Peridure* be King,
His brothers death, in time, will make him odious
Unto his subjects, and they may restore
Mild *Elidure* againe; and then I dye.   1670
   Sico. Withdraw, shes dead, as surely as you live.
   Lady. What, shall I never from this servitude
Receive releasant? Evermore be plagud
With this insulting Queen? Is there no change,
No other alteration in the state?

I know there is not. I am borne to be
A slave, to one baser than slavery.

   Sico. I will release you, by a speedy death.

   Lady. By death? alasse, what tongue pronounst that word?
What! my Lord weather-cocke? nay then I see   1680
Death in thy mouth is but base flattery.

   Sico. By heaven, I am sent to kill you.

   Lady. By whose meanes?

   Sico. By one that will avouch it, when tis done.

   Lady. Not the proud queene?

   Sico. Yes; but I am determined,
In full amends for all my flattery,
To save your life, and kill her instantly.

   La. Oh if a Divell would undertake that deed!
I card[1] not though she heard me, I would say   1690
He were a starre, more glorious than the day.

   Sicoph. And would you for that good deed pardon me?

   Lady. And quite all former injury.

   Sicoph. But let me tell your highnes, by the way,
The Queene is not so hasty of your death.

   Lady. No, for she had rather have my life prolongd.

   Sicoph. I do assure your highnes, on mine honor,
When I did say she sent me to destroy you,
I slaunderd her great mercy towards you;
For she had given me order to release you.   1700

   Lady. O monstrous lie!

   Sicoph. Beleeve it, for tis true.
And this moreover; she so much repents

            [1] cared,—G.

Her former pride and hardnes, towards you,
That she could wish it never had bin done.

Lady. Then, I repent me of my wrongs towards her;
And, in the stead of a reward proposd
To him that should destroy her, I do wish,
Death be his death, that undertakes the deed.

Sicoph. But will you not forget these princelie words,   1710
If any alteration should ensue?

Lady. Not I, I in my oths am true.

Sicoph. Except once more the Lords crowne *Elydure?*

Lady. Though that should chance, ile hold my promise sure.

Sicoph. And you, too, Madam?

Q. So thou muderst hir.

Sico. Know that Lord *Peridurus* and his brother
Are in the battell slaine: and by the nobles,
Her husband, Elidure, raisd to the state.
Setting aside all jesting, Queene, beleeve it,   1720
And truce with her, least she triumph againe.

Queeñe. For Gods sake make us friends.

Sicoph. Good Lord, how strange this reconciled foes
Behold each other!

Lady.   Sister.

Queene.   Kind Sister.

Sicoph. Then make me your brother. Say, are you friends?

Both. We are.

Sicoph.   Then, chance what can,
In this I have proovd myselfe an honest man.

Enter MALGO.

Malgo. The king your husband, madam, new releast,
Desires your presence at his Coronation.
  Lady. My *Elydure* a third time to be crownd!   1730
  Mal. True, Madam, and expects your company.
  Lady. And you knew this before?
  Sicoph. No, on mine honor.
  Lady. Neither you, Sister?
  Queene Neither.
  Lady. If you did,
My oath is past, and what I have lately sworne
Ile hold inviolate.   Here all stryfe ends:
Thy wit has made two proude shrewes perfect friends.   [*Exeunt*

Enter, in state, ELIDURE, CORNWELL, MARTIANUS, MORGAN *and all the Lords.*

  Corn. A third time live our gratious soveraigne!   1740
Monarch of England, crowned by these hands!
  Elid. A third time, Lords, I do returne your love,
And wish it with my soule, so heaven were pleasd,
My ambitious Brothers had not died for this.
But we have given them honorable graves.

Enter QUEEN *and* LADY.

And mournd their most untimely funerall.
My loved Queen, come seat thee by my side,
Partner in all my sorrowes and my joyes;
And you, her reconciled Sister, sit

By her, in second place of majesty;
It joyes me that you have outworne your pride.

Lady. Methinks, my gratious husband and my King,
I never tooke more pleasure in my glasse,
Then I receive in her society.

Queen. Nor I in all my state as in her love.

Elid. My Lord of *Cornwell*, whose that whispers to you?
Or whats the newes?

Corn. My liege, he tells me heeres a great contention
Betwixt two noted persons of the land,
Much spoke of by all states; one *Somebody*
Hath brought before your highnes, and this presence,
An infamous and strange opiniond fellow
Cald *Nobody:* they would intreat your highnes
To heare their matters scand.

Elid. Weele sit in person on their controversies.
Admit them *Cornwell.*

Lady. Is that strange monster tooke, so much renownd
In Citty, Court and Country for lewd prancks?
Tis well, weel heare how he can purge himselfe.

Enter SOMEBODY, *bringing in* NOBODY *and his man, with Billes and staves.*

Som. Now, sirrha, we have brought you before the King.
Wheres your hart now?

Nob. My harts in my hose; but my face was never ashamed to
shew itselfe yet, before king or keyser.

Som. And where's your hart, sirrha?

Clowne. My harts lower then my hose, for mine is at my heel;
but whersoever it is, it is a true hart, and so is not *somb.*

Som. Health to your Majestie, and to the Queene!
With a hart lower than this humble earth,
Whereon I kneele, I beg against this fellow
Justice, my liege. 1780

Elid. Against whom?

Som. Against *Nobody.*

No. My liege, his words wel sute unto his thoughts;
He wishes no man Justice, being composd
Of all deceit, of subtilty and slight.
For mine own part, if in this royall presence,
And before all these true judiciall Lords,
I cannot with sincerenes cleare myselfe
Of all suggestions falsly coynd against me,
Let me be hangd up sunning in the ayre, 1790
And made a scar-crow.

Mar. Lets heare his accusations;
And then how well thou canst aquit thy selfe.

Som. First: when this monster made his residence
Within the country, and disperst his shape
Through every shire and country of the Land,
Where plenty had before a quiet seat,
And the poore commons of the Land were full
With rich abundance and society,[1]
At his arrive, great dearths, and scarsity, 1800
By ingrosing corne, and racking poore mens rents.
This makes so many poore and honest Farmers

[1] satiety.

To sell their leases, and to beg their bread;
This makes so many beggers in the Land.

Corn. I, but what proofe, or lawfull evidence,
Can you bring forth that this was done by him?

Som. My Lord, I tras't him, and so found him out;
But should your Lordship not beleeve my proofe,
Examine all the rich and wealthy chuffes,
Whose full cramd Garners to the roofes are fild, 1810
In every dearth, who makes this scarsitye,
And every man will clearely quit himselfe:
Then, consequently, it must be *Nobody*.
[1] Base copper money is stampt, the mint disgrast—
Make search who doth this, every man cleares one:
So, consequently, it must be *Nobody*.
Besides, whereas the nobles of the land
And Gentlemen built goodly manner houses,
Fit to receive a king and all his traine,
And there kept royall hospitality: 1820
Since this intestine monster, No-body,
Dwels in these goodly houses, keepes no traine —
A hundred Chimnies, and not one cast smoke—
And now the cause of these, mock-begger Hal,
Is this, they are dwelt in by *Nobody*.
For this out of the countrey he was chast.

No. My royall liedge, whie am I thus disgrast?
Ile prove that slandrous wretch hath this al done.

Elid. Tis good you can acquit you. Such abuses

---

[1] Is this a skit upon the Government coining base money for Ireland in 1598 or 1599, or does it only refer to the coiners?

Grow in the countrey, and unknowne to us! 1830
Nay then, no marvell that so manie poore
Starve in the streets, and beg from doore to doore.
Then, sirha, purge you from this countrey blame,
Or we will make thee the worlds publike shame.
   Corn. Now, *Nobody*, what can you say to this?
   Clo. My M. hath good cards on his side, Ile warrant him.
   No. My Lord, you know that slanders are no proofes:
Nor words, without their present evidence.
If things were done, they must be done by *Somebody*,
Else could they have no being. Is corne hoorded? 1840
Somebody hords it, else it would be delt
In mutual plentie throughout all the land.
Are their rents raisd? If *Nobody* should doe it,
Then should it be undone. Is
Base money stampt, and the kings letters forgd?
Somebody needes must doe it, therefore not I.
And where he saies, great houses long since built
Lye destitute and wast, because inhabited
By *Nobody;* my liedge, I answer thus.
If Somebody dwelt therein I would give place: 1850
Or wold he but alow those chimnies fire—
They would cast cloudes to heaven; the kitchin, foode—
It would releeve the poore; the sellers beere[1]—
It would make strangers drinke. But he commits
These outrages, then laies the blame on me;
And for my good deeds I am made a scorne.
I onely give the tired a refuge seat,

   [1] Beer in the cellars.—G.

The unclothed, garments, and the starved, meate.

Clow. How say you by this maister Somebody? I beleeve you will be found out by and by. 1860

Corn. If this be true my liedge, as true it is,
Somebody will be found an arrant cheater,
Unlesse he better can acquit himselfe..

Sich. Touch him with the citty, since you have taken the foile in the countrey.

Mar. Sirha, what can you say to this?

Someb. What should I saie, my Lord? see heare complaints
Made in the citty against *no-body*,
As well as in the countrey. See their bils;
Heeres one complaines his wife hath bin abroad, 1870
And asking where she revels night by night:
She answers she hath bin with *nobody*.
Heares queanes maintaind in every suburb streete;
Aske who maintaines them, and tis *nobody*.
Watches are beaten, and constables are scoft
In dead of night; men are made drunke in tavernes,
Girles loose their maiden heads at thirteene yeares,
Pockets pickt, and purses cut in throngs—

Queene. Inough, inough! Doth *nobody* all this?
Though he hath cleard himselfe from country crimes, 1880
He cannot scape the citty.

No. Yes, dread Queene,
I must confesse these things are daily done,
For which I heere accuse this Somebody,
That everywhere with slaunders dogs my steps,
And cunningly assumes my borrowed shape.

Women lie out; if they be tooke and found
With *somebody*, then *Nobody* goes cleere;
Else the blames mine. He doth these faults unknowne,
Then slanders my chast innocence for proofe.
Somebody doth maintaine a common strumpet   1890
Ith Garden-allies, and undid himselfe;
Somebody swaggered with the watch last night,
Was carried to the counter; *Somebody*
Once pickt a pocket in this Play-house yard,
Was hoysted on the stage, and shamd about it.

   Clow. Ha, ha! hath my maister met with you?

   No. Alasse, my liege, your honest Nobodie
Builds Churches, in these dayes, and Hospitals;
Releeves the severall prisons in the Citty;
Redeemes the needy debtor from the hole—   1900
And when this *somebody* brings infant children,
And leaves them in the night at strangers doores,
Nobody fathers them, provides them nurses—
What should I say? Your highnes love I crave,
That am all just!

   Corn.   Then *somebodies* a knave.

   Sicoph. If neither citty nor countrie will prevaile, to him
With the court ma.[1] *somebody*, and there you will match him.

   Som. Then touching his abuses in the court—

   Corn. I, marrie, Nobody, what say you to this?
See, heere are dangerous Libils gainst the state,   1910
And no name to them, therefore *nobodies*.

   Mar. Besides, strange rumors and false buzzing tales

[1] Maister.—G.

Of mutinous leesings raisd by *Nobody.*

Malg. False dice and cheating brought even to the presence!
And who dares be so impudently knavish,
Unlesse some fellow of your name and garbe?

Morg. Cards of advantage, with such cheating tricks,
Brought even amongst the noblest of the land,
And when these cosening shifts are once discovered
There is no cheater found save Nobody.   1920

Som. How canst thou answer these?

Nobo.   Even as the rest.
Are libels cast? If *nobody* did make them
And *nobodies* name to them, they are no libels.
For he that sets his name to any slander
Makes it by that no libell. This aproves [1]
He forgd those slanderous writs to scandall me;
And for false cards and dice, let my great slops,
And his big bellied dublet both be sercht,
And see which harbors most hipocrisie.   1930

Queene. Let them both be sercht.

Sico. Ile take my leave of the presence.

Clow. Nay, M. *Sicophant,* weele have the inside of your pockets translated to, weele see what stuffyng they have; Ile take a little paines with you.

Elid. What have you there in *nobodyes* pockets?

Corn. Here are, my liedge, bonds, forfeit by poore men,
Which he releast out of the usurers hands,
And canceld. Leases, likewise forfeited,
By him repurchast. These petitions,   1940

[1] proves.—G.

Of many poore men, to preferre their sutes
Unto your highnesse.

   Elid. Thou art just, we know;
All great mens pockets should be lined so.

   Queene. What bumbast beares his gorge?

   Mor. False Cards, false Dice;
The kings hand, counterfeit;
Bonds put in sute, to gaine the forfitures;
Forgd deedes, to cheate men of their ancient land;
And thousand such like trashe.   1950

   Clo. Nay, looke you heere! heares one that, for his bones, is pretily stuft. Heares fulloms and gourds; heeres tall-men and low-men; Heere trayduce ace, passedge comes a pace.

   Som. Mercy, great King!

   Sicoph.   Mercy, my Soveraigne!

   Corn. My liedge, you cannot to be[1] severe in punishing
Those monstrous crimes, the onely staine and blemish
To the weale-publike.

   Eli. Villaines, heare your doome.
Thou that hast bin the oppressyon of the poore,
Shalt bee more poore than penury itselfe.   1960
All that thou hast, is forfit to the Law.
For thy extortion, I will have thee branded
Upon the forhead with the letter F;
For cheating, whipt; for forging, loose thine eares;
Last, for abasing of thy Soveraignes Coyne,
And traitrous impresse of our Kingly seale,
Suffer the death of traitors. Beare him hence.

               [1] *orig.* to be = be too.

Som. Since I must needs be marterd, graunt me this;
That *Nobody* may whip, or torture, me,
Or hang me for a traitor.

Morg.   Away with him.   1970

Som. Or if needs I must dye a traitors death;
That *Nobody* may see me when I dye.

Malg. Hence with the traitor.

Clo. I know by your complexion, you were ripe for the hangman;
but now to this leane Gentleman.

Lady. Let me doome him, smoth spaniel, soothing grome,
Slicke, oyly knave, egregious parasite!
Thou turning vane, and changing Weather-cocke,
My sentence is, thou shalt be naked stript,
And by the citty beadles soundly whipt.   1980

Clow. Ile make bold to see the execution.

No. Well hath the king decreed. Now, by your highnesse
patience, let *Nobody* borrow a word or two of Every-body.

The Epilogue.

Heer, if you wonder why the king *Elidurus* bestowes nothing on
me, for all my good services in his land—if the multitude shuld
say he hath preferd Nobody, *Somebody* or other would say it were
not well done, for, in doing good to *Nobody*, he should but get himselfe an il name. Therefore, I will leave my sute to him, and turne
to you. Kinde Gentleman, if any-body heere dislike No-body,
then I hope Every-body have pleased you, for being offended with
nobody, [1] nor Anybody can-finde himselfe agrieved. Gentlemen,

---

[1] not.

they have a cold sute that have *no-body* to speak in their cause, and therefore blame us not to feare. Yet our comfort is this. If *nobody* have offended, you cannot blame Nobody for it, or rather we will find Somebody hereafter, shall make good the fault that nobody hath done; and so, I crave the generall grace of Every-body.

Eli. Now forward, Lords, long may our glories stand,
Three sundry times Crownd King of this faire land. *Exeunt.*

FINIS.

NOTES.

1.—*The German Collection of English Plays*, 1620.

TIECK thought that the German translation of *Nobody and Somebody* was made from a lost primitive play, of which the English published copy is a correction and amplification. But it is more natural to suppose, either that the changes were made by the English comedians themselves, who adapted the plays both to their own diminished numbers when travelling on the continent, and to the supposed tastes of their somewhat rude audience, or else that they were made by the German translators, who, in the very infancy of their art, could not as yet endure the refinements of the English state, but ever tended to reduce the plays to a more archaic form. Among English plays we see the same thing. Colley Cibber was in reality not much less a barbarizer of Shakspere than the German translator is of *Nobody and Somebody.*

The first drama of this collection is the history of *Esther and Haman.* An interlude called *Queen Hester* was published, 4°,

1561, by Wm. Pickering and Thomas Hacket.—' A new Interlude, drawen out of the holy Scripture of godly Queen Hester, very necessary, newly made and imprinted this present year, 1561.' The characters are King Assuerus, III. Gentlemen, Aman, Mardocheus, Hester, Pursuivant, Pride, Adulation, Ambition, Hardydardy, a Jew, Arbona Sziba.

Also in June 1594, when the Lord Chamberlain's men played for a few days alternately with the Lord Admiral's men at Newington, *Hester and Ahasuerus* was played twice, evidently by the former company, on June 3 and June 10. The plays belonging to the Chamberlain's men then registered, are *Hester*, *Andronicus*, *Hamlet*, and probably *The taming of a shrowe*. (Henslowe's diary, pp. 35, 36.)

Titus Andronicus seems to be from an older edition than any we have in English. It may be the same as the *Titus and Vespasian*, played so often by the Lord Strange's men in 1591-92 (see Henslowe's diary, 20—30). Vespasian is one of the chief characters in the German play.

It appears by Henslowe's diary, that he paid Decker in earnest of a book called 'The whole history of Fortunatus,' 40s., 9 Nov., 1599. But the Lord Admiral's men had a play called the 1st part of *Fortunatus*, Feb. 3, 1596. It is not then marked as new, though it does not occur previously in Henslowe. Chapman's *Blind Beggar* was new on the 12th of the same month. *Fortunatus* was a very popular play.

Decker's *Old Fortunatus* belonged to the Lord Admiral's men. But this was only in its new form. It was thus registered to W. Apsley in 1599—*A comedy called Old Fortunatus in his new livery*. It was published by him in 1600, 'as it was played before the

Queen's Majesty this Christmas, by the Right Hon. the E. of Nottingham, Lord High Admiral of England, his servants.' So that the Christmas when the Lord Chamberlain's men were in disgrace, not only was their place at Court filched by the opposition, but their play likewise. In a similar way B. Jonson refurbished Jeronymo, which belonged to the Lord Chamberlain's men, for the Lord Admiral's.

A passage in Taine's *History of English literature*, tr., vol. i. p. 247, on the theatrical poets gives a foreigner's view of the diction of our theatre :—

'There are none of those solid pleadings, none of those probing discussions, which moment by moment add reason to reason, objection to objection; one would say that they only *knew how to scold, to repeat themselves, to mark time.*'

The German translator of the English comedies evidently felt this. He wished to find the logical and general meaning hidden under each metaphor; and so he reduced about half of them to such a form as this :—

$$\text{I am so} \begin{Bmatrix} \text{mad,} \\ \text{angry,} \\ \text{hungry,} \\ \text{joyful,} \\ \text{in love,} \\ \text{\&c.,} \end{Bmatrix} \text{that I know not what to do.}^{1}$$

2.—*You cannot choose a man, not you!* p. 162, l. 116.—Compare with the Nurse's words—'You know not how to choose a man.'—*Romeo and Juliet*, II. v. 39.—G.

[1] The MS. of the opening of this Note by Mr Simpson on the German Collection of Plays is lost; other notes on the subject, however, will be found in the Introductions, &c., to the several plays. *See* Index.—G.

3.—*Mix not my forward summer*, p. 188, l. 754.—Compare with 'This goodly summer with your winter mixed,' *Titus Andronicus*, V. ii. 140.

4.—*I will once trust an Englishman on his word*, p. 215, l. 1412.—Compare with 'Thus once I mean to try a Frenchman's faith,' in a similar situation in *Edward III* (1596), sig. G. 3, l. 29.—G.

5.—*Chorus* in Play of *Stucley*: her speeches are very like those of the Chorus in *Henry V*: e.g., p. 248, l. 2260, *et seq*.—G.

6.—*Reach me my glove*, p. 291, l. 365.—Compare with *Henry VI*, Part 1, I. iii., l. 141.

6.—*Stage Directions*: Two are evidently omitted, viz., something giving the sense of 'Strikes him,' at both p. 292, l. 388, and p. 297, l. 515.—G.

Bungay:
CLAY AND TAYLOR, PRINTERS.

www.ingramcontent.com/pod-product-compliance
Lightning Source LLC
Chambersburg PA
CBHW030347230426
43664CB00007BB/563